Liberalism and the Limits of Justice

SECOND EDITION

A liberal society seeks not to impose a single way of life but to leave its citizens as free as possible to choose their own values and ends. It therefore must govern by principles of justice that do not presuppose any particular vision of the good life. But can any such principles be found? And if not, what are the consequences for justice as a moral and political ideal?

These are the questions Michael Sandel takes up in this penetrating critique of contemporary liberalism. He locates modern liberalism in the tradition of Kant, and focuses on its most influential recent expression in the work of John Rawls. In the most important challenge yet to Rawls's theory of justice, Sandel traces the limits of liberalism to the conception of the person that underlies it, and argues for a deeper understanding of community than liberalism allows.

For this second edition Sandel has addressed criticisms of the first edition in a new preface, and has written a new chapter considering Rawls's latest work.

Liberalism
and the
Limits of Justice

SECOND EDITION

MICHAEL J. SANDEL

CAMBRIDGE
UNIVERSITY PRESS

PUBLISHED BY THE PRESS SYNDICATE OF THE UNIVERSITY OF CAMBRIDGE
The Pitt Building, Trumpington Street, Cambridge CB2 1RP, United Kingdom

CAMBRIDGE UNIVERSITY PRESS
The Edinburgh Building, Cambridge CB2 2RU, UK   http://www.cup.cam.ac.uk
40 West 20th Street, New York, NY 10011-4211, USA   http://www.cup.org
10 Stamford Road, Oakleigh, Melbourne 3166, Australia

First edition published 1982
Second edition first published 1998

Printed in the United States of America

Typeset in New Baskerville 10.5/13, using QuarkXPress for the Macintosh [BB]

*A catalog record for this book is available from
the British Library.*

Library of Congress Cataloging-in-Publication Data applied for.

ISBN 0-521-56298-8 hardback
ISBN 0-521-56741-6 paperback

To my parents

Contents

Contents

Preface to the Second Edition
The Limits of Communitarianism

Much has changed in the landscape of political philosophy since this book first appeared. The 1980s and 1990s brought an avalanche of books and articles devoted to what now goes by the name of the 'liberal-communitarian' debate. Meanwhile, John Rawls, whose deservedly celebrated work *A Theory of Justice* was the primary focus of my critique, has recast his theory in important ways. In the new final chapter for this second edition, I examine the revised version of liberalism that Rawls presents in his recent work. In this preface, I wish to register some unease with the 'communitarian' label that has been applied to the view advanced in *Liberalism and the Limits of Justice (LLJ)*.

WHERE COMMUNITARIANISM GOES WRONG

Along with the works of other contemporary critics of liberal political theory, notably Alasdair MacIntyre,[1] Charles Taylor,[2] and Michael Walzer,[3] *LLJ* has come to be identified with the 'communitarian' critique of rights-oriented liberalism. Since part of my argument is that contemporary liberalism offers an inadequate account of community, the term fits to some extent. In many respects, however, the label is misleading. The 'liberal-communitarian' debate that has raged among political philosophers in recent years describes a range of issues, and I do not always find myself on the communitarian side.

The debate is sometimes cast as an argument between those who prize individual liberty and those who think the values of the community or the will of the majority should always prevail, or between those who believe in universal human rights and those who insist

---

1 See Alasdair MacIntyre, *After Virtue* (Notre Dame: University of Notre Dame Press, 1981).
2 See Charles Taylor, *Philosophical Papers, vol. I: Human Agency and Language; vol. II: Philosophy and the Human Sciences* (Cambridge: Cambridge University Press, 1985); and Taylor, *Sources of the Self: The Making of Modern Identity* (Cambridge, Mass.: Harvard University Press, 1989).
3 See Michael Walzer, *Spheres of Justice: A Defense of Pluralism and Equality* (New York: Basic Books, 1983).

there is no way to criticize or judge the values that inform different cultures and traditions. Insofar as 'communitarianism' is another name for majoritarianism, or for the idea that rights should rest on the values that predominate in any given community at any given time, it is not a view I would defend.

What is at stake in the debate between Rawlsian liberalism and the view I advance in *LLJ* is not whether rights are important but whether rights can be identified and justified in a way that does not presuppose any particular conception of the good life. At issue is not whether individual or communal claims should carry greater weight but whether the principles of justice that govern the basic structure of society can be neutral with respect to the competing moral and religious convictions its citizens espouse. The fundamental question, in other words, is whether the right is prior to the good.

For Rawls, as for Kant, the priority of the right over the good stands for two claims, and it is important to distinguish them. The first is the claim that certain individual rights are so important that even the general welfare cannot override them. The second is the claim that the principles of justice that specify our rights do not depend for their justification on any particular conception of the good life or, as Rawls has put it more recently, on any 'comprehensive' moral or religious conception. It is the second claim for the priority of right, not the first, that *LLJ* seeks to challenge.

The notion that justice is relative to the good, not independent of it, connects *LLJ* to writings by others commonly identified as the 'communitarian critics' of liberalism. But there are two versions of the claim that justice is relative to good, and only one of them is 'communitarian' in the usual sense. Much of the confusion that has beset the liberal-communitarian debate arises from failing to distinguish the two versions.

One way of linking justice with conceptions of the good holds that principles of justice derive their moral force from values commonly espoused or widely shared in a particular community or tradition. This way of linking justice and the good is communitarian in the sense that the values of the community define what counts as just or unjust. On this view, the case for recognizing a right depends on showing that such a right is implicit in the shared understandings that inform the tradition or community in question. There can be disagreement, of course, about what rights the shared understandings of a particular tradition actually support; social critics and political reformers can interpret traditions in ways that challenge prevailing practices. But these arguments always take the form of recalling a community to itself, of appealing to ideals implicit but unrealized in a common project or tradition.

A second way of linking justice with conceptions of the good holds that principles of justice depend for their justification on the moral worth or intrinsic good of the ends they serve. On this view, the case for recognizing a right depends on showing that it honors or advances some important human good. Whether this good happens to be widely prized or implicit in the traditions of the community would not be decisive. The second way of tying justice to conceptions of the good is therefore not, strictly speaking, communitarian. Since it rests the case for rights on the moral importance of the purposes or ends rights promote, it is better described as teleological, or (in the jargon of contemporary philosophy) perfectionist. Aristotle's political theory is an example: Before we can define people's rights or investigate 'the nature of the ideal constitution', he writes, 'it is necessary for us first to determine the nature of the most desirable way of life. As long as that remains obscure, the nature of the ideal constitution must also remain obscure.'[4]

Of the two ways of linking justice to conceptions of the good, the first is insufficient. The mere fact that certain practices are sanctioned by the traditions of a particular community is not enough to make them just. To make justice the creature of convention is to deprive it of its critical character, even if allowance is made for competing interpretations of what the relevant tradition requires. Arguments about justice and rights have an unavoidably judgmental aspect. Liberals who think the case for rights should be neutral toward substantive moral and religious doctrines and communitarians who think rights should rest on prevailing social values make a similar mistake; both try to avoid passing judgment on the content of the ends that rights promote. But these are not the only alternatives. A third possibility, more plausible in my view, is that rights depend for their justification on the moral importance of the ends they serve.

---

4 *The Politics of Aristotle*, 1323a14, ed. and trans. by Ernest Barker (London: Oxford University Press, 1958), p. 279.

THE RIGHT TO RELIGIOUS LIBERTY

Consider the case of religious liberty. Why should the free exercise of religion enjoy special constitutional protection? The liberal might reply that religious liberty is important for the same reason individual liberty in general is important – so that people may be free to live autonomously, to choose and pursue their values for themselves. According to this view, government should uphold religious liberty in order to respect persons as free and independent selves, capable of choosing their own religious convictions. The respect the liberal invokes is not, strictly speaking, respect for religion, but respect for the self whose religion it is, or respect for the dignity that consists in the capacity to choose one's religion freely. On the liberal view, religious beliefs are worthy of respect, not in virtue of their content but instead in virtue of being 'the product of free and voluntary choice'.[5]

This way of defending religious liberty puts the right before the good; it tries to secure the right to religious freedom without passing judgment on the content of people's beliefs or on the moral importance of religion as such. But the right to religious liberty is not best understood as a particular case of a more general right to individual autonomy. Assimilating religious liberty to a general right to choose one's own values misdescribes the nature of religious conviction and obscures the reasons for according the free exercise of religion special constitutional protection. Construing all religious convictions as products of choice may miss the role that religion plays in the lives of those for whom the observance of religious duties is a constitutive end, essential to their good and indispensable to their identity. Some may view their religious beliefs as matters of choice, others not. What makes a religious belief worthy of respect is not its mode of acquisition – be it choice, revelation, persuasion, or habituation – but its place in a good life, or the qualities of character it promotes, or (from a political point of view) its tendency to cultivate the habits and dispositions that make good citizens.

To place religious convictions on a par with the various interests and ends an independent self may choose makes it difficult to distinguish between claims of conscience, on the one hand, and mere pref-

---

5 The phrase is from *Wallace v. Jaffree*, 472 U.S. 38, 52–53 (1985): "Religious beliefs worthy of respect are the product of free and voluntary choice by the faithful."

erences, on the other. Once this distinction is lost, the right to demand of the state a special justification for laws that burden the free exercise of religion is bound to appear as nothing more weighty than 'a private right to ignore generally applicable laws'.[6] If an orthodox Jew is granted the right to wear a yarmulke while on duty in an air force health clinic, then what about servicemen who want to wear other head coverings prohibited by military dress codes?[7] If Native Americans have a right to the sacramental use of peyote, then what can be said to those who would violate state drug laws for recreational purposes?[8] If Sabbath observers are granted the right to schedule their day off from work on the day corresponding to their Sabbath, does not the same right have to be accorded those who want a certain day off to watch football?[9]

Assimilating religious liberty to liberty in general reflects the liberal aspiration to neutrality. But this generalizing tendency does not always serve religious liberty well. It confuses the pursuit of preferences with the performance of duties. It therefore ignores the special concern of religious liberty with the predicament of conscientiously encumbered selves – claimed by duties they cannot choose to renounce, even in the face of civil obligations that may conflict.

But why, it might be asked, should the state accord special respect to conscientiously encumbered selves? Part of the reason is that for government to burden practices central to the self-definition of its citizens is to frustrate them more profoundly than to deprive them of interests less central to the projects that give meaning to their lives. But encumbrance as such is not a sufficient basis for special respect. Defining projects and commitments can range from the admirable and heroic to the obsessive and demonic. Situated selves can display solidarity and depth of character or prejudice and narrow-mindedness.

The case for according special protection to the free exercise of religion presupposes that religious belief, as characteristically practiced in a particular society, produces ways of being and acting that are worthy of honor and appreciation – either because they are admirable in themselves or because they foster qualities of character

---

6 The phrase is from *Employment Division v. Smith*, 494 U.S. 872, 886 (1990).

7 See *Goldman v. Weinberger*, 475 U.S. 503 (1986).

8 See *Employment Division v. Smith*, 494 U.S. 872 (1990).

9 See *Thornton v. Caldor, Inc.*, 474 U.S. 703 (1985).

that make good citizens. Unless there were reason to think religious beliefs and practices contribute to morally admirable ways of life, the case for a right to religious liberty would be weakened. Pragmatic considerations would, of course, remain; upholding religious liberty could still be justified as a way of avoiding the civil strife that can result when church and state are too closely intertwined. But the moral justification for a right to religious liberty is unavoidably judgmental; the case for the right cannot wholly be detached from a substantive judgment about the moral worth of the practice it protects.

THE RIGHT TO FREE SPEECH

The link between rights and the goods rights protect is also illustrated by recent debates about free speech and hate speech. Should neo-Nazis have the right to march in Skokie, Illinois, a community with large numbers of Holocaust survivors?[10] Should white-supremacist groups be allowed to promulgate their racist views?[11] Liberals argue that government must be neutral toward the opinions its citizens espouse. Government can regulate the time, place, and manner of speech – it can ban a noisy rally in the middle of the night – but it cannot regulate the content of speech. To ban offensive or unpopular speech imposes on some the values of others and so fails to respect each citizen's capacity to choose and express his or her own opinions.

Liberals can, consistent with their view, restrict speech likely to cause significant harm – violence, for example. But in the case of hate speech, what counts as harm is constrained by the liberal conception of the person. According to this conception, my dignity consists not in any social roles I inhabit but instead in my capacity to choose my roles and identities for myself. But this means that my dignity could never be damaged by an insult directed against a group with which I identify. No hate speech could constitute harm in itself, for on the liberal view, the highest respect is the self-respect of a self independent of its aims and attachments. For the unencumbered self, the grounds of self-respect are antecedent to any particular ties and attachments, and so beyond the reach of an insult to 'my people'. The liberal would therefore oppose restrictions on hate speech, except

10 See *Collin v. Smith*, 447 F. Supp. 676 (1978); *Collin v. Smith*, 578 F.2d 1198 (1978).
11 See *Beauharnais v. Illinois*, 343 U.S. 250 (1952).

where it is likely to provoke some actual physical harm – some harm independent of the speech itself.

The communitarian might reply that the liberal conception of harm is too narrow. For people who understand themselves as defined by the ethnic or religious group to which they belong, an insult to the group can inflict a harm as real and as damaging as some physical harms. For Holocaust survivors, the neo-Nazi march was aimed at provoking fears and memories of unspeakable horrors that reached to the core of their identities and life stories.

But to acknowledge the harm that hate speech can inflict does not establish that the speech should be restricted. The harm such speech inflicts has to be weighed against the good of upholding free speech. With speech as with religion, it is not enough simply to invoke the claims of thickly constituted selves. What matters is the moral importance of the speech in relation to the moral status of the settled identities the speech would disrupt or offend. If Skokie could keep out the Nazis, why could not the segregationist communities of the South keep out civil-rights marchers of the 1950s and 1960s? The Southern segregationists did not want Martin Luther King, Jr., to march in their communities any more than the residents of Skokie wanted the neo-Nazis to march in theirs. Like the Holocaust survivors, the segregationists could claim to be thickly constituted selves, bound by common memories that would be deeply offended by the marchers and their message.

Is there a principled way of distinguishing the two cases? For liberals who insist on being neutral with respect to the content of speech, and for communitarians who define rights according to the prevailing values of the communities in question, the answer must be no. The liberal would uphold free speech in both cases, and the communitarian would override it. But the need to decide both cases in the same way displays the folly of the nonjudgmental impulse liberals and communitarians share.

The obvious ground for distinguishing the cases is that the neo-Nazis promote genocide and hate, whereas Martin Luther King, Jr., sought civil rights for blacks. The difference consists in the content of the speech, in the nature of the cause. There is also a difference in the moral worth of the communities whose integrity was at stake. The shared memories of the Holocaust survivors deserve a moral deference that the solidarity of the segregationists does not. Moral discriminations such as these are consistent with common sense but at odds with the version of liberalism that asserts the priority of the right over the good and the version of communitarianism that rests the case for rights on communal values alone.

If the right to free speech depends for its justification on a substantive moral judgment about the importance of speech in relation to the risks it entails, it does not follow that judges should try, in each particular case, to assess the merits of the speech for themselves. Nor, in every case involving religious liberty, should judges undertake to assess the moral importance of the religious practice at issue. On any theory of rights, certain general rules and doctrines are desirable to spare judges the need to recur to first principles in every case that comes before them. But sometimes, in hard cases, judges cannot apply such rules without appealing directly to the moral purposes that justify rights in the first place.

One striking example is the opinion of Judge Frank Johnson in the 1965 case that permitted Martin Luther King's historic march from Selma to Montgomery. Alabama Governor George Wallace tried to prevent the march. Judge Johnson acknowledged that the states had the right to regulate the use of their highways, and that a mass march along a public highway reached 'to the outer limits of what is constitutionally allowed.' Nevertheless, he ordered the state to permit the march, on grounds of the justice of its cause: 'The extent of the right to assemble, demonstrate and march peaceably along the highways', he wrote, 'should be commensurate with the enormity of the wrongs that are being protested and petitioned against. In this case, the wrongs are enormous. The extent of the right to demonstrate against these wrongs should be determined accordingly.'[12]

Judge Johnson's decision was not content-neutral; it would not have helped the Nazis in Skokie. But it aptly illustrates the difference between the liberal approach to rights and the approach that would rest rights on a substantive moral judgment of the ends rights advance.

Cambridge, Massachusetts
December, 1997

12 *Williams v. Wallace*, 240 F. Supp. 100, 108, 106 (1965).

Acknowledgments

This book began life in Oxford in the late 1970s, a stimulating time for the study of political philosophy, especially so at Balliol College. I am indebted to teachers and friends of those years and since, who taught me much of what I have written here. Thanks are due first of all to William Connolly, Richard Fallon, Donald Herzog, Steven Lukes, David Miller, Alan Montefiore, Judith Shklar, and Charles Taylor, all of whom read an earlier version of this essay and offered valuable comments and criticisms. Their advice was all to the good, and does not account for whatever weaknesses remain. Some, however, are implicated a little more deeply. Among my contemporaries while abroad, Ronald Beiner, Richard Fallon, and Scott Matheson bear a special responsibility. Discussions and travels with them helped shape these thoughts, and made for intellectual comradeship of the highest order. I owe my deepest debt to those among my teachers whose influence is most present in this work: Ronald Dworkin, whose arguments demanded a better answer than I could offer at the time; Charles Taylor, who broadened Anglo-American horizons and taught the relevance of Aristotle and Hegel; and especially Alan Montefiore, who made philosophy inescapable, and set me on this path six years ago.

In preparing the material for the second edition, I am indebted to critics and friends (in some cases, one and the same) who have responded to the arguments presented in the first edition. I would like to record a special debt to John Rawls. His powerful statement of liberal political philosophy inspired this book from a distance. In the years since, I have had the good fortune to know him as a kind and generous colleague.

Introduction
Liberalism and the Primacy of Justice

This is an essay about liberalism. The liberalism with which I am concerned is a version of liberalism prominent in the moral and legal and political philosophy of the day: a liberalism in which the notions of justice, fairness, and individual rights play a central role, and which is indebted to Kant for much of its philosophical foundation. As an ethic that asserts the priority of the right over the good, and is typically defined in opposition to utilitarian conceptions, the liberalism I have in mind might best be described as 'deontological liberalism', a formidable name for what I think will appear a familiar doctrine.

'Deontological liberalism' is above all a theory about justice, and in particular about the primacy of justice among moral and political ideals. Its core thesis can be stated as follows: society, being composed of a plurality of persons, each with his own aims, interests, and conceptions of the good, is best arranged when it is governed by principles that do not *themselves* presuppose any particular conception of the good; what justifies these regulative principles above all is not that they maximize the social welfare or otherwise promote the good, but rather that they conform to the concept of *right*, a moral category given prior to the good and independent of it.

This is the liberalism of Kant and of much contemporary moral and political philosophy, and it is this liberalism that I propose to challenge. Against the primacy of justice, I shall argue for the limits of justice, and, by implication, for the limits of liberalism as well. The limits I have in mind are not practical but conceptual. My point is not that justice, however noble in principle, is unlikely ever fully to be realized in practice, but rather that the limits reside in the ideal itself. For a society inspired by the liberal promise, the problem is not simply that justice remains always to be achieved, but that the vision is flawed, the aspiration incomplete. But before exploring these limits, we must see more clearly what the claim for the primacy of justice consists in.

THE FOUNDATIONS OF LIBERALISM: KANT VERSUS MILL

The primacy of justice can be understood in two different but related ways. The first is a straightforward moral sense. It says that justice is primary in that the demands of justice outweigh other moral and political interests, however pressing these others may be. On this view, justice is not merely one value among others, to be weighed and considered as the occasion arises, but the highest of all social virtues, the one that must be met before others can make their claims. If the happiness of the world could be advanced by unjust means alone, not happiness but justice would properly prevail. And when justice issues in certain individual rights, even the general welfare cannot override them.

But the primacy of justice, in its moral sense alone, hardly distinguishes this liberalism from other well-known varieties. Many liberal thinkers have emphasized the importance of justice and insisted on the sanctity of individual rights. John Stuart Mill called justice 'the chief part, and incomparably the most sacred and binding part, of all morality' (1863: 465), and Locke held man's natural rights to be stronger than any commonwealth could override (1690). But neither was a deontological liberal in the deeper sense that concerns us here. For the full deontological ethic is not only about morals but also about the foundation of morals. It concerns not just the weight of the moral law, but also the means of its derivation, what Kant would call its 'determining ground' (1788).

On the full deontological view, the primacy of justice describes not only a moral priority but also a privileged form of justification; the right is prior to the good not only in that its claims take precedence, but also in that its principles are independently derived. This means that, unlike other practical injunctions, principles of justice are justified in a way that does not depend on any particular vision of the good. To the contrary: given its independent status, the right constrains the good and sets its bounds. 'The concept of good and evil is not defined prior to the moral law, to which, it would seem, the former would have to serve as foundation; rather the concept of good and evil must be defined after and by means of the law' (Kant 1788: 65).

From the standpoint of moral foundations, then, the primacy of justice amounts to this: the virtue of the moral law does not consist in the fact that it promotes some goal or end presumed to be good. It is instead an end in itself, given prior to all other ends, and regulative with respect to them. Kant distinguishes this second-order, foundational sense of primacy from the first-order, moral sense as follows:

By primacy between two or more things connected by reason, I understand the prerogative of one by virtue of which it is the prime ground of determination of the combination with the others. In a narrower practical sense it refers to the prerogative of the interest of one so far as the interest of the others is subordinated to it and is not itself inferior to any other (1788: 124).

The contrast might also be drawn in terms of two different senses of deontology. In its moral sense, deontology opposes *consequentialism;* it describes a first-order ethic containing certain categorical duties and prohibitions which take unqualified precedence over other moral and practical concerns. In its foundational sense, deontology opposes *teleology;* it describes a form of justification in which first principles are derived in a way that does not presuppose any final human purposes or ends, nor any determinate conception of the human good.

Of the two strands of the deontological ethic, the first is no doubt the more familiar. Many liberals, not only deontological ones, have given special weight to justice and individual rights. This raises the question of how the two aspects of deontology are related. Can liberalism of the first kind be defended without recourse to the second? Mill, for one, thought so, and argued for the possibility, indeed for the necessity, of detaching the two.

To have a right, says Mill, is 'to have something which society ought to defend me in the possession of' (1863: 459). So strong is society's obligation that my claim 'assumes that character of absoluteness, that apparent infinity, and incommensurability with all other considerations, which constitute the distinction between the feeling of right and wrong and that of ordinary expediency and inexpediency' (1863: 460). But if it be asked why society must meet this obligation, it is for 'no other reason than general utility' (1863: 459). Justice is properly regarded as 'the chief part, and incomparably the most sacred and binding part, of all morality', not by reason of abstract right, but simply because the requirements of justice 'stand higher in the scale of social utility, and are therefore of more paramount obligation, than any others' (1863: 465, 469).

It is proper to state that I forego any advantage which could be derived to my argument from the idea of abstract right, as a thing independent of utility. I regard utility as the ultimate appeal on all ethical questions; but it must be utility in the largest sense, grounded on the permanent interests of man as a progressive being (1849: 485).

The overriding importance of justice and rights makes them 'more absolute and imperative' than other claims, but what makes them important in the first place is their service to social utility, their ultimate ground. 'All action is for the sake of some end, and rules of action, it seems natural to suppose, must take their whole character and color from the end to which they are subservient' (1863: 402). On the utilitarian view, principles of justice, like all other moral principles, take their character and color from the end of happiness. For 'questions of ends are . . . questions about what things are desirable', and happiness is desirable, in fact 'the only thing desirable as an end', because 'people do actually desire it' (1863: 438). In this the teleological foundation and psychological assumptions of Mill's liberalism become clear.

For Kant, by contrast, the two aspects of deontology are closely connected, and his ethics and metaphysics argue powerfully against the possibility of having one without the other. Against a position such as Mill's (and that of modern-day 'rule utilitarians') the Kantian view suggests at least two compelling objections. One says that utilitarian foundations are unreliable, the other that unreliable foundations, where justice is concerned, can be coercive and unfair.

Utilitarianism is unreliable in that no merely empirical foundation, utilitarian or otherwise, can secure absolutely the primacy of justice and the sanctity of individual rights. A principle that must presuppose certain desires and inclinations can be no less conditional than the desires themselves. But our desires and the means of satisfying them typically vary, both between persons and, over time, within individual persons. And so any principle that depends on them must be similarly contingent. Thus 'all practical principles which presuppose an object (material) of the faculty of desire as the determining ground of the will are without exception empirical and can furnish no practical laws' (Kant 1788: 19). Where utility is the determining ground – even 'utility in the largest sense' – there must in principle be cases where the general welfare overrides justice rather than secures it.

Mill in effect concedes the point, but would question whether justice should be *that* unconditionally privileged anyhow. He acknowledges that the utilitarian account does not make justice absolutely prior, that there may be particular cases 'in which some other social duty is so important as to overrule any one of the general maxims of justice' (1863: 469). But if, by this qualification, the happiness of mankind is advanced, what grounds could there be for affirming the primacy of justice more completely?[1]

Kant's answer would be that even exceptions in the name of human happiness must be rejected, for the failure to affirm absolutely the primacy of justice leads to unfairness and coercion. Even if the desire for happiness were universally shared, it could not serve as basis for the moral law. Persons would still differ in their conceptions of what happiness consists in, and to install any particular conception as regulative would impose on some the conceptions of others, and so deny at least to some the freedom to advance their own conceptions. It would create a society where some were coerced by the values of others, rather than one where the needs of each harmonized with the ends of all. 'Men have different views on the empirical end of happiness and what it consists of, so that as far as happiness is concerned, their will cannot be brought under any common principle nor thus under any external law harmonizing with the freedom of everyone' (Kant 1793: 73–4).

For Kant, the priority of right is 'derived entirely from the concept of *freedom* in the mutual external relationships of human beings, and has nothing to do with the end which all men have by nature (i.e. the aim of achieving happiness) or with the recognized means of attaining this end' (1793: 73). As such, it must have a basis prior to all empirical ends. Even a union founded on some common end which all members share will not do. Only a union 'as an end in itself which they all ought to share and which is thus an absolute and primary duty in all external relationships whatsoever among human beings' can

---

1 Mill goes on to claim that justice just *is* whatever utility requires. Where the general maxims of justice are outweighed, 'we usually say, not that justice must give way to some other moral principle, but that what is just in ordinary cases is, by reason of that other principle, not just in the particular case. By this useful accommodation of language, the character of indefeasibility attributed to justice is kept up, and we are saved from the necessity of maintaining that there can be laudable injustice' (1863: 469).

secure justice and avoid the coercion of some by the convictions of others. Only in such a union can no one 'compel me to be happy in accordance with his conception of the welfare of others' (1793: 73–4). Only when I am governed by principles that do not presuppose any particular ends am I free to pursue my own ends consistent with a similar freedom for all.

On the Kantian view, the two strands of the deontological ethic hang together. The moral priority of justice is made possible (and necessary) by its foundational priority. Justice is more than just another value, because its principles are independently derived. Unlike other practical principles, the moral law is not implicated in advance in various contingent interests and ends; it does not presuppose any particular conception of the good. Given its basis prior to all merely empirical ends, justice stands privileged with respect to the good, and sets its bounds.

But this raises the question what the basis of the right could possibly be. If it must be a basis prior to all purposes and ends, unconditioned even by 'the special circumstances of human nature' (1785: 92), where could such a basis conceivably be found? Given the stringent demands of the deontological ethic, the moral law would seem almost to require a foundation in nothing, for any material precondition would undermine its priority. 'Duty!' asks Kant at his most lyrical, 'What origin is there worthy of thee, and where is to be found the root of thy noble descent which proudly rejects all kinship with the inclinations?' (1788: 89).

His answer is that the basis of the moral law is to be found in the subject, not the object of practical reason, a subject capable of an autonomous will. No empirical end but rather 'a subject of ends, namely a rational being himself, must be made the ground for all maxims of action' (1785: 105). Nothing other than 'the subject of all possible ends himself' can give rise to the right, for only this subject is also the subject of an autonomous will. Only such a subject could be that 'something which elevates man above himself as a part of the world of sense' and enables him to participate in an ideal, unconditioned realm wholly independent of our social and psychological inclinations. And only this thoroughgoing independence can afford us the detachment we need if we are ever freely to choose for ourselves, unconditioned by the contingencies of circumstance. On the deontological view, what matters above all is not the ends we choose but our capacity to choose them. And this capacity, being prior to any particular end it may affirm, resides in the subject. 'It is nothing else than personality, i.e., the freedom and independence from the mechanism of nature regarded as a capacity of a being which is subject to special laws (pure practical laws given by its own reason)' (1788: 89).

The concept of a subject given prior to and independent of its objects offers a foundation for the moral law that, unlike merely empirical foundations, awaits neither teleology nor psychology. In this way, it powerfully completes the deontological vision. As the right is prior to the good, so the subject is prior to its ends. For Kant, these parallel priorities explain 'once and for all the reasons which occasion all the confusions of philosophers concerning the supreme principle of morals. For they sought an object of the will in order to make it into the material and the foundation of a law.' But this was bound to leave their first principles mired in heteronomy. 'Instead, they should have looked for a law which directly determined the will a priori and only then sought the object suitable to it' (1788: 66). Had they done so, they would have arrived at the distinction between a subject and an object of practical reason, and thus a basis of right independent of any particular object.

If the claim for the primacy of justice is to succeed, if the right is to be prior to the good in the interlocking moral and foundational senses we have distinguished, then some version of the claim for the primacy of the subject must succeed as well. This much seems clear. What remains to be shown is whether this last claim can be defended. How do we know that there is any such subject, identifiable apart from and prior to the objects it seeks? This question assumes special interest once it is recalled that the claim for the priority of the subject is not an empirical claim. If it were, it could hardly do the work that recommends it to the deontological ethic in the first place.

THE TRANSCENDENTAL SUBJECT

Kant offers two arguments in support of his notion of the subject – one epistemological, the other practical. Both are forms of 'transcendental' arguments, in that they proceed by seeking out the presuppositions of certain apparently indispensable features of our experience. The epistemological argument inquires into the presuppositions of self-knowledge. It begins with the thought that I cannot know

everything there is to know about myself just by looking, or intro-
specting. For when I introspect, all I can see are the deliverances of
my senses; I can know myself only *qua* object of experience, as
the bearer of this or that desire, inclination, aim, disposition, and so
on. But this kind of self-knowledge is bound to be limited. For it can
never enable me to get behind the stream of appearances to see
what they are appearances *of*. 'So far as man is acquainted with himself by inner sensation . . . he cannot claim to know what he is in himself' (Kant 1785: 119). Introspection, or 'inner sense' alone, could
never deliver knowledge of anything standing behind these appearances, for any such deliverance would instantly dissolve into yet
another appearance. None the less, we must presume something further. 'Beyond this character of himself as a subject made up, as it is, of
mere appearances he must suppose there to be something else which
is its ground – namely his Ego as this may be constituted in itself' (Kant
1785: 119).

This something further, which we cannot know empirically but
must none the less presuppose as the condition of knowing anything
at all, is the subject itself. The subject is the something 'back there',
antecedent to any particular experience, that unifies our diverse perceptions and holds them together in a single consciousness. It provides the principle of unity without which our self-perceptions would
be nothing more than a stream of disconnected and everchanging
representations, the perceptions of no one. And while we cannot
grasp this principle empirically, we must presume its validity if we are
to make sense of self-knowledge at all.

The thought that the representations given in intuition one and all
belong to me, is therefore equivalent to the thought that I unite them in
one self-consciousness, or can at least so unite them; and although this
thought is not itself the consciousness of the *synthesis* of the representations, it presupposes the possibility of that synthesis. In other words, only
in so far as I can grasp the manifold of the representations in one consciousness, do I call them one and all *mine*. For otherwise I should have
as many-coloured and diverse a self as I have representations of which I
am conscious to myself (Kant 1787: 154).

The discovery that I must understand myself as a subject as well as
an object of experience suggests two different ways of conceiving the
laws that govern my actions. It thus leads from the epistemological

argument to a further, practical argument for the priority of the subject. *Qua* object of experience, I belong to the sensible world; my actions are determined, as the movements of all other objects are determined, by the laws of nature and the regularities of cause and effect. *Qua* subject of experience, by contrast, I inhabit an intelligible or super-sensible world; here, being independent of the laws of nature, I am capable of autonomy, capable of acting according to a law I give myself.

Only from this second standpoint can I regard myself as free, 'for to be independent of determination by causes in the sensible world (and this is what reason must always attribute to itself) is to be free' (Kant 1785: 120). Were I wholly an empirical being, I would not be capable of freedom, for every exercise of will would be conditioned by the desire for some object. All choice would be heteronomous choice, governed by the pursuit of some end. My will could never be a first cause, only the effect of some prior cause, the instrument of one or another impulse or inclination. In so far as we think of ourselves as free, we cannot think of ourselves as merely empirical beings. 'When we think of ourselves as free, we transfer ourselves into the intelligible world as members and recognize the autonomy of the will' (Kant 1785: 121). And so the notion of a subject prior to and independent of experience, such as the deontological ethic requires, appears not only possible but indispensable, a necessary presupposition of the possibility of self-knowledge and of freedom.

We can now see more clearly what, on the deontological ethic, the claim for the primacy of justice consists in. On the Kantian view, the priority of right is both moral and foundational. It is grounded in the concept of a subject given prior to its ends, a concept held indispensable to our understanding ourselves as freely choosing, autonomous beings. Society is best arranged when it is governed by principles that do not presuppose any particular conception of the good, for any other arrangement would fail to respect persons as beings capable of choice; it would treat them as objects rather than subjects, as means rather than ends in themselves.

Deontological themes find similar expression in much contemporary liberal thought. Thus 'the rights secured by justice are not subject to the calculus of social interests' (Rawls 1971: 4), but instead 'function as trump cards held by individuals' (Dworkin 1978: 136) against policies that would impose some particular vision of the good on society as a whole. 'Since the citizens of a society differ in their conceptions', the government fails to respect them as equals 'if it prefers one conception to the other, either because the officials believe that one is intrinsically superior, or because one is held by the more numerous or more powerful group' (Dworkin 1978: 127). By comparison with the good, the concepts of right and wrong 'have an independent and overriding status because they establish our basic position as freely choosing entities'. More important than any choice, the value of personhood 'is the presupposition and substrate of the very concept of choice. And that is why the norms surrounding respect for person may not be compromised, why these norms are absolute in respect to the various ends we choose to pursue' (Fried 1978: 8–9, 29).

By virtue of its independence from ordinary psychological and teleological assumptions, this liberalism, at least in its contemporary versions, typically presents itself as immune from most controversies to which political theories have traditionally been vulnerable, especially on questions of human nature and the meaning of the good life. Thus it is claimed that 'liberalism does not rest on any special theory of personality' (Dworkin 1978: 142), that its key assumptions involve 'no particular theory of human motivation' (Rawls 1971: 129), that 'liberals, as such, are indifferent' to the ways of life individuals choose to pursue (Dworkin 1978; 143), and that, in order to accept liberalism, one 'need not take a position upon a host of Big Questions of a highly controversial character' (Ackerman 1980: 361).

But if certain 'big questions' of philosophy and psychology are beside the point for deontological liberalism, it is only because it locates its controversy elsewhere. As we have seen, this liberalism avoids reliance on any particular theory of the person, at least in the traditional sense of attributing to all human beings a determinate nature, or certain essential desires and inclinations, such as selfishness or sociability, for example. But there is another sense in which this liberalism does imply a certain theory of the person. It concerns not the object of human desires but the subject of desire, and how this subject is constituted.

For justice to be primary, certain things must be true of us. We must be creatures of a certain kind, related to human circumstance in a certain way. In particular, we must stand to our circumstance always at a certain distance, conditioned to be sure, but part of us always antecedent to any conditions. Only in this way can we view ourselves as subjects as well as objects of experience, as agents and not just instruments of the purposes we pursue. Deontological liberalism supposes that we can, indeed must, understand ourselves as independent in this sense. I shall argue that we cannot, and that, in the partiality of this self-image, the limits of justice can be found. Where, then, does the deontological theory of the person go wrong? How do its shortcomings undermine the primacy of justice, and what rival virtue appears when the limits of justice are found? These are the questions this essay seeks to answer. To set the stage for my argument it will be helpful first to consider two other challenges that might be made to the Kantian view.

THE SOCIOLOGICAL OBJECTION

The first might be called the sociological objection, for it begins by emphasizing the pervasive influence of social conditions in shaping individual values and political arrangements. It claims that liberalism is wrong because neutrality is impossible, and that neutrality is impossible because try as we might we can never wholly escape the effects of our conditioning. All political orders thus embody *some* values; the question is *whose* values prevail, and who gains and loses as a result. The vaunted independence of the deontological subject is a liberal illusion. It misunderstands the fundamentally 'social' nature of man, the fact that we are conditioned beings 'all the way down'. There is no point of exemption, no transcendental subject capable of standing outside society or outside experience. We are at every moment what we have become, a concatenation of desires and inclinations with nothing left over to inhabit a noumenal realm. The priority of the subject can only mean the priority of the individual, thus biasing the conception in favor of individualistic values familiar to the liberal tradition. Justice only *appears* primary because this individualism typically gives rise to conflicting claims. The limits of justice would therefore consist in the possibility of cultivating those co-operative virtues, such as altruism and benevolence, that render conflict less pressing. But these are precisely the virtues least likely to flourish in a society founded on individualistic assumptions. In short, the ideal of a society governed by neutral principles is liberalism's false promise. It affirms individualistic values while pretending to a neutrality which can never be achieved.

But the sociological objection fails in various ways to appreciate the force of the deontological view. First, it misunderstands the neutrality this liberalism claims to offer. What is neutral about the principles of right is not that they admit all possible values and ends but rather that they are derived in a way that does not depend on any particular values or ends. To be sure, once the principles of justice, thus derived, are on hand, they rule out certain ends – they would hardly be *regulative* if they were incompatible with *nothing* – but only those that are unjust, that is, only those inconsistent with principles which do not themselves depend for their validity on the validity of any particular way of life. Their neutrality describes their foundation, not their effect.

But even their effect is in important ways less restrictive than the sociological objection suggests. Altruism and benevolence, for example, are wholly compatible with this liberalism, and there is nothing in its assumptions to discourage their cultivation. The priority of the subject does not say that we are governed by self-interest, only that whatever interests we have must be the interests of some subject. From the standpoint of the right, I am free to seek my own good or the good of others, so long as I do not act unjustly. And this restriction has not to do with egoism or altruism but rather with the overriding interest in assuring a similar liberty for others. The co-operative virtues are in no way inconsistent with this liberalism.

Finally, it is unclear how the sociological objection proposes to deny the deontological notion of independence. If it means to offer a psychological objection, then it cannot reach the deontological view, which makes an epistemological claim. The independence of the subject does not mean that I can, as a psychological matter, summon at any moment the detachment required to overcome my prejudices or step outside my convictions, but rather that my values and ends do not define my identity, that I must regard myself as the bearer of a self distinct from my values and ends, whatever they may be.

If, on the other hand, the sociological objection means to challenge this epistemological claim, it is unclear what the basis for this challenge could be. Hume perhaps came closest to portraying a wholly empirically conditioned self, such as the sociological view requires, when he described the self as 'a bundle or collection of different perceptions, which succeed each other with an inconceivable rapidity, and are in a perpetual flux and movement' (1739: 252). But as Kant would later argue, 'no fixed and abiding self can present itself in this flux of inner appearances'. To make sense of the continuity of the self through time, we must presume some principle of unity which 'precedes all experience, and makes experience itself possible' (1781: 136). Indeed Hume himself anticipated this difficulty when he admitted that he could not in the end account for those principles 'that unite our successive perceptions in our thought or consciousness' (1739: 636). Problematic though the Kantian transcendental subject may be, the sociological objection seems ill-equipped to offer an effective critique. The epistemology it must presuppose is hardly more plausible.

DEONTOLOGY WITH A HUMEAN FACE

The second challenge poses a deeper difficulty with the Kantian subject. Like the first, it comes from an empiricist direction. But unlike the first, it seeks to secure deontological liberalism rather than oppose it. In fact this second challenge is less an objection to the Kantian view than a sympathetic reformulation. It embraces the priority of the right over the good, and even affirms the priority of the self over its ends. Where this view departs from Kant is in denying that a prior and independent self can only be a transcendental, or noumenal subject, lacking altogether an empirical foundation. This 'revisionist' deontology captures the spirit of much contemporary liberalism, and finds its fullest expression in the work of John Rawls. 'To develop a viable Kantian conception of justice,' he writes, 'the force and content of Kant's doctrine must be detached from its background in transcendental idealism' and recast within the 'canons of a reasonable empiricism' (Rawls 1977: 165).

For Rawls, the Kantian conception suffers from obscurity and arbitrariness, for it is unclear how an abstract, disembodied subject could without arbitrariness produce determinate principles of justice, or how in any case the legislation of such a subject would apply to actual human beings in the phenomenal world. The idealist metaphysic, for all its moral and political advantage, cedes too much to the transcendent, and in positing a noumenal realm wins for justice its primacy only at the cost of denying it its human situation.

And so Rawls takes as his project to preserve Kant's deontological teaching by replacing Germanic obscurities with a domesticated metaphysic less vulnerable to the charge of arbitrariness and more congenial to the Anglo-American temper. His proposal is to derive first principles from a hypothetical choice situation (the 'original position'), characterized by conditions meant to yield a determinate outcome fit for actual human beings. Not the kingdom of ends but the ordinary circumstances of justice – as borrowed from Hume – prevail there. Not an ever-receding moral future but a present firmly planted in human circumstance provides justice its occasion. If deontology be the result, it will be deontology with a Humean face.[2]

The theory of justice tries to present a natural procedural rendering of Kant's conception of the kingdom of ends, and of the notions of autonomy and the categorical imperative. In this way the underlying structure of Kant's doctrine is detached from its metaphysical surroundings so that it can be seen more clearly and presented relatively free from objection (264).[3]

Whether Kant's metaphysics are detachable 'surroundings' or inescapable presuppositions of the moral and political aspirations Kant and Rawls share – in short, whether Rawls can have liberal politics without metaphysical embarrassment – is one of the central issues posed by Rawls' conception. This essay argues that Rawls' attempt does not succeed, and that deontological liberalism cannot be rescued from the difficulties associated with the Kantian subject. Deontology with a Humean face either fails as deontology or recreates in the original position the disembodied subject it resolves to avoid. Justice cannot be primary in the deontological sense, because we cannot coherently regard ourselves as the kind of beings the deontological ethic – whether Kantian or Rawlsian – requires us to be. But attending to this liberalism is of more than critical interest alone. For Rawls' attempt to situate the deontological self, properly reconstructed, carries us beyond deontology to a conception of community that marks the limits of justice and locates the incompleteness of the liberal ideal.

2 I am indebted to Mark Hulbert for suggesting this phrase.
3 All page numbers given alone in round brackets refer to Rawls 1971. *A Theory of Justice*, Oxford.

Justice and the Moral Subject

Like Kant, Rawls is a deontological liberal. His book takes the main thesis of the deontological ethic as its central claim. That this claim has received little direct discussion in the voluminous critical literature on *A Theory of Justice* may attest to its fixed place in the moral and political assumptions of the time. It concerns not the principles of justice but the status of justice itself. It is the assertion that both opens the book and concludes it, the core conviction Rawls seeks above all to defend. It is the claim that 'justice is the first virtue of social institutions', the single most important consideration in assessing the basic structure of society and the overall direction of social change.

Justice is the first virtue of social institutions, as truth is of systems of thought. A theory however elegant and economical must be rejected or revised if it is untrue; likewise laws and institutions no matter how efficient and well-arranged must be reformed or abolished if they are unjust. . . . Being first virtues of human activities, truth and justice are uncompromising (3–4).

I have tried to set forth a theory that enables us to understand and to assess these feelings about the primacy of justice. Justice as fairness is the outcome: it articulates these opinions and supports their general tendency (586).

It is this claim for the primacy of justice that I propose to examine.

THE PRIMACY OF JUSTICE AND THE PRIORITY OF THE SELF

Now the primacy of justice is a powerful claim, and there is a danger that the familiarity of the thought is apt to blind us to its boldness. To understand why it is intuitively appealing but at the same time deeply puzzling and problematic, we might consider the following reconstruction of the claim, designed to capture both its familiarity and its force: justice is not merely one important value among others, to be weighed and considered as the occasion requires, but rather the *means* by which values are weighed and assessed. It is in this sense the 'value of values',[1] so to speak, not subject itself to the same kind of trade-offs as the values it regulates. Justice is the standard by which conflicting values are reconciled and competing conceptions of the good accommodated if not always resolved. As such, it must have a certain priority with respect to those values and those goods. No conception of the good could possibly defeat the requirements of justice, for these requirements are of a qualitatively different order; their validity is established in a different way. With respect to social values generally, justice stands detached and aloof, as a fair decision procedure stands aloof from the claims of the disputants before it.

But what exactly is the sense in which justice, as the arbiter of values, 'must' be prior with respect to them? One sense of this priority is a *moral* 'must' which emerges from Rawls' critique of utilitarian ethics. From this point of view, the priority of justice is a requirement of the essential plurality of the human species and the integrity of the individuals who comprise it. To sacrifice justice for the sake of the general good is to violate the inviolable, to fail to respect the distinction between persons.

Each person possesses an inviolability founded on justice that even the welfare of society as a whole cannot override. For this reason justice denies that the loss of freedom for some is made right by a greater good shared by others. It does not allow that the sacrifices imposed on a few are outweighed by the larger sum of advantages enjoyed by many. Therefore in a just society the liberties of equal citizenship are taken as settled; the rights secured by justice are not subject to political bargaining or to the calculus of social interests (3–4).

But there is another sense in which justice 'must' be prior to the values it appraises – prior in the sense of independently derived – and this has to do with a problematic feature of standards of judgment generally. It is an epistemological rather than a moral requirement, and arises from the problem of distinguishing a standard of assessment from the thing being assessed. As Rawls insists, we need an 'Archimedean point' from which to assess the basic structure of society. The

---

1 The phrase is that of Alexander Bickel, who attributes to law a primacy comparable to the status accorded justice here. 'The irreducible value, though not the exclusive one, is the idea of law. Law is more than just another opinion; not because it embodies all right values ... but because it is the value of values. Law is the principal institution through which a society can assert its values' (1975: 5).

problem is to give an account of where such a point could conceivably be found. Two possibilities seem to present themselves, each equally unsatisfactory: if the principles of justice are derived from the values or conceptions of the good current in the society, there is no assurance that the critical standpoint they provide is any more valid than the conceptions they would regulate, since, as a product of those values, justice would be subject to the same contingencies. The alternative would seem a standard somehow external to the values and interests prevailing in society. But if our experience were disqualified entirely as the source of such principles, the alternative would seem to be reliance on a priori assumptions whose credentials would appear equally suspect, although for opposite reasons. Where the first would be arbitrary because contingent, the second would be arbitrary because groundless. Where justice derives from existing values, the standards of appraisal blur with the objects of appraisal and there is no sure way of picking out the one from the other. Where justice is given by a priori principles, there is no sure way of connecting them up.

These then are the perplexing and difficult demands of the Archimedean point – to find a standpoint neither compromised by its implication in the world nor dissociated and so disqualified by detachment. 'We need a conception that enables us to envision our objective from afar' (22), but not *too* far; the desired standpoint is 'not a perspective from a certain place beyond the world, nor the point of view of a transcendent being; rather it is a certain form of thought and feeling that rational persons can adopt within the world' (587).

Before we consider Rawls' response to this challenge, it may be worth noting how Rawls' case for the primacy of justice is related to several parallel claims throughout his theory which, taken together, reveal a structure of argument characteristic of the deontological ethic as a whole. Closely tied to the primacy of justice is the more general notion of the priority of the right over the good. Like the primacy of justice, the priority of the right over the good appears initially as a first-order moral claim, in opposition to utilitarian doctrine, but comes ultimately to assume a certain meta-ethical status as well, particularly when Rawls argues more generally for deontological ethical theories as opposed to teleological ones.

As a straightforward moral claim the priority of right over good means that principles of right invariably outweigh considerations of welfare or the satisfaction of desire, however intense, and constrain in advance the range of desires and values properly entitled to satisfaction.

The principles of right, and so of justice, put limits on which satisfactions have value; they impose restrictions on what are reasonable conceptions of one's good. . . . We can express this by saying that in justice as in fairness the concept of right is prior to that of the good. . . . The priority of justice is accounted for, in part, by holding that the interests requiring the violation of justice have no value. Having no merit in the first place, they cannot override its claim (31).

In justice as fairness, unlike utilitarianism, the individual's right to equal liberty in the face of majority preferences to the contrary is unconditionally affirmed.

The intense convictions of the majority, if they are indeed mere preferences without any foundation in the principles of justice antecedently established, have no weight to begin with. The satisfaction of these feelings has no value that can be put in the scales against the claims of equal liberty. . . . Against these principles neither the intensity of feeling nor its being shared by the majority counts for anything. On the contract view, then, the grounds of liberty are completely separate from existing preferences (450).

Although Rawls argues first against utilitarian conceptions, his overall project is more ambitious, for justice as fairness stands not only against utilitarianism, but against all teleological theories as such. As a second-order, meta-ethical claim, the priority of right means that, of the 'two concepts of ethics', the right is derived independently from the good, rather than the other way around. This foundational priority allows the right to stand aloof from prevailing values and conceptions of the good, and makes Rawls' conception deontological rather than teleological (24–5, 30).

One of the first-order consequences of the deontological ethic is a firmer foundation for the equal liberty of individuals than could be available on teleological assumptions. In this, the importance of deontology to familiar liberal concerns most clearly appears. Where the right is instrumental to the advancement of some end held to be prior, the denial of liberty for some may be justified in the name of an overriding good for others. The liberties of equal citizenship are thus 'insecure when founded upon teleological principles. The argument for them relies upon precarious calculations as well as controversial and uncertain premises' (211). On the deontological view, 'equal liberties have a different basis altogether'. No longer mere means for maximizing satisfactions or realizing some overriding aim, 'these rights are assigned to fulfill the principles of co-operation that citizens would acknowledge when each is fairly represented as a moral person' (211), as an end in himself.

But the failure to secure the rights of equal liberty betrays a deeper flaw in the teleological conception. In Rawls' view, teleology confuses the relation of the right to the good because it misconceives the relation of the self to its ends. This leads Rawls to assert yet another deontological priority. Teleology to the contrary, what is most essential to our personhood is not the ends we choose but our capacity to choose them. And this capacity is located in a self which must be prior to the ends it chooses.

The structure of teleological doctrines is radically misconceived; from the start they relate the right and the good in the wrong way. We should not attempt to give form to our life by first looking to the good independently defined. It is not our aims that primarily reveal our nature but rather the principles that we would acknowledge to govern the background conditions under which these aims are to be formed and the manner in which they are to be pursued. *For the self is prior to the ends which are affirmed by it;* even a dominant end must be chosen from among numerous possibilities. . . . We should therefore reverse the relation between the right and the good proposed by teleological doctrines and view the right as prior. The moral theory is then developed by working in the opposite direction [emphasis added] (560).

The priority of the self over its ends means that I am not merely the passive receptacle of the accumulated aims, attributes, and purposes thrown up by experience, not simply a product of the vagaries of circumstance, but always, irreducibly, an active, willing agent, distinguishable from my surroundings, and capable of choice. To identify any set of characteristics as *my* aims, ambitions, desires, and so on, is always to imply some subject 'me' standing behind them, and the shape of this 'me' must be given prior to any of the ends or attributes I bear. As Rawls writes, 'even a dominant end must be chosen from among numerous possibilities'. And before an end can be chosen, there must be a self around to choose it.

But what exactly is the sense in which the self, as an agent of choice, 'must' be prior to the ends it chooses? One sense of the priority is a moral 'must' which reflects the imperative to respect above all the autonomy of the individual, to regard the human person as the bearer of a dignity beyond the roles that he inhabits and the ends he may pursue. But there is another sense in which the self 'must' be prior to the ends it affirms – prior in the sense of independently identifiable – and this is an epistemological requirement.

Here the account of the self reproduces the perplexities we encountered in the case of justice. There, we needed a standpoint of appraisal independent of prevailing social values. In the case of the person, we need a notion of the subject independent of its contingent wants and aims. As the priority of justice arose from the need to distinguish the standard of appraisal from the society being appraised, the priority of the self arises from the parallel need to distinguish the subject from its situation. Although this account is not offered by Rawls himself, I believe it to be implicit in his theory, and a reasonable reconstruction of the perplexities he seeks to address.

If all the self consisted in were a concatenation of various contingent desires, wants, and ends, there would be no non-arbitrary way, either for the self or for some outside observer, to identify *these* desires, interests, and ends, as the desires of any particular subject. Rather than be *of* the subject, they would *be* the subject. But the subject they would *be* would be indistinguishable from the sea of undifferentiated attributes of an unarticulated situation, which is to say it would be no subject at all, at least no subject we could recognize or pick out as resembling a human person.

Any theory of the self of the form 'I *am x, y,* and *z*', rather than 'I *have x, y,* and *z*', (where *x, y,* and *z* are desires, etc.) collapses the distance between subject and situation which is necessary to any coherent conception of a particular human subject. This space, or measure of detachment, is essential to the ineliminably *possessive* aspect of any coherent conception of the self. The possessive aspect of the self means that I can never fully be constituted by my attributes, that there must always be some attributes I *have* rather than am. Otherwise, just *any* change in my situation, however slight, would change the person I am. But taken literally, and given that my situation changes in some respect at least with every passing moment, this would mean that my identity would blur indistinguishably into 'my' situation. Without some distinction between the subject and the object of possession, it becomes impossible to distinguish what is me from what is mine, and we are left with what might be called a *radically situated subject*.

Now a radically situated subject is inadequate to the notion of the person in the same way a standard of appraisal thoroughly implicated in existing values is inadequate to the notion of justice; the impulse to priority reflected in the search for an Archimedean point is the response to both predicaments.

But in both cases, the alternatives are seriously constrained, the possible sites for the Archimedean point severely restricted. In the case of justice, the alternative to a situated conception would seem an appeal beyond experience to a priori principles. But this would be to assert the desired priority with a vengeance, and would achieve the necessary detachment only at the price of arbitrariness. A similar difficulty arises in the case of the subject. For a self totally detached from its empirically given features would seem no more than a kind of abstract consciousness (conscious of what?), a radically situated subject given way to a radically disembodied one. Here again, 'we need a conception that enables us to envision our objective from afar', but not so far that our objective fades from view and our vision dissolves into abstraction.

Thus we can see, in rough outline at least, how the argument hangs together, how the primacy of justice, the rejection of teleology, and the priority of the self are related, and finally, how these claims lend support to familiar liberal positions. The connection between the meta-ethical view and the conception of the self can be seen in the fact that teleological and deontological conceptions account for the unity of the self in different ways. Where, according to Rawls, teleological conceptions suppose that the unity of the self is achieved in the course of experience – in the case of hedonism, through maximizing the sum of pleasurable experiences within its 'psychic boundaries' (561) – justice as fairness reverses this perspective and conceives the unity of the self as something antecedently established, fashioned prior to the choices it makes in the course of its experience.

The parties [in the original position] regard moral personality and not the capacity for pleasure and pain as the fundamental aspect of the self. . . . The main idea is that given the priority of right, the choice of our conception of the good is framed within definite limits. . . . *The essential unity of the self is already provided by the conception of right* [emphasis added] (563).

Here, as in the case of equal liberty and the priority of right discussed above, deontological assumptions can be seen to generate familiar liberal conclusions and to ground them more firmly than traditional empiricist or utilitarian metaphysics allowed. The theme common to much classical liberal doctrine that emerges from the deontological account of the unity of the self is the notion of the human subject as a sovereign agent of choice, a creature whose ends are chosen rather than given, who comes by his aims and purposes by acts of will, as opposed, say, to acts of cognition. 'Thus a moral person is a subject with ends he has chosen, and his fundamental preference is for conditions that enable him to frame a mode of life that expresses his nature as a free and equal rational being as fully as circumstances permit' (561).

The antecedent unity of the self means that the subject, however heavily conditioned by his surroundings, is always, irreducibly, prior to his values and ends, and never fully constituted by them. Though there may be times when conditions are formidable and choices few, man's sovereign agency as such is not dependent on any particular conditions of existence, but guaranteed in advance. On the deontological conception, we could never be so thoroughly conditioned that our self became fully constituted by our situation, our ends fully determined in such a way that the self ceased to be prior with respect to them. The consequences of such a view for politics and justice are considerable. As long as it is assumed that man is by nature a being who chooses his ends rather than a being, as the ancients conceived him, who discovers his ends, then his fundamental preference must necessarily be for conditions of choice rather than, say, for conditions of self-knowledge.

The full force of the claim for the primacy of justice in both its moral and epistemological dimensions can more clearly be appreciated in the light of Rawls' discussion of the self. Since the self owes its constitution, its antecedent status, to the concept of right, we can only express our true nature when we act out of a sense of justice. This is why the sense of justice cannot be regarded as merely one desire among others but must be seen as a motivation of a qualitatively higher order, why justice is not merely one important value among others but truly the first virtue of social institutions.

The desire to express our nature as a free and equal rational being can be fulfilled only by acting on the principles of right and justice as having first priority. . . . It is acting from this precedence that expresses our freedom from contingency and happenstance. Therefore in order to realize our nature we have no alternative but to plan to preserve our sense of justice as governing our other aims. This sentiment cannot be fulfilled if it is compromised and balanced against other ends as but one desire among the rest. It is a desire to conduct oneself in a certain way above all else, a striving that contains within itself its own priority (574).

What we cannot do is express our nature by following a plan that views the sense of justice as but one desire to be weighed against others. For this sentiment reveals what the person is, and to compromise it is not to achieve for the self free reign but to give way to the contingencies and accidents of the world (575).

The connection between the primacy of justice and other central features of Rawls' conception – the priority of right, the deontological meta-ethic, and the antecedent unity of the self – reveals something of the overall structure of Rawls' theory, and indicates how deep and powerful a claim the primacy of justice is intended to be. It also suggests how this cluster of assertions, if they can be defended, provides an impressive foundation, at once moral and epistemological, for certain central liberal doctrines. We have sought to understand these claims and to clarify their connections by seeing them as answers to perplexities posed by two related reconstructions; the first seeks a standard of appraisal neither compromised by existing standards nor arbitrarily given, and the second seeks an account of the self as neither radically situated and therefore indistinguishable from its surroundings nor radically disembodied and therefore purely formal. Each reconstruction poses a set of unacceptable alternatives and requires for its solution a kind of Archimedean point that manages to detach itself from the contingent without lapsing into arbitrariness.

To this point, Rawls' project looks much like Kant's. But notwithstanding their roughly common agenda and deontological affinities, Rawls' proposed solution departs radically from Kant's. The difference reflects Rawls' concern to establish the required deontological priorities – including the priority of the self – without recourse to a transcendent or otherwise disembodied subject. This contrast assumes special interest given that Kant's idealism – the dimension

Rawls seeks above all to avoid – would lead much nineteenth- and twentieth-century Continental philosophy in a direction largely alien to the Anglo-American tradition of moral and political thought in which Rawls' work is firmly installed.

For Kant, the priority of right, or the supremacy of the moral law, and the unity of the self, or the synthetic unity of apperception, could only be established by means of a transcendental deduction and the positing of a noumenal or intelligible realm as the necessary presupposition of our capacity for freedom and self-knowledge. Rawls rejects Kant's metaphysics, but believes he can preserve their moral force 'within the scope of an empirical theory' (Rawls 1979: 18). This is the role of the original position.

LIBERALISM WITHOUT METAPHYSICS: THE ORIGINAL POSITION

The original position is Rawls' answer to Kant; it is his alternative to the route represented by the *Critique of Pure Reason* and the key to Rawls' solution to the perplexities we have considered. It is the original position that 'enables us to envisage our objective from afar', but not so far as to land us in the realm of transcendence. It aims to satisfy these demands by describing an initial situation of fairness and defining as just those principles that rational parties subject to its conditions would agree to.

Two crucial ingredients equip the original position to solve the dilemmas described by the reconstructions and to answer the need for an Archimedean point. Each takes the form of an assumption about the parties to the original position: one says what they do not know, the other, what they do know. What they do not know is any information that would distinguish any one of them from any other as the particular human beings they are. This is the assumption of the veil of ignorance. It means that the parties are assumed to be deprived of any knowledge of their place in society, their race, sex, or class, their wealth or fortune, their intelligence, strength, or other natural assets and abilities. Nor even do they know their conceptions of the good, their values, aims, or purposes in life. They know that they do in fact possess such conceptions and deem them worthy of advancement, whatever they are, but must choose the principles of justice in temporary ignorance of them. The purpose of this restriction is to prevent the choice of principles from being prejudiced by the contingency of natural and social circumstances, to abstract from all considerations deemed irrelevant from a moral point of view. It is the veil of ignorance that assures that the principles of justice will be chosen under conditions of equality and fairness. Since the parties to the contract are not distinguished by different interests, a further consequence of the veil of ignorance is to assure that the initial agreement be unanimous.

What the parties do know is that they, like everyone else, value certain primary social goods. Primary goods are 'things which it is supposed a rational man wants whatever else he wants', and include such things as rights and liberties, opportunities and powers, income and wealth. Regardless of a person's values, plans, or ultimate aims, it is assumed there are certain things of which he would prefer more rather than less, on the grounds that they are likely to be useful in advancing all ends, whatever ends they happen to be. So while the parties to the original position are ignorant of their particular ends, they are all assumed to be motivated by the desire for certain primary goods.

The precise content of the list of primary goods is given by what Rawls calls the thin theory of the good. It is thin in the sense that it incorporates minimal and widely shared assumptions about the kinds of things likely to be useful to all particular conceptions of the good, and therefore likely to be shared by persons whatever their more specific desires. The thin theory of the good is distinguished from the full theory of the good in that the thin theory can provide no basis for judging or choosing between various particular values or ends. So while the veil of ignorance provides that the parties deliberate in conditions of fairness and unanimity, the account of primary goods generates the minimal motivations necessary to get a problem of rational choice going, and to make possible a determinate solution. Together, the two assumptions assure that the parties act only on those interests that are common interests, that is, common to all rational persons, the foremost of which turns out to be an interest in establishing terms of social co-operation such that each person will have the fullest liberty to realize his aims and purposes compatible with an equal liberty for others.

The principles of justice emerge from the original position in what can be seen as a three-stage procedure. First comes the thin theory of the good embodied in the description of the initial choice situation.

From the thin theory are derived the two principles of justice, which define, in turn, the concept of good and provide an interpretation of such values as the good of the community. It is important to note that although the thin theory of the good is prior to the theory of right and the principles of justice, it is not substantial enough a theory to undermine the priority of the right over the good that gives the conception its deontological character. The priority of right on which the theory depends is with respect to the full theory of the good – the one having to do with particular values and ends – and the full theory of the good only appears after the principles of justice and in the light of them. As Rawls explains,

To establish [the principles of right] it is necessary to rely on some notion of goodness, for we need assumptions about the parties' motives in the original position. Since these assumptions must not jeopardize the prior place of the concept of right, the theory of the good used in arguing for the principles of justice is restricted to the bare essentials. This account of the good I call the thin theory: its purpose is to secure the premise about primary goods required to arrive at the principles of justice. Once this theory is worked out and the primary goods accounted for, we are free to use the principles of justice in the further development of what I shall call the full theory of the good (396).

This three-stage procedure seems to meet Rawls' deontological requirements in the following way: The priority of the right over the (full theory of the) good satisfies the requirement that the standard of appraisal be prior to and distinguishable from the objects of appraisal, uncompromised by implication in existing wants and desires. And the fact that the principles of right come not from nowhere but from a thin theory of the good related to actual (if very general) human desires gives the principles a determinate ground and prevents their being arbitrary and detached from the world. And so, without recourse to transcendental deductions, it seems possible to find an Archimedean point that is neither radically situated nor radically disembodied, neither 'at the mercy of existing wants and interests' nor dependent on a priori considerations.

The essential point is that despite the individualistic features of justice as fairness, *the two principles of justice are not contingent upon existing desires or present social conditions*. Thus we are able to derive a conception of a just basic structure, and an ideal of the person compatible with it, that can serve as a standard for appraising institutions and for guiding the overall direction of social change. In order to find an Archimedean point *it is not necessary to appeal to a priori or perfectionist principles.* By assuming certain general desires, such as the desire for primary social goods, and by taking as a basis the agreements that would be made in a suitably defined situation, we can achieve the requisite independence from existing circumstances [emphasis added] (263).

This, in brief, is the procedure by which the two principles of justice are derived. As Rawls notes, justice as fairness, like other contract views, consists of two parts, the first being the interpretation of the initial situation and the problem of choice posed there, the second involving the two principles of justice which, it is argued, would be agreed to. 'One may accept the first part of the theory (or some variant thereof), but not the other, and conversely' (15). Even short of taking up the actual principles of justice Rawls believes would be chosen, it is possible to identify two kinds of objections that would be likely to arise on the move from the first half of the theory to the second.

One set of objections would question whether the original position achieves genuine detachment from existing wants and desires. This sort of objection would be likely to fix on the account of primary goods or some other aspect of the thin theory of the good and argue that it is biased in favor of particular conceptions of the good and against others. It might contest Rawls' claim that the list of primary goods really is equally or nearly equally valuable to all ways of life. It might question the thinness of the thin theory of the good, claiming that it undermines the fairness of the initial situation, that it introduces assumptions not universally shared, that it is implicated too deeply in the contingent preferences of, say, Western liberal bourgeois life plans, and that the resulting principles are the product of prevailing values after all.

A second set of objections would argue, on the other hand, that the original position achieves too much detachment from human circumstances, that the initial situation it describes is too abstract to yield the principles Rawls says it would, or for that matter, any determinate principles at all. Such an objection would most likely take issue with the veil of ignorance on the grounds that it excludes morally relevant information, information necessary to generate any meaningful results. It would argue that the notion of the person embedded in the original position is too formal and abstract, too detached from contingency to account for the requisite motivations. Where the first objection complains that the thin theory of the good is too thick to be fair, the second contends that the veil of ignorance is too opaque to yield a determinate solution.

I shall not pursue either of these objections here. Given our concern with the deontological project as a whole, our interest in the original position is a more general one. Simply stated, it is this: If the original position is Rawls' answer to Kant, is it a satisfactory answer? Does it succeed in its aspiration to reformulate Kantian moral and political claims 'within the scope of an empirical theory'? Can it provide a foundation for deontological liberalism while avoiding the metaphysically contentious 'surroundings' of Kant's theory? More specifically, can the description of the original position accommodate and support the claim for the primacy of justice in the strong sense Rawls seeks to advance?

On one reading of the original position, a straightforward empiricist interpretation that Rawls himself invites, it cannot support the deontological claim. To see why this is so, we must examine its conditions more closely, in part with a view to understanding the kind of claim these conditions embody. We will not be concerned, therefore, with the question of whether the thin theory of the good is too thick or too thin to generate the principles of justice Rawls says it does, but rather with the question of what *makes* the theory of the good thick or thin, and how this account fits with the account of what *makes* justice primary. But perhaps we had best get down to examining the conditions that characterize the original position as Rawls describes them. For this we must turn to the circumstances of justice.

THE CIRCUMSTANCES OF JUSTICE: EMPIRICIST OBJECTIONS

The circumstances of justice are the conditions that engage the virtue of justice. They are the conditions that prevail in human societies and make human co-operation both possible and necessary. Society is seen as a co-operative venture for mutual advantage, which means that it is typically marked by a conflict as well as an identity of interests – an identity of interests in that all stand to gain from mutual co-operation, a conflict in that, given their divergent interests and ends, people differ over how the fruits of their cooperation are to be distributed. Principles are needed to specify arrangements by which such claims can be sorted out, and it is the role of justice to provide them. The background conditions that make such sorting-out arrangements necessary are the circumstances of justice.

Following Hume, Rawls notes that these circumstances are of two kinds – objective and subjective. The objective circumstances of justice include such facts as the moderate scarcity of resources, whereas the subjective circumstances concern the subjects of cooperation, most notably the fact that they are characterized by different interests and ends. This means that each person has a distinctive life plan, or conception of the good, which he regards as worthy of advancement. Rawls emphasizes this aspect by assuming that, as conceived in the original position at least, the parties are mutually disinterested, that they are concerned to advance their own conception of the good and no one else's, and that in advancing their ends they are not bound to each other by prior moral ties. The circumstances of justice are thus summarized:

One can say, in brief, that the circumstances of justice obtain whenever mutually disinterested persons put forward conflicting claims to the division of social advantages under conditions of moderate scarcity. Unless these circumstances existed there would be no occasion for the virtue of justice, just as in the absence of threats of injury to life and limb there would be no occasion for physical courage (128).

The circumstances of justice are the circumstances that give rise to the virtue of justice. In their absence, the virtue of justice would be nugatory; it would not be required nor for that matter even possible. 'But a human society *is* characterized by the circumstances of justice' [emphasis added] (129–30). Therefore the virtue of justice *is* required.

The conditions that occasion the virtue of justice are empirical conditions. About this Rawls is clear and unabashed. 'Moral philosophy must be free to use contingent assumptions and general facts as it pleases'. It can proceed in no other way. What matters is that the premises be 'true and sufficiently general' (51, 158).

The fundamental principles of justice quite properly depend upon the natural facts about men in society. This dependence is made explicit by the description of the original position: the decision of the parties is taken in the light of general knowledge. Moreover, the various elements of the original position presuppose many things about the circumstances of human life. . . . If these assumptions are true and suitably general, everything is in order, for without these elements the whole scheme would be pointless and empty (159, 160).

But an empiricist understanding of the original position seems deeply at odds with deontological claims. For if justice depends for its virtue on certain empirical preconditions, it is unclear how its priority could unconditionally be affirmed. Rawls says that he borrows his account of the circumstances of justice from Hume (126–8). But Hume's circumstances cannot support the priority of right in the deontological sense. They are after all empirical conditions. To establish the primacy of justice in the categorical sense Rawls' claim requires, he would have to show not only that the circumstances of justice prevail in all societies, but that they prevail to such an extent that the virtue of justice is always more fully or extensively engaged than any other virtue. Otherwise, he would be entitled to conclude only that justice is the first virtue of certain kinds of societies, namely those where conditions are such that the resolution of conflicting claims among mutually disinterested parties is the most pressing social priority.

To be sure, a sociologist might argue, for example, that given the increasing scarcity of energy and other basic resources facing modern advanced industrial societies, combined with the breakdown of consensus and the loss of common purposes (the objective and subjective circumstances respectively), the circumstances of justice have come to prevail with such intensity that justice has become, for these societies, the first virtue. But if Rawls means the primacy of justice to depend on a generalization such as this, he would need at least to provide the relevant sociological support. Just asserting that '*a* human society *is* characterized by the circumstances of justice' would not be enough [emphasis added] (129–30).

The notion that the primacy of justice could be grounded empirically becomes all the more implausible when we consider how unlikely the necessary generalization must be, at least when applied across the range of social institutions. For while we can easily enough imagine that certain large-scale associations such as the modern nation-state might meet its requirements in many cases, we can readily imagine a range of more intimate or solidaristic associations in which the values and aims of the participants coincide closely enough that the circumstances of justice prevail to a relatively small degree. As Hume himself observes, we need not have recourse to utopian visions or the fiction of poets to imagine such conditions, but 'may discover the same truth by common experience and observation' (1739: 495).

In the present disposition of the human heart, it would, perhaps, be difficult to find complete instances of such enlarged affections; but still we may observe that the case of families approaches towards it; and the stronger the mutual benevolence is among the individuals, the nearer it approaches; till all distinction of property be, in a great measure, lost and confounded among them. Between married persons, the cement of friendship is by the laws supposed so strong as to abolish all division of possessions; and has often, in reality, the force ascribed to it (1777: 17–18).

While the institution of the family may represent an extreme case in this respect, we can easily imagine a range of intermediate cases of social institutions, a continuum of human associations characterized in varying degrees by the circumstances of justice. These would include, at various points along the spectrum, tribes, neighborhoods, cities, towns, universities, trade unions, national liberation movements and established nationalisms, and a wide variety of ethnic, religious, cultural, and linguistic communities with more or less clearly defined common identities and shared purposes, precisely those attributes whose presence signifies the relative absence of the circumstances of justice. Although the circumstances of justice might well exist in all of these cases, they would not likely predominate, at least not to such an extent that justice was engaged in all cases in greater measure than any other virtue. On the empiricist interpretation of the original position, justice can be primary only for those societies beset by sufficient discord to make the accommodation of conflicting interests and aims the overriding moral and political consideration; justice is the first virtue of social institutions not absolutely, as truth is to theories, but only conditionally, as physical courage is to a war zone.

But this formulation suggests a further sense in which the primacy of justice is undermined by the empiricist account of the circumstances of justice. It fixes on the sense in which justice appears as a remedial virtue, whose moral advantage consists in the repair it works on fallen conditions. But if the virtue of justice is measured by the morally diminished conditions that are its prerequisite, then the *absence* of these conditions – however this state of affairs might be described – must embody a rival virtue of at least commensurate priority, the one that is engaged in so far as justice is not engaged. If physical courage is a virtue only in the face of injurious conditions, then the peace and tranquillity that would deny courage its occasion must surely be virtues of at least equivalent status. And so it is with justice. As Hume's account confirms, the remedial character of justice entails another set of virtues of at least a comparable order.

Justice takes it rise from human conventions . . . and these are intended as a remedy to some inconveniences, which proceed from the concurrence of certain qualities of the human mind with the situation of external objects. The qualities of the mind are selfishness and limited generosity; and the situation of external objects is their easy change, join'd to their scarcity in comparison of the wants and desires of men. . . . Encrease to a sufficient degree the benevolence of men, or the bounty of nature, and you render justice useless, by supplying its place with much nobler virtues, and more favourable blessings (1739: 494–5).

To invoke the circumstances of justice is simultaneously to concede, implicitly at least, the circumstances of benevolence, or fraternity, or of enlarged affections, whatever the description might be; such are the circumstances that prevail in so far as the circumstances of justice do not prevail, and the virtue to which they give definition must be a virtue of at least correlative status.

One consequence of the remedial aspect of justice is that we cannot say in advance whether, in any particular instance, an increase in justice is associated with an overall moral improvement. This is because a gain in justice can come about in one of two ways; it can arise where before there was injustice, or it can occur where before there was neither justice nor injustice but a sufficient measure of benevolence or fraternity such that the virtue of justice had not been extensively engaged. Where justice replaces injustice, other things being equal, the overall moral improvement is clear. On the other hand, where an increase in justice reflects some transformation in the quality of pre-existing motivations and dispositions, the overall moral balance might well be diminished.

When fraternity fades, more justice may be done, but even more may be required to restore the moral status quo. Furthermore, there is no guarantee that justice and its rival virtues are perfectly commensurable. The breakdown of certain personal and civic attachments may represent a moral loss that even a full measure of justice cannot redeem. Does it go without saying that a rent in the fabric of implicit understandings and commitments is fully morally repaired so long as everyone 'does what he ought' in the aftermath?

Consider for example a more or less ideal family situation, where relations are governed in large part by spontaneous affection and where, in consequence, the circumstances of justice prevail to a relatively small degree. Individual rights and fair decision procedures are seldom invoked, not because injustice is rampant but because their appeal is pre-empted by a spirit of generosity in which I am rarely inclined to claim my fair share. Nor does this generosity necessarily imply that I receive out of kindness a share that is equal to or greater than the share I would be entitled to under fair principles of justice. I may get less. The point is not that I get what I would otherwise get, only more spontaneously, but simply that the questions of what I get and what I am due do not loom large in the overall context of this way of life.

Now imagine that one day the harmonious family comes to be wrought with dissension. Interests grow divergent and the circumstances of justice grow more acute. The affection and spontaneity of previous days give way to demands for fairness and the observance of rights. And let us further imagine that the old generosity is replaced by a judicious temper of unexceptionable integrity and that the new moral necessities are met with a full measure of justice, such that no injustice prevails. Parents and children reflectively equilibriate, dutifully if sullenly abide by the two principles of justice, and even manage to achieve the conditions of stability and congruence so that the good of justice is realized within their household. Now what are we to make of this? Are we prepared to say that the arrival of justice, however full, restores to the situation its full moral character, and that the only difference is a psychological one? Or consider again the parallel of physical courage. Imagine a society once tranquil but with little courage (not out of cowardice but quietude), now turned violent and precarious, but where the virtue of courage is on bold, even plentiful display. Is it obvious we would prefer the second from a moral point of view?

To be sure, the incommensurabilities, if they exist, could pull in the opposite direction as well. It may be that despite the harshness of the circumstances of courage, there is a certain nobility that flourishes in the new way of life unavailable to the human spirit under more protected conditions and that this goes uncompensated by even the most blissful peace. And if the demise of familial or communal *Gemeinschaft* reflects not the onset of material meanness but the flowering of diversity, or the children outgrowing the parochial ways of their parents' home, we might be inclined to view the advent of justice in a more favorable light. The general point remains. An increase in justice can fail to be associated with an overall moral improvement in at least two different ways: either by failing fully to meet an increase in the circumstances of justice, or by an inability, however full, to compensate the loss of certain 'nobler virtues, and more favourable blessings'.

If an increase in justice does not necessarily imply an unqualified moral improvement, it can also be shown that in some cases, justice is not a virtue but a vice. This can be seen by considering what we might call the reflexive dimension of the circumstances of justice. The reflexive dimension refers to the fact that what the parties know about their condition is an ingredient of their condition. Rawls acknowledges this feature when he writes, 'I shall, of course, assume that the persons in the original position know that these circumstances of justice obtain' (128).

The circumstances of justice, and more specifically the subjective aspect of these circumstances, consist partly in the motivations of the participants and in the way they perceive their motivations. If the parties one day came to regard their circumstances differently, if they came to believe that the circumstances of justice (or of benevolence) obtained to a greater or lesser extent than before, this very shift would amount to a change in those circumstances. As Rawls points out in his discussion of the good of justice, acting out of a sense of justice can be contagious; it reinforces the assumptions it presupposes and enhances its own stability by encouraging and affirming like motivations in others.

But what is the effect of this 'contagion' when it is applied to a situation where, or in so far as, the circumstances of justice do not obtain? When I act out of a sense of justice in inappropriate circumstances, say in circumstances where the virtues of benevolence and fraternity rather than justice are relevantly engaged, my act may not merely be superfluous, but might contribute to a reorientation of prevailing understandings and motivations, thereby transforming the circumstances of justice in some degree. And this can be true even where the 'act' I perform out of justice is 'the same act' as the one I would have performed out of benevolence or fraternity, except in a different spirit. As in Rawls' account of stability, my act and the sense of justice that informs it have the self-fulfilling effect of bringing about the conditions under which they *would* have been appropriate. But in the case of the inappropriate act of justice, the result is to render the circumstances of justice more pressing without necessarily evoking an increase in the incidence of justice to a similar degree.

Gratuitous displays of physical courage in the midst of tranquil conditions can prove disruptive of the very tranquillity they fail to appreciate and quite possibly can fail to replace. It is similar with justice. If, out of a misplaced sense of justice, a close friend of long standing repeatedly insists on calculating and paying his precise share of every common expenditure, or refuses to accept any favor or hospitality except at the greatest protest and embarrassment, not only will I feel compelled to be reciprocally scrupulous but at some point may begin to wonder whether I have not misunderstood our relationship. The circumstances of benevolence will to this extent have diminished, and the circumstances of justice grown. This follows as a consequence of the reflexive dimension of the (subjective aspect of the) circumstances of justice. But as we have already seen, there is no guarantee that the new sense of justice can fully replace the old spontaneity, even in those cases where no injustice results. Since the exercise of justice in inappropriate conditions will have brought about an overall decline in the moral character of the association, justice in this case will have been not a virtue but a vice.

So the circumstances of justice fit badly with the primacy of justice and the related deontological themes Rawls seeks to defend. Given the contrasting philosophical pedigrees of the two accounts, it is little wonder that the inconsistencies arise. Where the circumstances of justice are explicitly Humean – 'Hume's account of them is especially perspicuous and the preceding summary adds nothing essential to his much fuller discussion' (127–8) – the deontological conception at the heart of Rawls' theory finds its primary formulation in Kant, whose epistemology and ethics were directed in large part against the very empiricist and utilitarian tradition that Hume represents. For Kant, the deontologically given notion of right which Rawls seeks to recapture derives its force from a moral metaphysic that rules out precisely the appeal to contingent human circumstances on which Hume's account of the virtue of justice is based.

For Hume, justice is the product of human conventions and 'derives its existence entirely from its necessary *use* to the intercourse and social state of mankind'.

Thus, the rules of equity or justice depend entirely on the particular state and condition in which men are placed, and owe their origins and existence to that utility, which results to the public from their strict and regular observance. Reverse, in any considerable circumstance, the condition of men: Produce extreme abundance or extreme necessity: Implant in the human breast perfect moderation and humanity, or perfect rapaciousness and malice: By rendering justice totally *useless,* you thereby totally destroy its essence, and suspend its obligation upon mankind (1777: 20).

For Kant, by contrast,

Empirical principles are always unfitted to serve as a ground for moral laws. The universality with which these laws should hold for all rational beings without exception – the unconditioned practical necessity which they thus impose – falls away if their basis is taken from the *special constitution of human nature* or from the accidental circumstances in which it is placed (1785:109).

If, as it appears, a Humean account of the circumstances of justice can neither support nor accommodate the privileged status of justice and right required by Rawls and derived from Kant, the question naturally arises why Rawls does not adopt instead a Kantian account of the circumstances of justice. The answer is that Kant, strictly speaking, has none, at least none that situates the virtue of justice in circumstances characteristic of human society. Nor is it obvious that he could provide one. To do so would be to contradict the essential point of Kantian ethics – that man acts morally only in so far as he is able to rise above the heteronomous influences and contingent determinations of his natural and social conditions and act according to a principle given by pure practical reason. For Kant, the circumstances of justice do not consist in those conditions of human society that make justice necessary, but rather in an ideal realm abstracted from human society that makes justice, and morality in general, a possibility. This realm is the kingdom of ends. It is a realm beyond the phenomenal world – as Kant acknowledges, 'it is certainly only an ideal' – where human beings are admitted not as permanent residents but more likely as fleeting visitors. Admission to *these* circumstances of justice is not a precondition of moral virtue but a measure of its achievement, a place where human beings arrive only in so far as they are able to act out of conformity to the autonomously given moral law, in so far, that is, as they can abstract from their situation to will and act as un-situated beings, from a universal point of view. This is why the categorical imperative can enjoin only that man act *as though* he were a legislating member of the kingdom of ends.

We shall be able – if we abstract from the personal differences between rational beings, and also from all the content of their private ends – to conceive a whole of all ends in systematic conjunction ... that is, we shall be able to conceive a kingdom of ends which is possible in accordance with the above principles (Kant 1785: 100–1).

Now a kingdom of ends would actually come into existence through maxims which the categorical imperative prescribes as a rule for all rational beings, *if these maxims were universally followed.* Yet even if a rational being were himself to follow such a maxim strictly, he cannot count on everybody else being faithful to it on this ground. . . . But in spite of this the law 'Act on the maxims of a member who makes universal laws for a merely possible kingdom of ends' remains in full force, since its command is categorical (Kant 1785: 106).

As we have already seen, Rawls parts company with Kant where ideal realms and transcendental subjects enter the conception, and the account of the kingdom of ends is one such point. Rawls finds such a notion unsatisfactory as a basis for human justice, since it seems to apply to human beings only in so far as they are detached from actual human circumstances, which is to say only in so far as they cease to be human beings. Such a notion is at least obscure, and may fall subject to the strictures against a priori standards of appraisal and radically disembodied conceptions of the self. Rawls expresses these worries, especially concerning the problem of arbitrariness, by suggesting with Sidgwick that Kant's doctrine requiring abstraction from all contingency may be unable to distinguish between the lives of the saint and the scoundrel, as long as both are lived by a consistent set of principles freely chosen and conscientiously acted upon. The choice of the noumenal self may – in fact might necessarily – be arbitrary in this sense. 'Kant did not show that acting from the moral law expresses our nature in identifiable ways that acting from contrary principles does not' (255). This criticism reflects Rawls' more general difference with Kant on the role of the empirical and the a priori in moral theory, in particular Rawls' view that 'the analysis of moral concepts and the a priori, however traditionally understood, is too slender a basis' for a substantive theory of justice. 'Moral philosophy must be free to use contingent assumptions and general facts as it pleases' (51).

To overcome these difficulties, while at the same time preserving the priority of right, Rawls seeks to reformulate the notion of the kingdom of ends in a way that accommodates an empirical account of the circumstances of justice but rules out the contingent differences between persons that would otherwise prevail there.

The description of the original position interprets the point of view of noumenal selves, of what it means to be a free and equal rational being. Our nature as such beings is displayed when we act from the principles we would choose when this nature is reflected in the conditions determining the choice. Thus men exhibit their freedom, their independence from the contingencies of nature and society, by acting in ways they would acknowledge in the original position (255–6).

Like the kingdom of ends, the original position, with the veil of ignorance, has the effect of 'abstract[ing] from the personal differences between rational beings, and also from all the content of their private ends'. But unlike the Kantian version, it has the purported advantage of applying to actual human beings subject to the ordinary conditions of human circumstance.

The original position may be viewed, then, as a procedural interpretation of Kant's conception of autonomy and the categorical imperative. The principles regulative of the kingdom of ends are those that would be chosen in this position, and the description of this situation enables us to explain the sense in which acting from these principles expresses our nature as free and equal rational persons. *No longer are these notions purely transcendent and lacking explicable connections with human conduct, for the pro-*

cedural conception of the original position allows us to make these ties [emphasis added] (256).

The aim of the original position is to provide a means of deriving principles of justice that abstracts from contingent and therefore morally irrelevant social and natural influences – this is the Kantian aspiration – without having to rely on a noumenal realm or on the notion of a transcendent subject wholly beyond experience. Rawls' solution is to restrict the description of the parties in the original position to those characteristics which all human beings share as free and equal rational beings. Roughly speaking, these are that each is a being who chooses his ends and who values certain primary goods as instrumental to their realization, whatever those ends might be. These features are assumed to be common to all human beings as such, and are in this sense non-contingent.

Thus, given human nature, wanting them [primary goods] is part of being rational. . . . The preference for primary goods is derived, then, from only the most general assumptions about rationality and the conditions of human life. To act from the principles of justice is to act from categorical imperatives in the sense that they apply to us whatever in particular our aims are. This simply reflects the fact that no such contingencies appear as premises in their derivation (253).

Rawls acknowledges that notwithstanding its Kantian affinities, the original position departs from Kant's views in several respects (256). Among them must surely be the reliance of Rawls on certain generalized human preferences or desires for the derivation of the principles of justice. For Kant, to found the moral law on generalized preferences and desires, however widespread across human beings, would be merely to substitute a wider heteronomy for a narrower one (1788: 25–8). It would not be to escape from contingency in his more exacting sense, which applies to the constitution of human nature as well as to the constitution of particular human beings. Even the 'thin theory of the good' would be too thick to satisfy the Kantian conception of autonomy.

For Rawls, this more global contingency is not a problem. His concern is to develop a theory of justice that is fair between persons, and so only those contingencies that differentiate persons from each other need be ruled out. Contingent attributes common to human beings as such are not only not a problem for Rawls, but are essential ingredients of his moral theory. 'Moral philosophy must be free to use contingent assumptions and general facts as it pleases.' Among these general facts are the facts of the circumstances of justice. Although Kant's view does not admit them, Rawls' theory relies on them; these facts assure that the principles of justice the theory produces apply to human beings in the real world rather than to disembodied or transcendent beings beyond the world.

Being in the circumstances of justice [the parties] are situated in the world with other men who likewise face limitations of moderate scarcity and competing claims. Human freedom is to be regulated by principles chosen in the light of these natural restrictions. Thus justice as fairness is a theory of human justice and among its premises are the elementary facts about persons and their place in nature (257).

We can see, then, why Rawls cannot simply adopt a Kantian account of the circumstances of justice to go conveniently with his other Kantian positions, why he is pressured instead to resort to the notion of an original position which includes as part of its description an empirical account of characteristic human circumstances. It is this uneasy combination that gives rise to the objections we have considered. As a Kantian conception of the moral law and the kingdom of ends seems to deny justice its human situation, the Humean account of the human situation seems unable to accommodate strong claims on behalf of the primacy of justice. But understanding how the inconsistencies arise is not to dissolve them but if anything to confirm them. And so it would appear that the two aspirations of Rawls' theory, to avoid both the contingency of existing desires and the alleged arbitrariness and obscurity of the transcendent, are uncombinable after all, the Archimedean point wiped out in a litany of contradictions.

THE CIRCUMSTANCES OF JUSTICE:
DEONTOLOGICAL REJOINDER

To all of this, Rawls might make the following reply: The apparent incompatibilities between the primacy of justice and the circumstances of justice are based on a misunderstanding of the original position and the role it plays in the conception as a whole. The objections are too quick. They fail to appreciate that the account of the circumstances of justice is an account within the account of the original position, which, it must be recalled, is hypothetical to begin with. The conditions described there are meant to be the conditions in which the parties to the original position carry out their deliberations, not the actual conditions in which ordinary human beings live their lives.

The objections depend in large part on the mistaken assumption that the facts of the circumstances of justice are meant to be facts of life in the real, phenomenal world in which the principles of justice would actually apply, and that their validity therefore depends on the same empirical considerations on which all ordinary factual claims depend. But the description of the circumstances of justice cannot be regarded as a straightforward empirical generalization, to be established or refuted by the best evidence of sociology, psychology, and so on. Since the entire account of the circumstances of justice is located within the account of the original position, the conditions and motivations it describes are asserted only of the parties to the original position and not necessarily of real human beings. Once installed as a premise of the original position, the account of the circumstances of justice ceases to work as a simple empirical account which can be checked for accuracy against actual human conditions. Its validity depends instead on the extent to which the conception of which it is a part yields principles of justice that successfully capture our settled convictions in reflective equilibrium. 'It seems best to regard these conditions simply as reasonable stipulations to be assessed eventually by the whole theory to which they belong. . . . Justification rests upon the entire conception and how it fits in with and organizes our considered judgments in reflective equilibrium' (578–9).

The description of the circumstances of justice, then, does not need to be true in any literal, empirical sense. The original position that contains it is in any case an admitted fiction, a heuristic device designed to constrain our reasoning about justice in certain ways. The distinction between provisions of the circumstances of justice and the motivations that actually prevail in human societies is for Rawls a constant theme; 'We must keep in mind that the parties to the original position are theoretically defined individuals' (147). 'The account of these conditions [i.e. the circumstances of justice] involves no particular theory of human motivations' (130). 'The motivation of the persons in the original position must not be confused with the motivation of persons in everyday life who accept the principles that would be chosen and who have the corresponding sense of justice' (148).

Rawls emphasizes in particular that the assumption of mutual disinterest and the absence of prior moral ties in the original position does not imply a judgment that people really are mutually disinterested or without moral ties.

We need not suppose of course that persons never make substantial sacrifices for one another, since moved by affection and ties of sentiment they often do (178).

There is no inconsistency in supposing that once the veil of ignorance is removed, the parties find that they have ties of sentiment and affection, and want to advance the interests of others and to see their ends attained (129).

Although the assumption of mutual disinterest and the presumed preference for primary goods are the main motivational premises of the original position, this implies neither that these motivations hold for persons in real life, nor that they would hold for persons living in a well-ordered society governed by the two principles of justice.

As for the scope of the motivation assumption, one must keep in mind that *it holds only for the parties in the original position;* they are to deliberate as if they prefer more rather than less primary goods. . . . *The assumption may not characterize the general motivation of people in society, however, and in particular it may fail for the citizens of a well-ordered society* (a society effectively regulated by the public principles adopted in the original position) [emphasis added] (Rawls 1975: 543–4).

So Rawls might reply, and to considerable advantage. To renounce the straightforward empiricist reading of the circumstances of justice is to rescue the claim for the primacy of justice from the more obvious empiricist objections at least. It would also go some way toward making sense of such enigmatic locutions as '*a* human society *is* characterized by the circumstances of justice' [emphasis added] (129–30), which in the context of Rawls' account seems more than a merely empirical generalization and yet something short of a stipulative definition. But the rejection of the empiricist interpretation raises a more difficult question: if the descriptive premises of the original position are not subject in any straightforward sense to empirical tests, to what sort of test are they subject? If the constraints on the motivational assumptions are not empirical constraints, then what kinds of constraints are they?

All we have been able to say so far about the grounds for a premise of the original position is that its validity depends on whether, or to what extent, the conception of which it is a part yields principles of justice that successfully capture our considered judgments in reflective equilibrium. But this does not tell us enough. For what keeps the method of reflective equilibrium from being circular is the availability of independent criteria of judgment at each end, however provisional, in the light of which we adjust and correct the other. In the case of justice, this means that we must have some (independent if provisional) way of judging *both* the desirability of the principles of justice a particular description may yield *and* the plausibility or reasonableness of the motivational assumptions that generate them. ('Each of the presumptions should by itself be natural and plausible' (18).) The independent yet provisional criteria on the side of the desirability of the principles are given by our intuitions about what is just. But what is the corresponding ground on the descriptive side? What we are looking for is that *with reference to which* the plausibility of the premises of the original position might be assessed. One is tempted to say, in line with the normative side, that the criteria of plausibility are given by our 'intuitions' about what is empirically true. But as we have found, the empiricist temptation to think that the actual conditions and motivations of human beings provide the standard of plausibility leads to unacceptable consequences.

To put our problem another way: as the account of reflective equilibrium makes clear, the conditions of the original position cannot be *so* immune from actual human circumstance that just *any* assumptions producing attractive principles of justice would do. Unless the premises of such principles bear *some* resemblance to the condition of creatures discernibly human, the success of the equilibrium is, to that extent, undermined. If we could match our convictions about justice only by appealing to premises that struck us as eccentric or outlandish or metaphysically extreme, we would rightly be led to question the convictions those principles happened to fit. This, after all, comes close to being Rawls' case against Kant, that he was able to establish morally compelling conclusions only at the expense of an account of moral circumstance that bore little resemblance to anything discernibly human.

To summarize: the validity of a premise of the original position is not given empirically, but by a method of justification known as reflective equilibrium. This method involves two different kinds of justification coming together to provide mutual correction and support. One aspect of the justification appeals to our considered convictions about justice; the other appeals to a standard of descriptive but not strictly empirical plausibility which we are searching to define.

Rawls himself seems unclear on what he takes the descriptive standard to be. Both in his general remarks on justification and in his defense of specific premises of the original position, his language reflects his equivocation, and is worth examining closely:

But how are we to decide what is the most favored interpretation [of the initial situation]? I assume, for one thing, that there is a broad measure of agreement that principles of justice should be chosen under certain conditions. To justify a particular description of the initial situation one shows that it incorporates these *commonly shared presumptions.* One argues from *widely accepted but weak premises* to more specific conclusions. Each of the presumptions should by itself be *natural and plausible;* some of them may seem *innocuous or even trivial* [emphasis added] (18).

In searching for the most favored description of this situation we work from both ends. We begin by describing it so that it represents *generally shared and preferably weak conditions.* We then see if these conditions are strong enough to yield a significant set of principles. If not, we look for further premises *equally reasonable* [emphasis added] (20).

In his specific defense of the assumption of mutual disinterest, Rawls appeals to similar criteria:

The postulate of mutual disinterest in the original position is made to insure that the principles of justice do not depend upon strong assumptions. Recall that the original position is meant to incorporate *widely shared and yet weak conditions.* A conception of justice should not presuppose, then, extensive ties of natural sentiment. At the basis of the theory, one tries to *assume as little as possible* [emphasis added] (129).

In arguing for mutual disinterest over benevolence as the appropriate motivational premise, Rawls argues that the combined assumptions of mutual disinterest and the veil of ignorance have 'the merits of simplicity and clarity' while at the same time insuring the beneficent aspects of seemingly more generous motivations. If it is asked why not postulate benevolence with the veil of ignorance, 'the answer is that there is no need for *so strong a condition*. Moreover, it would defeat the purpose of grounding the theory of justice on *weak stipulations,* as well as being incongruous with the circumstances of justice' [emphasis added] (149). Finally, Rawls states in his concluding remarks on justification, 'I have several times noted the *minimal nature of the conditions* on principles when taken singly. For example, the assumption of mutually disinterested motivation is *not a demanding stipulation.* Not only does it enable us to base the theory upon a reasonably precise notion of rational choice, but *it asks little of the parties*' [emphasis added] (583).

Rawls seems to offer two basic answers to the question of how, from the descriptive point of view, an assumption of the original position is to be justified, neither of which takes us very far. The first answer is that it should be widely accepted and commonly shared, the second that it should be a weak as opposed to a strong assumption, and if possible, natural, reasonable, innocuous and even trivial. Yet it is unclear what these considerations amount to, or how in any case they help us know whether to describe the parties as mutually disinterested or benevolent.

First, it is unclear what *about* a motivational assumption should be commonly shared or widely accepted, and why this should count in its favor. Should we look for the *motive* that is most commonly shared (in which case we would have to generalize about the motives people have)? Or the one that is most widely regarded to be the prevailing motive (in which case we would have to generalize about the generalizations people make about other people's motives)? Or the one that is most widely agreed to be an appropriate condition on principles of justice (in which case we would have to generalize about how people are likely to interpret the requirement of common agreement that we are struggling to interpret)? But these interpretations are either empirical or question-begging or both, and in any case are not obviously relevant to the validity of a premise such as mutual disinterest or benevolence as a condition of the original position.

The requirement that the assumption be weak rather than strong begs precisely the question we seek to answer: weak or strong with respect to *what?* We might say an assumption is weak from a conceptual point of view, and therefore likely to be innocuous or trivial or otherwise unobjectionable, when it depends for its validity on the validity of relatively few related propositions, and where those it does rely on are themselves weak and uncontroversial. An assumption is strong in these terms when, for it to be true, many other things, including controversial things, have also to be true. But surely the assumptions of mutual disinterest and benevolence cannot be distinguished on the grounds that either is weaker or stronger an assumption in the conceptual sense; neither relies on a premise which is *conceptually* more contentious or problematic than the other.

If neither is more nor less conceptually demanding than the other, the alternative sense would seem to refer to statistical probabilities. When welfare economists, for example, refer to motivational assumptions as strong or weak, they mean to describe the likelihood that the motivation applies to a large proportion of the population. Much of Rawls' language seems to suggest this general probabilistic usage. What else could he mean when he says that assuming the parties to be mutually disinterested is assuming 'less' than to assume that extensive ties of natural sentiment prevail? How does he know that assuming mutual disinterest is not a demanding stipulation in that 'it asks little of the parties'? Does this assume that we are inclined by nature toward selfishness rather than benevolence? Maybe for some it is asking much more to ask that they act selfishly rather than benevolently. Is it then a matter of statistical probabilities which way people are naturally inclined to behave? And how could such a question even be formulated precisely enough to get a reasonable estimate without specifying the range of situations involved? In any case, if all Rawls means by the distinction between weak and strong assumptions is that the premises should be more realistic rather than less realistic, then we are back to the merely empirical understanding of the conditions in the original position which has already been rejected.

Although Rawls' own account of the original position and the status of its descriptive premises is unclear, some account of these matters is essential if we are to make sense of his theory at all. Unless we can overcome the apparent obstacles to explicating the original position and its premises, the coherence of the entire conception will be in doubt. What we need is an account of what exactly constrains the descriptive assumptions appropriate to the initial situation, that is, what constrains them *besides* the constraints imposed from the normative side, which consist of our considered convictions about justice. More generally, we need to know something more precise about the status of the original position, phenomenal or otherwise; what *is* the original position, anyhow?

IN SEARCH OF THE MORAL SUBJECT

I believe these questions can be answered, if not in Rawls' explicit language at least in terms consistent with his conception as a whole. Finding the answers may therefore involve certain departures from the text in order to make sense of the text. The justification for this interpretation will be found in hints and traces of evidence scattered throughout the text and, more importantly, in the sense it enables us to make of Rawls' theory as a whole, and in particular its ability to resolve certain problematic features of the original position we have been unable to resolve in any other way.

But our point of departure is a point firmly within the text, in the notion of reflective equilibrium as the method of justification that governs the conception as a whole. The key is to see the original position as the fulcrum of reflective equilibrium, in so far as it can be achieved. The original position is the fulcrum of the justificatory process in that *it* is the device through which all justification must pass, the place at which all arguments must arrive and from which they must depart. This is why a premise of the original position can be defended or attacked from either of two directions, on grounds of its plausibility (in a sense yet to be determined) or on grounds of its fit with our considered convictions about justice.

In searching for the most favored description of this situation we work from both ends. . . . By going back and forth, sometimes altering the conditions of the contractual circumstances, at others withdrawing our judgments and conforming them to principle, I assume that eventually we shall find a description of the initial situation that both expresses reasonable conditions and yields principles which match our considered judgments duly pruned and adjusted. This state of affairs I refer to as reflective equilibrium (20).

The description of the original position is the product of two basic ingredients: our best judgments of 'reasonableness and plausibility' (yet to be explicated) from one side, and our considered convictions of justice from the other. From the raw materials of our intuitions,

47

properly filtered and shaped by the original position, a final product emerges. But it is a final product of dual dimensions, and in this lies the key to our account. For what issues at one end in a theory of justice must issue at the other in a theory of the person, or more precisely, a theory of the moral subject. Looking from one direction through the lens of the original position we see the two principles of justice; looking from the other direction we see a reflection of ourselves. If the method of reflective equilibrium operates with the symmetry Rawls ascribes to it, then the original position must produce not only a moral theory but also a philosophical anthropology.

Throughout most of his book, Rawls is concerned primarily with the former. His aim is to produce a theory of justice, and so most of his attention is devoted to the argument from the original position to the principles of justice, and to a description of the original position which adequately anticipates the requirements of justice. He is understandably less concerned to pursue the argument in the opposite direction, and accordingly less explicit about what would be found there. This may account in part for his greater clarity on the basis of our moral intuitions than on the origin and status of our 'descriptive' intuitions (what makes them reasonable or unreasonable, strong or weak, etc.). If this reconstruction is correct, then the independent yet provisional standard by which the reasonableness of our descriptive assumptions is assessed is given not by the laws of empirical psychology or sociology but instead by the nature of the moral subject as we understand it, which is to say by the constitutive understanding we have of ourselves.

Given that the aim of the conception is to produce a theory of justice, there is a tendency to dismiss the sometimes unattractive motivational assumptions of the original position as part of a merely heuristic device of no independent or continuing interest once the principles of justice have been fully worked out. But if reflective equilibrium truly works both ways, then the account of human circumstance that emerges once reflective equilibrium is achieved can no more be dispensed with as the incidental product of a fictive contrivance than can the principles of justice themselves. Given the methodological symmetry of the original position, we cannot regard one of its products as chaff to the other's wheat, to be chucked away once the flour has been ground. We must be prepared to live with the vision contained in the original position, mutual disinterest and all, prepared to live with it in the sense of accepting its description as an accurate reflection of human moral circumstance, consistent with our understanding of ourselves.

Finally, we may remind ourselves that the hypothetical nature of the original position invites the question: why should we take any interest in it, moral or otherwise? Recall the answer: *the conditions embodied in the description of this situation are ones that we do in fact accept. Or if we do not, then we can be persuaded to do so* by philosophical considerations of the sort occasionally introduced [emphasis added] (587).

As the concepts of pure speculative reason are to Kant's moral theory, so the conditions embodied in the original position are to Rawls' theory of justice. 'They are not like the props and buttresses which usually have to be put behind a hastily erected building, but they are rather true members making the structure of the system plain' (Kant 1788: 7).

These considerations powerfully suggest that implicit in Rawls' theory of justice is a conception of the moral subject that both shapes the principles of justice and is shaped in their image through the medium of the original position. It is this conception I propose to illuminate and explore. If it can somehow be made explicit, it should help not only to resolve the perplexities concerning the status of the original position, but also to assess the central claims of the conception as a whole. So where Rawls' main discussion tends to take the nature of the moral subject as given and argue through the original position to the principles of justice, I propose to work in the opposite direction, to take the principles of justice as provisionally given and argue back to the nature of the moral subject. In doing so, I take myself to be tracing the lineaments of an argument of the following kind: assuming we are beings capable of justice, and more precisely, beings for whom justice is primary, we must be creatures of a certain kind, related to human circumstances in a certain way. What then must be true of a subject for whom justice is the first virtue? And how is the conception of such a subject embodied in the original position?

Now the description of this subject will have a distinctive logical status. It will in some sense be necessary, non-contingent, and prior to any particular experience – the 'must' in the formulation is not for nothing – but it will not of course be an analytic claim. It will in some sense be empirical, but not 'merely' empirical. Given the reflexive

49

character of such descriptions, they are not merely descriptive but also partly constitutive of the kind of beings we are. Our knowing them is part of what makes them true, and makes us the reflexive, self-interpreting creatures that we are.

One might describe a general account of these constituent features of our self-understanding by a variety of names: a theory of the person, a conception of the self, a moral epistemology, a theory of human nature, a theory of the moral subject, a philosophical anthropology. These descriptions carry differing, sometimes conflicting connotations, usually associated with the philosophical traditions from which they derive. To speak of human nature, for example, is often to suggest a classical teleological conception, associated with the notion of a universal human essence, invariant in all times and places. Talk of the self, on the other hand, tends to bias the issue in favor of individualistic notions and to suggest that the self-understanding involved amounts merely to the coming to awareness of an individual person, as in psychotherapy, for example. These associations pose certain difficulties, for they threaten to beg the very question we seek to answer, namely, how the subject is constituted, in what terms and on what scale it is properly conceived. To avoid confusion on this count, I should say in advance that the account I have in mind is a philosophical anthropology in the broadest sense; philosophical in that it is arrived at reflectively rather than by empirical generalization, anthropology in that it concerns the nature of the human subject in its various possible forms of identity.

THE SELF AND THE OTHER: THE PRIORITY OF PLURALITY

With these qualifications as background, and with some reference to our earlier discussion of the problem of the self, we can proceed to reconstruct Rawls' reasoning about the nature of the moral subject as follows. For Rawls, the first feature of any creature capable of justice is that it be plural in number. Justice could not apply in a world where only one subject existed. It could only have place in a society of beings who were in some sense distinguishable one from another. 'Principles of justice deal with conflicting claims upon the advantages won by social co-operation; they apply to the relations among several persons or groups. The word "contract" suggests this plurality' (16). For there to be justice, there must be the possibility of conflicting claims, and for there to be conflicting claims, there must be more than a single claimant. In this way, the plurality of persons can be seen as a necessary presupposition of the possibility of justice.

Rawls insists on the essential plurality of the human subject when he faults utilitarianism for extending to society as a whole the principles of rational choice for one man. This is a fallacy, he argues, because it conflates diverse systems of justice into a single system of desire, and so fails to take seriously the distinction between persons. On utilitarianism, '*many persons* are fused into one', and '*separate individuals* are thought of as so many different lines'. But utilitarianism is mistaken, for 'there is no reason to suppose that the principles which should regulate an association of men is simply an extension of the principle of choice for one man. On the contrary: if we assume that the correct regulative principle for anything depends on *the nature of that thing*, and that *the plurality of distinct persons with separate systems of ends is an essential feature of human* societies, we should not expect the principles of social choice to be utilitarian' [emphasis added] (28–9).

Taking seriously 'the plurality and distinctiveness of individuals' means more than defending liberty and freedom of thought, and holding that the good of society consists in the advantages enjoyed by individuals, as the utilitarians did. It means understanding the plurality of persons to be an essential feature of any account of the moral subject, a postulate of philosophical anthropology. In this light, 'utilitarianism is not individualistic, at least when arrived at by the more natural course of reflection', for by conflating all systems of desires into one, it contradicts this essential postulate (29).

But in order for subjects to be plural, there must be something that differentiates them, some way of distinguishing one from another, some principle of individuation. For Rawls, our individuating characteristics are given empirically, by the distinctive concatenation of wants and desires, aims and attributes, purposes and ends that come to characterize human beings in their particularity. Each individual is located uniquely in time and place, born into a particular family and society, and the contingencies of these circumstances, together with the interests and values and aspirations to which they give rise, are what set people apart, what make them the particular persons they are.

Within any group of persons, especially those of similar circumstances, there will likely be found certain overlapping characteristics, certain interests held in common. But notwithstanding even the closest similarity of situation, no two persons could ever be said to be identically situated, nor could it be that any two persons had identical aims and interests in every respect, for if they did, it would no longer be clear how we could identify them as two distinguishable persons. In this way, the essential plurality of persons is assured, or perhaps better, defined. For Rawls, the fact of our fundamental plurality is a necessary presupposition of our being creatures capable of justice. What any particular person's individuality actually consists in, however, is an empirical matter. The fundamental feature of the moral subject is its plurality, and given the means of individuation, the number of its plurality corresponds to the number of empirically individuated human beings in the world. All of which is to say that on Rawls' view of the moral subject, every individual human being is a moral subject, and every moral subject is an individual human being.

At this point it might reasonably be asked whether, on Rawls' conception of the person, unity as well as plurality might appear as an essential feature of the moral subject, equally necessary a presupposition of the view that man is a creature capable of justice. Indeed, Rawls describes the circumstances of justice as 'the normal conditions under which human co-operation is both possible and necessary', and from this it might be thought that where the essential plurality of the moral subject makes human co-operation necessary, some essential unity of persons makes human co-operation possible. But this would misunderstand the logic of Rawls' conception, and threaten to undermine the priorities on which the deontological ethic depends. I believe he would answer roughly as follows:

While it is true that the principle of unity has an important place in justice as fairness (see in particular the account of the idea of social union, section 79), it is a mistake to accord it an equal priority with plurality; it is not essential to our nature in the same way. This is because any account of the unity of human subjectivity must *presuppose* its plurality, in a way that is not true in reverse. This can be seen if we consider the notion of a human society as a co-operative venture for mutual advantage, marked as it typically is by a conflict as well as an identity of interests. Now the conflict of interests arises, as we have seen, from the fact that the subjects of co-operation have different interests and ends, and *this* fact follows from the nature of a being capable of justice at all. The identity of interests, however, expresses the fact that the parties happen to have suitably similar needs and interests such that co-operation among them is mutually advantageous. And *this* fact, that their needs and interests happen to coincide in such a way, does not follow from the nature of their subjectivity, but merely from the happy accident of their circumstances. That they are able to come together to co-operate for mutual advantage presupposes an antecedent plurality. Co-operation is by its very nature co-operation between or among agents, whose plurality must therefore be antecedent to the identity of interests they realize in co-operative association.

The essential idea is that we want to account for the social values, for the intrinsic good of institutional, community, and associative activities, by a conception of justice that in its theoretical basis is individualistic. For reasons of clarity among others, we do not want to rely on an undefined concept of community, or to suppose that society is an organic whole with a life of its own distinct from and superior to that of all its members in their relations with one another. Thus the contractual conception of the original position is worked out first. . . . From this conception, however individualistic it might seem, we must eventually explain the value of community (264–5).

That we are distinct persons, characterized by separate systems of ends, is a necessary presupposition of a being capable of justice. What in particular our ends consist in, and whether they happen to coincide or overlap with the ends of others, is an empirical question that cannot be known in advance. This is the sense – epistemological rather than psychological – in which the plurality of subjects is given prior to their unity. We are distinct individuals first, and then (circumstances permitting) we form relationships and engage in co-operative arrangements with others. The point is not that persons co-operate out of selfish motives alone, but rather that our knowledge of the basis of plurality is given prior to experience, while our knowledge of the basis of unity or co-operation can only come in the light of experience. In any particular instance, we just have to see whether or not the basis for co-operation exists.

The priority of plurality over unity, or the notion of the antecedent individuation of the subject, describes the terms of relation between the self and the other that must obtain for justice to be primary. But before our reconstruction of Rawls' conception of the person can be complete, we must consider a parallel issue, and this is the relation of the self to its ends.

THE SELF AND ITS ENDS: THE SUBJECT OF POSSESSION

On the deontological ethic, 'the self is prior to the ends which are affirmed by it' (560). For Rawls, giving an account of this priority poses a special challenge, for his project rules out a self that achieves its priority by inhabiting a transcendent or noumenal realm. In Rawls' view, any account of self and ends must tell us not one thing but two things: how the self is distinguished from its ends, and also how the self is connected to its ends. Without the first we are left with a radically situated subject; without the second, a radically disembodied subject.

Rawls' solution, implicit in the design of the original position, is to conceive the self as a subject of possession, for in possession the self is distanced from its ends without being detached altogether. The notion of the self as a subject of possession can be located in the assumption of mutual disinterest. This assumption looks on the surface like a psychological assumption – it says the parties take no interest in one another's interests – but given its place in the original position it works instead as an epistemological claim, as a claim about the forms of self-knowledge of which we are capable. This is why Rawls can coherently maintain that the assumption of mutual disinterest is 'the main motivational condition of the original position' (189), and yet 'involves no particular theory of human motivations' (130).

We can now see how this is so. The assumption of mutual disinterest is not an assumption about what motivates people, but an assumption about the nature of subjects who possess motivations in general. It concerns the nature of the self (that is, how it is constituted, how it stands with respect to its situation generally), not the nature of the self's desires or aims. It concerns the *subject* of interests and ends, not the *content* of those interests and ends, whatever they may happen to be. As Kant argues that all experience must be the experience of some subject, Rawls' assumption of mutual disinterest holds that all interests must be the interests of some subject.

Although the interests advanced by these plans are not assumed to be interests *in the self,* they are interests *of a self* that regards its conception of the good as worthy of recognition [emphasis added] (127).

54

I make no restrictive assumptions about the parties' conceptions of the good except that they are rational long-term plans. While these plans determine the aims and interests *of a self,* the aims and interests are not presumed to be egoistic or selfish. Whether this is the case depends upon the kinds of ends which a person pursues. If wealth, position, and influence, and the accolades of social prestige are a person's final purposes, then surely his conception of the good is egoistic. His dominant interests are *in himself,* not merely, *as they must always be,* interests *of a self* [emphasis added] (129).

In the assumption of mutual disinterest, we find the key to Rawls' conception of the subject, the picture of the way we must be to be subjects for whom justice is primary. But the notion of the self as a subject of possession, taken alone, does not complete the picture. As the account of plurality suggests, not just any subject of possession will do, but only an antecedently individuated subject, the bounds of whose self are fixed prior to experience. To be a deontological self, I must be a subject whose identity is given independently of the things I have, independently, that is, of my interests and ends and my relations with others. Combined with the idea of possession, this notion of individuation powerfully completes Rawls' theory of the person. We can appreciate its full consequences by contrasting two aspects of possession – two different ways an interest can be 'of a self' – and seeing how the notion of antecedent individuation commits the deontological self to one of them.

In so far as I possess something, I am at once related to it and distanced from it. To say that I possess a certain trait or desire or ambition is to say that I am related to it in a certain way – it is *mine* rather than *yours* – and also that I am distanced from it in a certain way – that it is *mine* rather than *me.* The latter point means that if I lose a thing I possess, I am still the same 'I' who had it; this is the sense, paradoxical at first but unavoidable on reflection, in which the notion of possession is a distancing notion. This distancing aspect is essential to the continuity of the self. It preserves for the self a certain dignity and integrity by saving it from transformation in the face of the slightest contingency. Preserving this distance, and the integrity it implies, typically requires a certain kind of self-knowledge. To preserve the distinction between what is *me* and what is (merely) *mine,* I must know, or be able to sort out when the occasion demands, something about who I am. Thus, Odysseus was able to survive his treacherous journey home by donning various disguises, and his ability to do so presupposed an understanding of who he was, to being with, so to speak. Since his self-knowledge preceded his experience in this sense, he was able to return home the same person who had left, familiar to Penelope, untransfigured by his journey, unlike Agamemnon, who returned a stranger to his household and met a different fate.[2]

It is a consequence of the dual aspect of possession that it can fade or diminish in two different ways. I gradually lose possession of a thing not only as it is distanced from my person, but also as the distance between my self and the thing narrows and tends toward collapse. I lose possession of a desire or an ambition as my commitment to it fades, as my hold on it becomes more attenuated, but also, after a certain point, as my attachment to it grows, as it gradually becomes attached to me. As the desire or ambition becomes increasingly constitutive of my identity, it becomes more and more *me,* and less and less *mine.* Or as we might say in some cases, the less I possess it, and the more I am possessed *by* it. Imagine that a desire, held tentatively at first, gradually becomes more central to my overall aims, until finally it becomes an overriding consideration in all I think and do. As it grows from a desire into an obsession, I possess it less and it possesses me more, until finally it becomes indistinguishable from my identity.

A different sort of example: in so far as the American Declaration of Independence is correct, that man is endowed by his Creator with certain inalienable rights that among them are life, liberty, and the pursuit of happiness, its famous litany describes not what we *have* as free men but rather what we *are.* The endowment is less a possession than a *nature* of a certain kind; he who would abnegate his liberty or pursue a miserable existence would experience these endowments not as possessions but as constraints. In so far as these rights are truly inalienable, a man is no more entitled to do away with them in his own case than to take them from another. Suicide is on a par with murder, and selling oneself into slavery is morally equivalent to enslaving another.

As these images suggest, possession is bound up with human agency and a sense of self-command. Dispossession, from both points

---

2 I am indebted for this example to Allen Grossman.

of view, can be understood as a kind of disempowering. When my possession of an object fades, whether because it slips from my grasp or looms so large before me that I am overwhelmed, disempowered in the face of it, my agency with respect to the object is diminished as well. Each challenge is associated with a different notion of agency, which implies, in turn, a different account of the relation of the self to its ends. We can think of the two dimensions of agency as different ways of repairing the drift toward dispossession, and distinguish them by the way they work to restore a sense of self-command.

The first kind of dispossession involves the distancing of the end from the self whose end it once was. It becomes increasingly unclear in what sense this is my end rather than yours, or somebody else's, or no one's at all. The self is disempowered because dissociated from those ends and desires which, woven gradually together into a coherent whole, provide a fixity of purpose, form a plan of life, and so account for the continuity of the self with its ends. Where the self is regarded as given prior to its ends, its bounds fixed once and for all such that they are impermeable, invulnerable to transformation by experience, such continuity is perpetually and inherently problematic; the only way it can be affirmed is for the self to reach beyond itself, to grasp as an object of its will the ends it would possess, and hold them, as it always must, external to itself.[3]

The second kind of dispossession disempowers in another way. Here, the problem is not to overcome the distance created by the drift of the end from the self, but rather to recover and preserve a space that increasingly threatens to collapse. Crowded by the claims and pressures of various possible purposes and ends, all impinging indiscriminately on my identity, I am unable to sort them out, unable to mark out the limits or the boundaries of my self, incapable of saying where my identity ends and the world of attributes, aims, and desires begins. I am disempowered in the sense of lacking any clear grip on who, in particular, I am. Too much is too essential to my identity. Where the ends are given prior to the self they constitute, the bounds of the subject are open, its identity infinitely accommodating

3 Compare Kant (1797: 62): 'Therefore, the relation of having something external to oneself as one's own (property) consists of a purely *de jure* union of the Will of the subject with that object, independently of his relationship to it in space and time and in accordance with the concept of intelligible possession.'

and ultimately fluid. Unable to distinguish what is mine from what is me, I am in constant danger of drowning in a sea of circumstance.

We might understand human agency as the faculty by which the self comes by its ends. This acknowledges its close connection with the notion of possession without begging the question which dimension of possession is at stake, nor the question of the relative priority of self and ends. For if I am a being with ends, there are at least two ways I might 'come by' them: one is by choice, the other by discovery, by 'finding them out'. The first sense of 'coming by' we might call the voluntarist dimension of agency, the second sense the cognitive dimension. Each kind of agency can be seen as repairing a different kind of dispossession.

Where the self is disempowered because detached from its ends, dispossession is repaired by the faculty of agency in its voluntarist sense, in which the self is related to its ends as a willing subject to the objects of choice. The relevant agency involves the exercise of will, for it is the will that is able to transcend the space between the subject and its object without requiring that it be closed.

Where the self is disempowered because undifferentiated from its ends, dispossession is repaired by agency in its cognitive sense, in which the self is related to its ends as a knowing subject to the objects of understanding. Where the ends of the self are given in advance, the relevant agency is not voluntarist but cognitive, since the subject achieves self-command not by choosing that which is already given (this would be unintelligible) but by reflecting on itself and inquiring into its constituent nature, discerning its laws and imperatives, and acknowledging its purposes as its own. Where the faculty of will seeks to reverse the drifting apart of self and ends by restoring a certain continuity between them, reflexivity is a distancing faculty, and issues in a certain detachment. It succeeds by restoring the shrunken space between self and ends. In reflexivity, the self turns its lights inward upon itself, making the self its own object of inquiry and reflection. When I am able to reflect on my obsession, able to pick it out and make it an object of my reflection, I thereby establish a certain space between it and me, and so diminish its hold. It becomes more an attribute and less a constituent of my identity, and so dissolves from an obsession to a mere desire.

Where the subject is regarded as prior to its ends, self-knowledge is not a possibility in this sense, for the bounds it would define are taken as given in advance, unreflectively, by the principle of antecedent individuation. The bounds of the self are fixed and within them all is transparent. The relevant moral question is not 'Who am I?' (for the answer to this question is given in advance) but rather 'What ends shall I choose?' and this is a question addressed to the will.

For the self whose identity is constituted in the light of ends already before it, agency consists less in summoning the will than in seeking self-understanding. The relevant question is not what ends to choose, for my problem is precisely that the answer to this question is already given, but rather who I am, how I am to discern in this clutter of possible ends what is me from what is mine. Here, the bounds of the self are not fixtures but possibilities, their contours no longer self-evident but at least partly unformed. Rendering them clear, and defining the bounds of my identity are one and the same. The self-command that is measured in the first case in terms of the scope and reach of my will is determined in the second by the depth and clarity of my self-awareness.

We can now see how the cluster of assumptions associated with the voluntarist notion of agency and the distancing aspect of possession fill out Rawls' theory of the person. The notion of a subject of possession, individuated in advance and given prior to its ends, seems just the conception required to redeem the deontological ethic without lapsing into transcendence. In this way, the self is distinguished from its ends – it stands beyond them, at a distance, with a certain priority – but is also related to its ends, as willing subject to the objects of choice.

The voluntarist notion of agency is thus a key ingredient in Rawls' conception, and plays a central role in the deontological ethic as a whole. 'It is not our aims that primarily reveal our nature' (560), but rather our capacity to choose our aims that matters most, and this capacity finds expression in the principles of justice. 'Thus a moral person is a subject with ends he has chosen, and his fundamental preference is for conditions that enable him to frame a mode of life that expresses his nature as a free and equal rational being as fully as circumstances permit' (561). This, finally, is why we cannot regard justice as just one value among others. 'In order to realize our nature we have no alternative but to plan to preserve our sense of justice as governing our other aims' (574).

INDIVIDUALISM AND THE CLAIMS OF COMMUNITY

In our reconstruction of the deontological subject we find at last the standard by which the descriptive premises of the original position may be assessed, the counterweight to our moral intuitions that provides Rawls' reflective equilibrium with a test at both ends. It is this conception of the subject, and no particular account of human motivations, that the assumption of mutual disinterest conveys.

We may recall that on Rawls' account, 'the postulate of mutual disinterest in the original position is made to insure that the principles of justice do not depend upon strong assumptions' (129), and the point of avoiding strong assumptions is to make possible the derivation of principles that do not presuppose any particular conception of the good. 'Liberty in adopting a conception of the good is limited only by principles that are deduced from a doctrine which imposes no prior constraints on these conceptions. Presuming mutual disinterest in the original position carries out this idea' (254). Strong or controversial assumptions would threaten to impose a particular conception of the good, and so bias the choice of principles in advance.

How strong or weak, then, *are* the assumptions that form Rawls' conception of the person? With what range of values and ends are they compatible? Are they weak and innocent enough to avoid ruling out any conceptions of the good in advance? We have already seen that the empiricist reading of the original position produces a litany of objections on this score; the circumstances of justice and especially the assumption of mutual disinterest are thought to introduce an individualistic bias, and to rule out or otherwise devalue such motives as benevolence, altruism, and communitarian sentiments. As one critic has written, the original position contains 'a strong individualistic bias, which is further strengthened by the motivational assumptions of mutual disinterest and absence of envy. . . . The original position seems to presuppose not just a neutral theory of the good, but a liberal, individualistic conception according to which the best that can be wished for someone is the unimpeded pursuit of his own path, provided it does not interfere with the rights of others' (Nagel 1973: 9–10).

But as Rawls rightly insists, his theory is not the 'narrowly individualistic doctrine' that the empiricist objection supposes. 'Once the point of the assumption of mutual disinterest is understood, the objection seems misplaced' (584). Notwithstanding its individualist dimension, justice as fairness does not defend private society as an ideal (522f), or presuppose selfish or egoistic motivations (129), or oppose communitarian values. 'Although justice as fairness begins by taking the persons in the original position as individuals . . . this is no obstacle to explicating the higher-order moral sentiments that serve to bind a community of persons together' (192).

Rawls has emphasized in particular that the assumption of mutual disinterest does not bias the choice of principles in favor of individualistic values at the expense of communitarian ones. Those who suppose that it does overlook the special status of the original position, and mistakenly assume that the motives attributed to the parties are meant to apply generally to actual human beings or to persons in a well-ordered society. But neither is the case. The motives attributed to the parties in the original position neither reflect the actual motivations current in society nor determine directly the motives of persons in a well-ordered society.

Given the restricted scope of these assumptions, Rawls argues, 'there seems to be no reason offhand why the ends of people in a well-ordered society should be predominantly individualistic' (1975: 544). Communitarian values, like any other values individuals might choose to pursue, would likely exist, and possibly even flourish in a society governed by the two principles of justice.

There is no reason why a well-ordered society should encourage primarily individualistic values if this means ways of life that lead individuals to pursue their own way and to have no concern for the interest of others (although respecting their rights and liberties). Normally one would expect most people to belong to one or more associations and to have at least some collective ends in this sense. The basic liberties are not intended to keep persons in isolation from one another, or to persuade them to live private lives, even though some no doubt will, but to secure the right of free movement between associations and smaller communities (1975: 550).

On Rawls' conception of the person, my ends are benevolent or communitarian when they take as their object the good of another, or of a group of others with whom I may be associated, and indeed there is nothing in his view to rule out communitarian ends in this sense. All interests, values, and conceptions of the good are open to the

Rawlsian self, so long as they can be cast as the interests of a subject individuated in advance and given prior to its ends, so long, that is, as they describe the objects I seek rather than the subject I am. Only the *bounds* of the self are fixed in advance.

But this suggests a deeper sense in which Rawls' conception is individualistic. We can locate this individualism and identify the conceptions of the good it excludes by recalling that the Rawlsian self is not only a subject of possession, but an antecedently individuated subject, standing always at a certain distance from the interests it has. One consequence of this distance is to put the self beyond the reach of experience, to make it invulnerable, to fix its identity once and for all. No commitment could grip me so deeply that I could not understand myself without it. No transformation of life purposes and plans could be so unsettling as to disrupt the contours of my identity. No project could be so essential that turning away from it would call into question the person I am. Given my independence from the values I have, I can always stand apart from them; my public identity as a moral person 'is not affected by changes over time' in my conception of the good (Rawls 1980: 544–5).[4]

But a self so thoroughly independent as this rules out any conception of the good (or of the bad) bound up with possession in the constitutive sense. It rules out the possibility of any attachment (or obsession) able to reach beyond our values and sentiments to engage our identity itself. It rules out the possibility of a public life in which, for good or ill, the identity as well as the interests of the participants could be at stake. And it rules out the possibility that common purposes and ends could inspire more or less expansive self-understandings and so define a community in the constitutive sense, a community describing the subject and not just the objects of shared aspirations. More generally, Rawls' account rules out the possibility of what we might call 'intersubjective' or 'intrasubjective' forms of self-understanding, ways of conceiving the subject that do not assume its bounds to be given in advance. Unlike Rawls' conception, intersubjective and intrasubjective conceptions do not assume that to speak of the self, from a moral point of view, is necessarily and unproblematically to speak of an antecedently individuated self.

4 Rawls suggests at one point that my *private* identity as a moral person might not be similarly immune from constitutive attachments (1980: 545). See p. 182, below.

Intersubjective conceptions allow that in certain moral circumstances, the relevant description of the self may embrace more than a single, individual human being, as when we attribute responsibility or affirm an obligation to a family or community or class or nation rather than to some particular human being. Such conceptions are presumably what Rawls has in mind when he rejects, 'for reasons of clarity among others', what he calls 'an undefined concept of community' and the notion that 'society is an organic whole' (264), for these suggest the metaphysically troubling side of Kant which Rawls is anxious to replace.

Intrasubjective conceptions, on the other hand, allow that for certain purposes, the appropriate description of the moral subject may refer to a plurality of selves within a single, individual human being, as when we account for inner deliberation in terms of the pull of competing identities, or moments of introspection in terms of occluded self-knowledge, or when we absolve someone from responsibility for the heretical beliefs 'he' held before his religious conversion. On intrasubjective conceptions, to speak of selves within a(n) (antecedently individuated empirical) self is not merely metaphorical but sometimes of genuine moral and practical import.

While Rawls does not reject such notions explicitly, he denies them by implication when he assumes that to every individual person there corresponds a single system of desires, and that utilitarianism fails as a social ethic in mistakenly applying to society the principles of choice appropriate for one man. Since he takes for granted that every individual consists of one and only one system of desires, the problem of conflating desires does not arise in the individual case, and the principle of rational prudence can properly govern one's conduct toward oneself. 'A person quite properly acts, at least when others are not affected, to achieve his own greatest good, to advance his rational ends as far as possible' (23). Whereas society consists of a plurality of subjects and so requires justice, in private morality, utilitarianism seems to suffice; where others are not involved, I am free to maximize my good without reference to the principle of right.[5] Here again

5 In his discussion of deliberative rationality, Rawls stops just short of acknowledging an intrasubjective dimension and admitting the concept of right as a constraint on private moral choice: 'One who rejects equally the claims of his future self and the interests of others is not only irresponsible with respect to them but in regard to his own person as

Rawls departs from Kant, who emphasized the concept of 'necessary duty to oneself,' and applied the category of right to private as well as public morality (Kant 1785: 89–90, 96–7 101, 105).

The assumptions of the original position thus stand opposed in advance to any conception of the good requiring a more or less expansive self-understanding, and in particular to the possibility of community in the constitutive sense. On Rawls' view, a sense of community describes a possible aim of antecedently individuated selves, not an ingredient or constituent of their identity as such. This guarantees its subordinate status. Since 'the essential unity of the self is already provided by the concept of right' (563), community must find its virtue as one contender among others within the framework defined by justice, not as a rival account of the framework itself. The question then becomes whether individuals who happen to espouse communitarian aims can pursue them within a well-ordered society, antecedently defined by the principles of justice, not whether a well-ordered society is *itself* a community (in the constitutive sense). 'There is, to be sure, one collective aim supported by state power for the whole well-ordered society, a just society wherein the common conception of justice is publicly recognized; but within this framework communitarian aims may be pursued, and quite possibly by the vast majority of persons' (Rawls 1975: 550).

We can see now more clearly the relation between Rawls' theory of the person and his claim for the primacy of justice. As a person's values and ends are always attributes and never constituents of the self, so a sense of community is only an attribute and never a constituent of a well-ordered society. As the self is prior to the aims it affirms, so a well-ordered society, defined by justice, is prior to the aims – communitarian or otherwise – its members may profess. This is the sense, both moral and epistemological, in which justice is the first virtue of social institutions.

Our reconstruction of Rawls' conception of the person now complete, it remains to assess this conception and the deontological ethic

---

well. He does not see himself as one enduring individual. Now looked at in this way, the principle of responsibility to self *resembles* a principle of right. . . . The person at one time, *so to speak,* must not be able to complain about actions of the person at another time' [emphasis added] (423).

it must support. We have seen that the assumptions contained in the original position are strong and far-reaching rather than weak and innocuous, though not for the reasons the empiricist objection suggests. These assumptions do not admit all ends, but rule out in advance any end whose adoption or pursuit could engage or transform the identity of the self, and they reject in particular the possibility that the good of community could consist in a constitutive dimension of this kind.

If it therefore cannot be said that Rawls' principles derive 'from a doctrine which imposes no prior constraints' on conceptions of the good, still it might be argued that the conceptions he excludes are somehow dispensable, that it is possible to account for justice and to arrive at a conception of a well-ordered society without them. Rawls' theory of justice is just such an attempt. In order to assess it, we must descend from deontological meta-ethics to consider first-order principles. In the chapters that follow, I shall argue that Rawls' conception of the person can neither support his theory of justice nor plausibly account for our capacities for agency and self-reflection; justice cannot be primary in the way deontology requires, for we cannot coherently regard ourselves as the sort of beings the deontological ethic requires us to be.

2

Possession, Desert, and Distributive Justice

Having clarified the status of Rawls' motivational assumptions, we can now put his theory of the person and his theory of justice side by side to check for the fit between them. In this way we can work within the argument from reflective equilibrium, by asking whether the theory of the person contained in the original position corresponds to the principles of justice it must both shape and reflect. Of special interest for this purpose is the difference principle, the principle that permits only those inequalities that work to the benefit of the least advantaged members of society. We shall see in this chapter that an adequate defense of the difference principle must presuppose a conception of the person unavailable on deontological assumptions, that we cannot be subjects for whom justice is primary and also be subjects for whom the difference principle is a principle of justice. A central focus will be on the role of desert in distributive justice, and on the conception of possession it requires. To explore these issues, we begin by contrasting Rawls' views with various competing distributive theories, and in particular the rival, but in some ways strikingly similar theory defended by Robert Nozick (1974).

LIBERTARIANISM TO EGALITARIANISM

From a practical political point of view, the positions of Rawls and Nozick are clearly opposed. Rawls, the welfare-state liberal, and Nozick, the libertarian conservative, define between them the clearest alternatives the American political agenda has to offer, at least where issues of distributive justice are concerned. And yet, from a philosophical point of view, they have much in common. Both define their positions in explicit opposition to utilitarianism, which each rejects on the grounds that it denies the distinction between persons. Both offer instead a rights-based ethic said to secure the liberty of individuals more completely. Although Nozick's account of rights owes much to Locke, both appeal to Kant's precept to treat every person as an end and not merely as a means, and seek principles of justice that embody it. Both deny that there exists any social entity above or beyond the individuals who comprise it. As Nozick writes, echoing Rawls in both principle and rhetoric,

Side constraints upon action [that is, unqualified prohibitions] reflect the underlying Kantian principle that individuals are ends and not merely means. . . . Side constraints express the inviolability of other persons. But why may not one violate persons for the greater social good? Individually, we each sometimes choose to undergo some pain or sacrifice for a greater benefit or to avoid a greater harm. . . . But there is no *social entity* with a good that undergoes some sacrifice for its own good. There are only individual people, different individual people, with their own individual lives. Using one of these people for the benefit of others, uses him and benefits the others. Nothing more. . . . To use a person in this way does not sufficiently respect and take account of the fact that he is a separate person, that his is the only life he has (1974: 30–3).

The moral side constraints upon what we may do, I claim, reflect the fact of our separate existences. They reflect the fact that no moral balancing act can take place among us; there is no moral outweighing of one of our lives by others so as to lead to a greater overall social good. There is no justified sacrifice of some of us for others (1974: 33).

Both theorists emphasize what Rawls calls 'the plurality and distinctness of persons' and what Nozick calls 'the fact of our separate existences'. This is the central moral fact that utilitarianism denies and that an individualistic, rights-based ethic affirms. On this moral fact, and on the importance of rights, Rawls and Nozick emphatically agree. And yet Rawls arrives at a theory of justice on which social and economic inequalities are permitted only in so far as they benefit the least well off, while Nozick holds justice to consist in voluntary exchanges and transfers alone, ruling out redistributive policies altogether. How then do their theories of justice come so sharply to diverge? Fortunately, the point of divergence can be located with some precision, since Rawls, in developing his second principle of justice (the one containing the difference principle), lays out a line of reasoning that begins with a position similar to Nozick's and ends with his own.

Rawls considers three possible principles by which the distribution of social and economic benefits might be regulated or assessed: natural liberty (similar to Nozick's 'entitlement theory'), liberal equality (akin to a standard meritocracy), and democratic equality (based on the difference principle). The system of natural liberty defines as just whatever distribution results from an efficient market economy in which a formal (i.e. legal) equality of opportunity prevails, such that positions are open to those with the relevant talents. Rawls finds this principle inadequate on the grounds that the distribution it sanctions tends simply to reproduce the initial distribution of talents and assets; those substantially endowed will wind up with substantial shares, and those with meager assets will end with meager results. Where the outcome tends simply to reproduce the initial distribution, it is possible to call it just only on the additional assumption that initial endowments were justly distributed. But this assumption cannot be established. 'The initial distribution of assets for any period of time is strongly influenced by natural and social contingencies', and as such is neither just nor unjust but simply arbitrary. And since there is nothing to recommend the justice of initial endowments, to install them in the name of justice is to incorporate the arbitrariness of fortune, nothing more. 'Intuitively, the most obvious injustice of the system of natural liberty is that it permits distributive shares to be improperly influenced by these factors so arbitrary from a moral point of view' (72).

The principle of liberal equality seeks to remedy the injustice of natural liberty by going beyond formal equality of opportunity and correcting, where possible, for social and cultural disadvantages. The aim is a kind of 'fair meritocracy', in which social and cultural inequalities are mitigated by equal educational opportunities, certain redistributive policies, and other social reforms. On the principle of liberal equality, the ideal is to provide all an 'equal start', so that those with similar native talents and capacities and a similar willingness to exercise them would have 'the same prospects of success regardless of their initial place in the social system, that is, irrespective of the income class into which they are born. In all sectors of society there should be roughly equal prospects of culture and achievement for everyone similarly motivated and endowed. The expectations of those with the same abilities and aspirations should not be affected by their social class' (73).

But while liberal equality represents an improvement over the system of natural liberty, 'intuitively it still appears defective'. Fair opportunity, however full, is too weak an assault on the arbitrariness of fortune.

Even if it works to perfection in eliminating the influence of social contingencies, it still permits the distribution of wealth and income to be determined by the natural distribution of abilities and talents. Within the limits allowed by the background arrangements, distributive shares are decided by the outcome of the natural lottery; and this outcome is arbitrary from a moral perspective. There is no more reason to permit the distribution of income and wealth to be settled by the distribution of natural assets than by historical and social fortune (73–4).

Once we are struck by the arbitrariness of initial endowments determining life prospects generally, we are bound on reflection to be as disturbed by the influence of natural contingencies as social and cultural ones. 'From a moral standpoint, the two seem equally arbitrary' (75). The same reasoning that leads us to favor a 'fair meritocracy' (as in liberal equality) over a purely formal equality of opportunity (as in natural liberty) naturally leads us further to seek what Rawls calls the democratic conception. But it seems clear that the democratic conception cannot be found in a simple extension of the principle of fair opportunity. For one thing, it would be virtually impossible to extend opportunity so completely as to eradicate even those inequalities stemming from social and cultural conditions alone. The institution of the family, for one, makes it 'impossible in practice to secure equal chances of achievement and culture for those similarly endowed' (74). But even if compensatory education and other reforms could fully, or even nearly, correct for social and cultural deprivation, it is difficult if not vaguely forbidding to imagine what kind of social policies would be required to 'correct' in a comparable way for the contingencies of natural fortune. What is needed, then, is a conception that nullifies the *effect* of these differences while at the same time acknowledging their intractability.

Some commentators, and particularly those hostile to the principle of democratic equality, describe the next logical step as a move from equality of opportunity to equality of result. In their view, any theory of justice that rejects a meritocratic conception for the moral arbitrariness of its distributive consequences must necessarily be committed to a kind of levelling equality requiring constant readjustment of distributive shares to correct for persisting differences of native talent and ability (Bell 1973: 441–3). But equality of result is by no means the only democratic alternative to a meritocratic regime, nor is it the principle adopted by Rawls. The difference principle is not synonymous with equality of result, nor does it require the levelling of all differences between persons. 'It does not follow that one should eliminate these distinctions,' writes Rawls. 'There is another way to deal with them' (102). Rawls' way is not to eradicate unequal endowments but to arrange the scheme of benefits and burdens so that the least advantaged may share in the resources of the fortunate. This is the arrangement that the difference principle seeks to achieve. It defines as just only those social and economic inequalities that work to the benefit of the least advantaged members of society. Taken together with the principle of offices and positions open to all under fair equality of opportunity, the difference principle defines Rawls' conception of democratic equality.

The difference principle is not simply a fuller version of the principle of fair opportunity; it attacks the problem of arbitrariness in a fundamentally different way. Rather than transform the conditions under which I exercise my talents, the difference principle transforms the moral basis on which I claim the benefits that flow from them. No longer am I to be regarded as the sole proprietor of my assets, or privileged recipient of the advantages they bring. 'The difference principle represents, in effect, an agreement to regard the distribution of natural talents as a common asset and to share in the benefits of this distribution whatever it turns out to be.' In this way, the difference principle acknowledges the arbitrariness of fortune by asserting that I am not really the owner but merely the guardian or repository of the talents and capacities that happen to reside in me, and as such have no special moral claim on the fruits of their exercise.

Those who have been favored by nature, whoever they are, may gain from their good fortune only on terms that improve the situation of those who have lost out. The naturally advantaged are not to gain merely because they are more gifted, but only to cover the costs of training and education and for using their endowments in ways that help the less fortunate as well. No one deserves his greater natural capacity nor merits a more favorable starting place in society (101–2).

By regarding the distribution of talents and attributes as a common asset rather than as individual possessions, Rawls obviates the need to 'even out' endowments in order to remedy the arbitrariness of social and natural contingencies. When 'men agree to share one another's fate' (102), it matters less that their fates, individually, may vary. This is why, although the difference principle tends to 'redress the bias of contingencies in the direction of equality', it 'does not require society to try to even out handicaps as if all were expected to compete on a fair basis in the same race' (101).

Rawls acknowledges that the difference principle and in particular the notion of endowments as 'common assets' clash with traditional conceptions of individual desert. 'There is a natural inclination to object that those better situated deserve their greater advantages whether or not they are to the benefit of others' (103). Rawls' response is that this conception of individual desert is a mistake, as the general argument from arbitrariness suggests. 'It seems to be one of the fixed points of our considered judgments that no one deserves his place in the distribution of native endowments, any more than one deserves one's initial starting place in society' (104). The claim that a person deserves at least what he achieves through his own effort is more intuitively plausible, but even the willingness to strive conscientiously may largely be determined by social and natural contingencies. 'The assertion that a man deserves the superior character that enables him to make the effort to cultivate his abilities is equally problematic; for his character depends in large part upon fortunate family and social circumstances for which he can claim no credit. The notion of desert seems not to apply to these cases' (104).

This is not to deny the role of individual entitlements altogether. Certain kinds of entitlements are consistent with the difference principle, but here it is necessary to distinguish between desert and legitimate expectations. Since it is in the general interest that I cultivate and exercise (some of) the talents and assets in my charge, rather than have them lie dormant, society is typically arranged to provide resources for their cultivation and incentives for their exercise. To be sure, I am entitled to my share of these benefits when I have qualified for them under the terms specified. What is important to stress, however, is that *these* claims honor the legitimate expectations created by institutions designed to elicit my efforts, not a primordial right or claim of desert in virtue of qualities I possess.

It is perfectly true that given a just system of co-operation as a scheme of public rules and the expectations set up by it, those who, with the prospect of improving their condition, have done what the system announces that it will reward are entitled to their advantages. In this sense the more fortunate have a claim to their better condition; their claims are legitimate expectations established by social institutions, and the community is obligated to meet them. But this sense of desert presupposes the existence of the cooperative scheme; it is irrelevant to the question whether in the first place the scheme is to be designed in accordance with the difference principle or some other criterion (103).

Although I am *entitled* to the benefits answering my legitimate expectations, I do not *deserve* them, for two reasons: first, given the assumption of common assets, I do not really *possess* the attributes that give rise to the benefits, or if I do possess them, it is only in the weak, accidental sense rather than the strong, constitutive sense, and this sense of possession is inadequate to establish desert in the strong, pre-institutional sense. And second, while I am entitled to my fair share under the rules, I am not entitled that *these* rules, rewarding *these* attributes, be in force rather than some others. For these reasons, the well-endowed 'cannot say that he deserves and therefore has a right to a scheme of co-operation in which he is permitted to acquire benefits in ways that do not contribute to the welfare of others. There is no basis for his making this claim' (104).

MERITOCRACY VERSUS THE DIFFERENCE PRINCIPLE

Before moving on to consider Nozick's answer to Rawls and his defense of natural liberty, it may be helpful to clarify further some of the contrasts between the difference principle (as in Rawls' 'democratic equality') and the meritocratic conception (as in 'liberal equality'). Perhaps the most striking difference is in the role of individual merit or desert, which is central in the meritocratic conception and absent, or at least seriously weakened, in justice as fairness.[1] In a 'fair meritocracy', that is, one in which discrimination and class biases are overcome, those who achieve favored positions have earned their status and so deserve the rewards that attach to it. Unequal distributive shares are allocated in recognition of superior achievement and not merely in satisfaction of legitimate expectations. As one defender of the meritocratic ethic explains,

---

1 I leave aside those versions of meritocracy that would allocate distributive shares for the sake of creating incentives and attracting the relevant talents alone, without reference to the moral worthiness of the recipients.

A meritocracy is made up of those who have earned their authority. . . . Meritocracy, in the context of my usage, is an emphasis on individual achievement and earned status as confirmed by one's peers. . . . While all men are entitled to respect, they are not all entitled to praise. The meritocracy, in the best meaning of that word, is made up of those worthy of praise (Bell 1973: 453–4).

A second, related difference concerns the distinction between genetic and cultural advantages. For Rawls, this distinction is virtually irrelevant to questions of justice. On meritocratic assumptions, however, the distinction is crucial; hence the intense debate among those committed to meritocratic ideals over the role of genetic and cultural factors in determining intelligence and life prospects generally. Where the justice of distributive arrangements is seen to depend on the 'fair opportunity' of all to compete equally for (ultimately) unequal rewards, the distinction of genetic from social and cultural obstacles becomes central to any assessment of the scheme. The more closely success can be traced to hereditary factors, the fewer inequalities social institutions can be presumed capable of (or responsible for) ameliorating, and the less scope seems available for the kind of individual effort on which desert is said to depend.

In the nature of meritocracy, as it has been traditionally conceived, what is central to the assessment of a person is the assumed relation of achievement to intelligence, and of intelligence to its measurement on the Intelligence Quotient scale. The first question, therefore, is what determines intelligence.

All this makes the question of the relation of intelligence to genetic inheritance very touchy. Is intelligence largely inherited? Can one raise intelligence by nurture? How does one separate native ability and drive from improvements in skill acquired through education? (Bell 1973: 411)

For justice as fairness, the debate over the determinants of intelligence and the extensive social scientific literature it has produced are more or less beside the point. Once one rejects the notions of individual desert and 'fair opportunity' as the primary bases of distributive shares, the distinction between genetic and cultural obstacles to success loses much of its moral interest. Once we agree to regard the distribution of talents as a common asset, it matters little how some came to reside in you and others in me.

Defenders of the meritocratic conceptions are not always explicit on the *grounds* for their distinction between natural and social advantages, but one can imagine at least two possible arguments, one moral and the other practical. The first would argue that genetic endowments are inviolable in a way that social or cultural characteristics are not, that a person's natural endowments are somehow more essentially *his,* more deeply constitutive of his identity than his socially conditioned attributes. Innate differences, however arbitrary, are not dispensable in the same way; they, and not the results of social and cultural conditioning, mark out the traits in the absence of which I would not be the particular person I am. On this view, whether I deserve the intelligence with which I am born, for example, is not the point; what matters is that my native intelligence is a fact irreducibly about *me,* and the integrity of my person requires that it not be tampered with, no matter how worthy the wider social purpose.

But this argument seems flawed once it appears that those qualities most plausibly regarded as essential to a person's identity – one's character, values, core convictions, and deepest loyalties, for example – are often heavily influenced by social and cultural factors, while many natural features – such as hair color and other trivial physical characteristics – are more readily dispensable. Even if some distinction between essential and merely accidental characteristics of the person is valid, there seems no obvious reason why it must correspond to the distinction between natural and social assets. Of course, Rawls' objection to the argument would be stronger still, for his theory of the person implies that no characteristic, whether social or natural, can be essential in this way. Even those attributes, such as a person's character and values, that intuitively seem closest to defining an essential self, are relegated to contingent status. As a person's character 'depends in large part upon fortunate family and social circumstances for which he can claim no credit' (104), so our values are accidental as well. 'That we have one conception of the good rather than another is not relevant from a moral standpoint. In acquiring it we are influenced by the same sort of contingencies that lead us to rule out a knowledge of our sex and class' (Rawls 1975: 537).

The practical argument would distinguish natural and social inequalities on the grounds that the first are intractable in a way that the second are not, and that society can therefore be held responsible for remedying social inequalities but not natural ones; the more inequality turns out to be genetic rather than culturally induced, the less society can 'do about it'. Given a fair system, some will advance more successfully than others, and there comes a point when even the most enlightened society can do nothing to alter this fact. At some point, even the most dogged reformers must acknowledge that life is unfair in a way that no social institutions can hope to set right. People are different, and these differences, sooner or later, will inevitably come to the fore, even – perhaps most assuredly – in a society where fair opportunity prevails. 'What is important is that the society, to the fullest possible extent, be a genuinely open one' (Bell 1973: 454).

To this Rawls would likely respond that society's role is naturally limited in this way only if one assumes that its only role in promoting justice consists in its efforts to even out the disadvantages of the least fortunate so that they may compete more fairly. But this assumption overlooks the equally significant social choice implicit in the aims institutions pursue and the attributes they reward in the process. Even if the vast majority of differences between persons turned out to be genetic rather than cultural, it would still remain for a society to determine *which* of these differences, if any, should properly be made the basis for differential distributive shares. To be sure, if the aim of social institutions is taken to be fixed, as maximizing the overall social product, for example, then the defenders of a 'fair meritocracy' are right, that the only remaining question of justice is how well people are equipped by the society to contribute to that purpose and to reap the benefits of their contribution. But the question must immediately arise as to why *that* aim should be primary, even if it can prevail only at the admitted expense of social injustice. In short, a society not only equips or fails to equip its members with the endowments relevant to its collective purpose, but also defines through its institutional arrangements the nature of that purpose and, derivatively, the attributes to be prized and installed as the basis of distributive shares. In a passage of some eloquence, Rawls writes:

In view of these remarks we may reject the contention that the ordering of institutions is always defective because the distribution of natural talents and the contingencies of social circumstances are unjust, and this injustice must inevitably carry over to human arrangements. Occasionally this reflection is offered as an excuse for ignoring injustice, as if the refusal to acquiesce in injustice is on a par with being unable to accept death. The natural distribution is neither just nor unjust; nor is it unjust that men are born into society at some particular position. These are simply natural facts. What is just and unjust is the way that institutions deal with these facts (102).

These considerations lead naturally to a third contrast between the meritocratic conception and the democratic one, which concerns the relation between the value of various assets and attributes on the one hand and the institutions that prize and reward them on the other. On the meritocratic conception, social institutions are bound to reward certain attributes rather than others. The qualities that a set of institutions calls forth have a worth antecedent to their institutional valuation, and so provide an independent test of the justice of the institutions themselves. Institutional arrangements that put a premium on noble qualities rather than base ones are, in virtue of *that,* the worthier, quite apart from other considerations relevant to justice, such as the purposes they advance.

On Rawls' view, institutions are not constrained in this way, for the virtues that would constrain them must themselves await institutional definition. 'The concept of moral worth does not provide a first principle of distributive justice', because it cannot be introduced until after the principles of justice are already on hand (312). Since no virtue has antecedent, or pre-institutional moral status, the design of institutions is open with respect to the qualities it may prize. As a result, the intrinsic worth of the attributes a society elicits and rewards cannot provide a measure for assessing its justice, for their worth only appears in the light of institutional arrangements to begin with. Rawls' rejection of pre-institutional notions of virtue reflects the priority of the right over the good and the refusal to choose in advance between competing conceptions of the good. A hunting society that rewards fleet-footedness over loquaciousness (as prized in a litigious society, for example) is not less just or worthy in virtue of *that,* for there are no antecedent grounds on which swiftness of foot could be shown as more or less virtuous than swiftness of tongue. The priority of just institutions with respect to virtue and moral worth provides a second reason why I cannot be said to deserve the benefits flowing from my natural attributes. In order for me to deserve the benefits associated with 'my' superior intelligence, say, it is necessary both that I possess my intelligence (in some non-arbitrary sense of possession), *and* that I have a right (in a strong, pre-institutional sense of right) that society value intelligence rather than something else. But on Rawls' account, neither condition holds. The argument from arbitrariness to common assets undermines the first, and the precedence of institutions over moral worth denies the second.

DEFENDING COMMON ASSETS

In developing our critique of Rawls' theory of the person and the difference principle, each in the light of the other, we shall take as our points of departure two strands of Nozick's critique of justice as fairness. The first attacks the difference principle and in particular the notion of possession on which it relies, and the second defends a version of natural liberty by fixing on the notions of desert and entitlement. Playing Nozick off against Rawls in this way will enable us to assess Rawls' conception and also to clarify some of the similarities and differences in their respective distributive theories.

Nozick's central objection to the argument producing the difference principle fixes on Rawls' view that the distribution of natural talents is best regarded as a 'common' or 'collective' possession to be shared across society as a whole. As Rawls writes,

The difference principle represents, in effect, an agreement to regard the distribution of natural talents as a common asset and to share in the benefits of this distribution whatever it turns out to be (101).

The two principles are equivalent, as I have remarked, to an undertaking to regard the distribution of natural abilities as a collective asset so that the more fortunate are to benefit only in ways that help those who have lost out (179).

Rawls believes the notion of common assets as embodied in the difference principle expresses the ideal of mutual respect deontological liberalism seeks to affirm.

By arranging inequalities for reciprocal advantage and by abstaining from the exploitation of the contingencies of natural and social circumstance within a framework of equal liberty, persons express their respect for one another in the very constitution of their society. . . . Another way of putting this is to say that the principles of justice manifest in the basic structure of society men's desire to treat one another not as means only but as ends in themselves (179).

Nozick argues, to the contrary, that to regard people's natural assets as common property is precisely to contradict all that deontological liberalism affirms in emphasizing the inviolability of the individual and the distinction between persons.

People will differ in how they view regarding natural talents as a common asset. Some will complain, echoing Rawls against utilitarianism, that this 'does not take seriously the distinction between persons'; and they will wonder whether any reconstruction of Kant that treats people's abilities and talents as resources for others can be adequate. 'The two principles of justice . . . rule out even the tendency to regard men as means to one another's welfare.' Only if one presses *very* hard on the distinction between men and their talents, assets, abilities and special traits (1974: 228).

Here Nozick goes to the heart of Rawls' theory of the subject. For as we have seen, Rawls presses very hard indeed on the distinction between the self and its various possessions. The severity of this distinction, problematic though it may be, is carefully fashioned to the requirements of the deontological project as a whole; it allows for the priority of the self over its ends, which supports in turn the priority of the right and the primacy of justice. A further feature of this conception is that it allows for the following defense against Nozick's objection to the difference principle.

Regarding the distribution of natural talents as a common asset does not violate the difference between persons nor regard some as means to others' welfare, because not *persons* but only 'their' *attributes* are being used as means to others' well-being. To say that *I* am somehow violated or abused when 'my' intelligence or even effort is used for the common benefit is to confuse the self with its contingently given and wholly inessential attributes (inessential, that is, to me being the particular self I am). Only on a theory of the person that held these endowments to be essential *constituents* rather than alienable *attributes* of the self could the sharing of assets be viewed as using *me* as a means to others' ends. But on Rawls' account all endowments are contingent and in principle detachable from the self, whose priority is assured by its ability constantly to recede before the swirl of circumstance. This is the feature that preserves its identity, by assuring its invulnerability to transformation by experience.

While this defense evades the inconsistency, it quickly invites a related objection of incoherence, for if Rawls must invoke the distinction between the self and its possessions in this thoroughgoing way, the question immediately arises whether, in avoiding a radically situated subject, Rawls does not lapse into the opposite extreme of a radically disembodied one. As Nozick presses the objection, 'Whether any coherent conception of a person remains when the distinction is so pressed is an open question. Why we, thick with particular traits, should be cheered that (only) the thus purified men within us are not regarded as means is also unclear' (1974: 228).

Nozick thus anticipates Rawls' defense and shows it to be too ingenious to redeem the theory. The notion that only *my assets* are being used as a means, not *me*, threatens to undermine the plausibility, even the coherence, of the very distinction it invokes. It suggests that on the difference principle, we can take seriously the distinction between persons only by taking metaphysically the distinction between a person and his attributes. But this has the consequence of leaving us with a subject *so* shorn of empirically identifiable characteristics (so 'purified', in Nozick's word), as to resemble after all the Kantian transcendent or disembodied subject Rawls set out to avoid. It would seem that Rawls escapes the charge of inconsistency only at the price of incoherence, and that Nozick's objection to the difference principle therefore succeeds.

But Rawls has an alternate defense available, this one unanticipated by Nozick. Although it rescues the difference principle from reliance on an apparently disembodied conception of the subject, it comes at some expense to other aspects of Rawls' doctrine, and so would likely be resisted by Rawls himself. Still, I shall try to show that only by somehow assuming it can the difference principle be sustained. On this second defense, Rawls might deny that the difference principle uses me as a means to others' ends, not by claiming that my *assets* rather than *person* are being used, but instead by questioning the sense in which those who share in 'my' assets are properly described as 'others'. Where the first defense presses the distinction between the self and its attributes, the second qualifies the distinction between the self and the other by allowing that, in certain moral circumstances, the relevant description of the self may embrace more than a single empirically individuated human being. The second defense ties the notion of common assets to the possibility of a common subject of possession. It appeals, in short, to an intersubjective conception of the self.

That the difference principle commits Rawls to an intersubjective conception he otherwise rejects seems the only way out of the difficulties Nozick raises. It also serves to highlight an unargued assumption in Rawls' theory of the subject. As we have seen, Rawls conceives the self as a subject of possession, bounded in advance, and given prior to its ends, and he assumes furthermore that the bounds of the subject unproblematically correspond to the bodily bounds between individual human beings. But this claim is never defended by Rawls, only assumed, its contestability hidden perhaps by its affinity with our unreflective common-sense view of the matter.[2] Rawls' emphasis on plurality as an essential feature of human society may be thought to lend some support to the assumption, but this can establish only that *some* principle of plurality or differentiation is essential to an account of the human subject, not necessarily a physical bodily one; nor can it show that the number of this plurality must correspond in all cases to the number of individual human beings in the world.

This in any case is the assumption that must give way if Nozick's objection to common assets is to be overcome. If the difference principle is to avoid using some as means to others' ends, it can only be possible under circumstances where the subject of possession is a 'we' rather than an 'I', which circumstances imply in turn the existence of a community in the constitutive sense.

The conclusion that Rawls' theory implicitly relies on an intersubjective conception he officially rejects finds further support in the discussions of desert and justification to follow, and is hinted at by various traces of intersubjective language to be found throughout the text. Such language first appears in the discussion of the difference principle when, as we have seen, the distribution of natural talents is described alternately as a 'common' or 'collective' or 'social' asset to be used for the 'common advantage' (101, 179, 107). 'In justice as fairness men agree to share one another's fate' (102). They resolve, that is, not to take seriously the differences between persons as the basis for differential life prospects, on the grounds that these differences arise from factors arbitrary from a moral point of view.

---

2 Still, Rawls' critique of utilitarianism makes especially perplexing his failure to defend his principle of individuation more completely, for it is precisely on this issue that he claims utilitarianism errs, by failing to recognize, or at any rate failing to take seriously, the distinction between persons.

In his discussion of the idea of social union, Rawls carries his inter-subjective language from common assets to common ends and purposes, and in rhetoric that comes perilously close to the teleological, speaks of human beings realizing their common nature as well. In his account of social union, Rawls shifts from distributive issues to a concern for self-realization, and seeks to show that justice as fairness can provide an interpretation of human sociability that is neither trivial nor purely instrumental. 'Thus human beings have in fact shared final ends and they value their common institutions and activities as goods in themselves' (522). The characteristics of social union are 'shared final ends and common activities valued for themselves' (525). Following Humboldt, a nineteenth-century liberal in the German idealist tradition, Rawls writes that 'it is through social union founded upon the needs and potentialities of its members that each person can participate in the total sum of the realized natural assets of the others. . . . *Only in the social union is the individual complete*' [emphasis added] (523, 525n). Social unions come in a variety of shapes and sizes; 'they range from families and friendships to much larger associations. Nor are there limits of time and space, for those widely separated by history and circumstance can nevertheless co-operate in *realizing their common nature*' [emphasis added] (527).

By their intersubjective dimensions, the difference principle and the idea of social union counter individualistic assumptions in two different ways, the difference principle by nullifying the arbitrariness that arises when natural assets are seen as individual possessions, the idea of social union by overcoming the partiality of persons that appears when individuals are thought to be complete in themselves. In a social union, 'the members of a community participate in one another's nature . . . [and] *the self is realized in the activities of many selves*' [emphasis added] (565).

It is a feature of human sociability that we are by ourselves but parts of what we might be. We must look to others to attain the excellences that we must leave aside, or lack altogether. The collective activity of society, the many associations and the public life of the largest community that regulates them, sustains our efforts and elicits our contribution. Yet the good attained from the common culture far exceeds our work in the sense that we *cease to be mere fragments:* that *part of ourselves* that we directly realize is joined to a wider and just arrangement the aims of which we affirm [emphasis added] (529).

THE BASIS OF DESERT

The notion of possession leads naturally to claims of desert and entitlement. The argument over what people possess, and on what terms, has a direct bearing on the question of what people deserve or are entitled to as a matter of justice. It is to the issues of desert and entitlement that we now turn, to consider the second strand of Nozick's critique of justice as fairness. Rawls rejects the principles of natural liberty and liberal equality on the grounds that they reward assets and attributes which, being arbitrary from a moral point of view, people cannot properly be said to deserve, and adopts the difference principle on the grounds that it nullifies this arbitrariness. Nozick attacks this line of reasoning by arguing first that arbitrariness does not undermine desert, and second that, even if it did, a version of natural liberty and not the difference principle would emerge as the preferred result.

Stated in terms of possession, Rawls' objection to natural liberty and liberal equality is that under these principles, persons are allowed unfairly to benefit (or suffer) from natural and social endowments that do not properly *belong* to them, at least not in the strong, constitutive sense of belonging. To be sure, the various natural assets with which I am born may be said to 'belong' to me in the weak, contingent sense that they reside accidentally within me, but this sense of ownership or possession cannot establish that I have any special rights with respect to these assets or any privileged claim to the fruits of their exercise. In this attenuated sense of possession, I am not really the owner but merely the guardian or repository of the assorted assets and attributes located 'here'. By failing to acknowledge the arbitrariness of fortune, the principles of natural liberty and liberal equality go wrong in assuming that 'my' assets belong to me in the strong, constitutive sense, and so allowing distributive shares to depend on them.

Expressed in terms of desert, Rawls' objection to the principles of natural liberty and liberal equality is that they reward assets and attributes that people cannot properly be said to deserve. Though some may think the fortunate deserve the things that lead to their greater advantage, 'this view is surely incorrect'.

It seems to be one of the fixed points of our considered judgments that no one deserves his place in the distribution of native endowments, any more than one deserves one's initial starting place in society. The assertion that a man deserves the superior character that enables him to make the effort to cultivate his abilities is equally problematic; for his character depends in large part upon fortunate family and social circumstances for which he can claim no credit. The notion of desert seems not to apply to these cases (104).

Because no one deserves his good luck in the genetic lottery, or his favored starting place in society, or for that matter the superior character that motivates him to cultivate his abilities conscientiously, no one can be said to deserve the benefits these assets produce. It is this deduction that Nozick disputes. 'It is not true,' he argues, 'that a person earns Y (a right to keep a painting he's made, praise for writing *A Theory of Justice,* and so on) only if he's earned (or otherwise *deserves*) whatever he used (including natural assets) in the process of earning Y. Some of the things he uses he just may *have,* not illegitimately. It needn't be that the foundations underlying desert are themselves deserved, *all the way down*' (1974: 225).

Now what are we to make of this claim? If I do not necessarily have to *deserve* everything I use in producing a thing in order to deserve the thing, what *does* my desert depend on? Nozick says that some of the things I use I 'just may *have,* not illegitimately' (and, presumably, possibly arbitrarily). Once again, the notion of possession enters the scene. To see whether my having a thing, not illegitimately, can enable me to deserve what it helps me produce, we must explore in greater detail the relation between possession and desert, and sort out once more the sense of possession being appealed to.

For this purpose, it may be helpful to consider a recent discussion of justice and personal desert by Joel Feinberg, who analyzes the bases of desert with an admirable clarity in terms suggestive for the arguments before us (1970). Feinberg begins with the observation that no one can deserve anything unless there is some basis for the desert. 'Desert without a basis is simply not desert'. But the question immediately arises what *kind* of basis is necessary. As Feinberg writes, 'Not any old basis will do'. Once again, the notion of possession provides the key. 'If a person is deserving of some sort of treatment, he must, necessarily, be so in virtue of some *possessed characteristic* or prior activity' [emphasis added] (1970: 48).

A characteristic of mine cannot be a basis for a desert of yours unless it somehow reveals or reflects some characteristic of yours. In general, the facts which constitute the basis of a subject's desert must be facts about that subject. If a student deserves a high grade in a course, for example, his desert must be in virtue of some fact about *him* – his earlier performances, say, or his present abilities. . . . It is necessary that a person's desert have a basis and that the basis consist in some fact about himself (1970: 58–9, 61).

Feinberg's analysis, tying a person's desert to some fact about the person, would appear to support Nozick's claim that 'the foundations underlying desert needn't themselves be deserved, *all the way down*'. In fact, the reliance of desert on some possessed characteristic of the person suggests a thesis even stronger than Nozick's: that the foundations underlying desert *cannot* themselves be deserved, *all the way down*, any more than the foundations underlying possession can themselves be possessed, *all the way down*. We have already seen how the notion of possession requires that somewhere, 'down there', there must be a subject of possession that is not *itself* possessed (for this would deny its agency), a subject 'doing the possessing', so to speak. The analogy for desert must be a *basis* of desert ultimately prior to desert. For consider: if desert presupposes some possessed characteristic, and if possessed characteristics presuppose some subject of possession which is not itself possessed, then desert must presuppose some subject of possession which is not itself possessed, and therefore some basis of desert which is not itself deserved. Just as there must be some subject of possession prior to possession, so there must be some basis of desert prior to desert. This is why the question whether someone deserves (to have) his sterling character, for example, is notoriously difficult (for it is unclear who or what is left to judge once his character has been removed), and why, beyond a certain point, asking just wholesale whether someone deserves to be the (kind of) person he is becomes incoherent altogether. Somewhere, 'down there', there must be a basis of desert that is not itself deserved. The foundations underlying desert cannot themselves be deserved, all the way down.

This result would seem amply to confirm Nozick's claim against Rawls that I do not necessarily have to *deserve* everything I use in producing a thing in order to deserve the thing, that some of what I use I 'just may *have*, not illegitimately'. And if this claim can be established, then it would appear that Rawls' argument from arbitrariness fails to undermine desert after all. To say, as Rawls does, that I do not deserve the superior character that led me to realize my abilities is no longer enough. To deny my desert, he must show that I do not *have* the requisite character, or alternatively, that I *have* it, but not in the requisite sense.

But this is precisely the argument Rawls' theory of the person allows him to make. For given his sharp distinction between the self, taken as the pure subject of possession, and the aims and attributes it possesses, the self is left bare of any substantive feature or characteristic that could qualify as a desert base. Given the distancing aspect of possession, the self *itself* is dispossessed. On Rawls' theory of the person, the self, strictly speaking, *has nothing*, nothing at least in the strong, constitutive sense necessary to desert. In a move similar to the one invoked to show that the difference principle does not use a *person* as a means, only a person's *attributes,* Rawls can accept that some undeserved desert base is necessary to desert, only to claim that, on an adequate understanding of the person, this condition could never in principle be met! On Rawls' conception, the characteristics I possess do not *attach* to the self but are only *related* to the self, standing always at a certain distance. This is what makes them attributes rather than constituents of my person; they are *mine* rather than *me*, things I *have* rather than *am*.

We can see in this light how Rawls' argument from arbitrariness undermines desert not directly, by claiming I cannot *deserve* what is arbitrarily given, but indirectly, by showing I cannot *possess* what is arbitrarily given, that is, that 'I', *qua* subject of possession, cannot possess it in the undistanced, constitutive sense necessary to provide a desert base. An arbitrarily given asset cannot be an essential constituent but only an accidental attribute of my person, for otherwise my identity would hang on a mere contingency, its continuity constantly vulnerable to transformation by experience, my status as a sovereign agent dependent on the conditions of my existence rather than epistemologically guaranteed. On Rawls' conception, no one can properly be said to deserve anything because no one can properly be said to possess anything, at least not in the strong, constitutive sense of possession necessary to the notion of desert.

A theory of justice without desert would seem a dramatic departure from traditional conceptions, but Rawls is at pains to show that it is not. In his opening pages, Rawls acknowledges that his approach 'may not seem to tally with tradition', but seeks to reassure that in fact it does.

The more specific sense that Aristotle gives to justice, and from which the most familiar formulations derive, is that of refraining from *pleonexia,* that is, from gaining some advantage for oneself by seizing *what belongs to another,* his property, his reward, his office, and the like, or by denying a person that which is due to him. . . . *Aristotle's definition clearly presupposes, however, an account of what properly belongs to a person, and of what is due to him. Now such entitlements are, I believe, very often derived from social institutions and the legitimate expectations to which they give rise.* There is no reason to think that Aristotle would disagree with this, and certainly he has a conception of social justice to account for these claims. . . . There is no conflict with the traditional notion [emphasis added] (10–11).

In comparing justice as fairness with traditional conceptions, Rawls confirms its novelty rather than denies it. What he presents as an incidental qualification to justice as classically conceived turns out on inspection to signal a striking departure. As Rawls suggests, traditional notions freely refer to 'what properly belongs to a person', institutions, presumably, aside; they presuppose thickly constituted persons with a fixity of character, certain features of which are taken to be essential, 'all the way down'. On Rawls' conception, however, none of these concepts is available. In so far as a theory of justice 'presupposes an account of what properly belongs to a person' (in the strong sense of 'belongs'), Rawls effectively acknowledges that he has none. Nor, he seems to imply, given the precedence of plurality, the priority of right, and the theory of the person they require, is it reasonable to think that such a theory of justice could be true. We are not essentially thick enough selves to bear rights and deserts antecedent to the institutions that define them. Given these constraints, the only alternative is to opt for a theory of justice based on entitlements to legitimate expectations, ruling out desert altogether. Rawls hedges this claim at first, saying only that 'such entitlements are, I believe, *very often* derived from social institutions and the legitimate expectations to which they give rise' [emphasis added] (10). But as the full consequences of Rawls' view emerge, 'very often' becomes 'always', for it becomes clear that 'such entitlements' can arise in no other way. While Aristotle might not disagree that entitlements can arise in this way, it seems far from his view that they can arise in no other way. In denying that justice has to do with giving people what they deserve, justice as fairness departs decisively from the traditional notion after all.

Rawls' apparent view that no one can properly be said to deserve anything, and the connection of this view with the notion of the self as 'essentially unencumbered', emerges more fully in his discussion of legitimate expectations and moral desert. He begins by acknowledging that justice as fairness, in rejecting desert, runs counter to common sense.

There is a tendency for common sense to suppose that income and wealth, and the good things in life generally, should be distributed according to moral desert. Justice is happiness according to virtue. While it is recognized that this ideal can never be fully carried out, it is the appropriate conception of distributive justice, at least as a prima facie principle, and society should try to realize it as circumstances permit. Now justice as fairness rejects this conception. Such a principle would not be chosen in the original position. There seems to be no way of defining the requisite criterion in that situation (310–11).

There seems to be no way of defining the requisite criterion of a person's virtue or moral worth in the original position because no substantive theory of the person antecedent to social institutions exists. For moral desert to provide an independent criterion of justice, there must be some substantive theory of the person, or of the worth of persons, to get it going. But for Rawls, the worth of persons is subsequent to institutions, not independent of them. And so a person's moral claims must await their arrival.

This leads to the distinction between moral desert and legitimate expectations. Once a person does the various things established institutions encourage him to do, he acquires certain rights, but not before. He is entitled that institutions honor the claims they announce they will reward, but he is not entitled that they undertake to reward any particular kind of claim in the first place.

A just scheme, then, answers to what men are entitled to; it satisfies their legitimate expectations as founded upon social institutions. But what they are entitled to is not proportional to nor dependent upon their intrinsic worth. The principles of justice that regulate the basic structure and specify the duties and obligations of individuals do not mention moral desert, and there is no tendency for distributive shares to correspond to it (311).

The principles of justice do not mention moral desert because, strictly speaking, no one can be said to deserve anything. Similarly, the reason people's entitlements are not proportional to nor dependent upon their intrinsic worth is that, on Rawls' view, *people have no intrinsic worth,* no worth that is intrinsic in the sense that it is theirs prior to or independent of or apart from what just institutions attribute to them.

The essential point is that the concept of moral worth does not provide a first principle of distributive justice. This is because it cannot be introduced until after the principles of justice and of natural duty and obligation have been acknowledged. . . . [T]he concept of moral worth is secondary to those of right and justice, and it plays no role in the substantive definition of distributive shares (312–13).

Rawls could agree with Feinberg that 'desert is a *moral* concept in the sense that it is logically prior to and independent of public institutions and their rules', but would deny that there is any 'antecedent standard for its definition' (313), and so disagree with Feinberg that 'one of the aims of [a system of public bestowals] is to give people what they deserve' (1970: 86). For Rawls, the principles of justice aim neither at rewarding virtue nor at giving people what they deserve, but instead at calling forth the resources and talents necessary to serve the common interest.

None of the precepts of justice aims at rewarding virtue. The premiums earned by scarce natural talents, for example, are to cover the costs of training and to encourage the efforts of learning, as well as to direct ability to where it best furthers the common interest. The distributive shares that result do not correlate with moral worth (311).

To illustrate the priority of just institutions with respect to virtue and moral worth, Rawls suggests an analogy to the relation between the rules of property and the law of robbery and theft.

These offenses and the demerits they entail presuppose the institution of property which is established for prior and independent social ends. For a society to organize itself with the aim of rewarding moral desert as a first principle would be like having the institution of property in order to punish thieves. The criterion to each according to his virtue would not, then, be chosen in the original position (313).

The analogy is intriguing, but one wonders whether it works entirely to Rawls' advantage. While it is apparent that the institution of property has a *certain* priority with respect to its correlative offenses, it is less clear why the dependence must run only in one direction, especially given Rawls' own commitment to the method of reflective equilibrium. For example, is our belief in the validity of the institution of property in no way enhanced by a conviction that robbery and theft are wrong? Would our confidence in the institution of property in no way be diminished if it turned out that those it defined as robbers and thieves were invariably good and virtuous men? And what of more extreme cases? While the norms and rules protecting human life can no doubt be defended on a variety of grounds, such as keeping people alive, avoiding suffering, and so on, is it logically mistaken to think that one justification of prohibitions against murder could be to punish murderers?

Rawls' position here appears especially perplexing in the light of a contrast he draws between distributive justice and retributive justice, suggesting that in the second case, some notion of moral desert may be appropriate after all. The view that distributive shares should match moral worth to the extent possible, writes Rawls, 'may arise from thinking of distributive justice as somehow the opposite of retributive justice'. But the analogy is mistaken. In a reasonably well-ordered society, 'Those who are punished for violating just laws have normally done something wrong. This is because the purpose of the criminal law is to uphold basic natural duties . . . and punishments are to serve the end'.

They are not simply a scheme of taxes and burdens designed to put a price on certain forms of conduct and in this way to guide men's conduct for mutual advantage. It would be far better if the acts prescribed by penal statutes were never done. *Thus a propensity to commit such acts is a mark of bad character,* and in a just society legal punishments will only fall upon those who display these faults.

It is clear that the distribution of economic and social advantages is entirely different. These arrangements are not the converse, so to speak, of the criminal law so that just as the one punishes certain offenses, the other rewards moral worth. The function of unequal distributive shares is to cover the costs of training and education, to attract individuals to places and associations where they are most needed from a social point of view, and so on. . . . *To think of distributive and retributive justice as converses of one another is completely misleading and suggests a moral basis of distributive shares where none exists* [emphasis added] (314–15).

Unlike the benefits that flow from distributive arrangements, the punishments and prohibitions associated with the criminal law are not simply a non-moral system of incentives and deterrents designed to encourage some forms of behavior and discourage others. For Rawls, the pre-institutional moral notions excluded in distributive justice somehow find meaning for retributive purposes, and there is a tendency for punishment to correspond to them.

The immediate puzzle is how this account can possibly fit with the analogy of property and theft. If retributive justice differs from distributive justice precisely in virtue of its prior moral basis, it is difficult to see how the example of property and theft could demonstrate the priority of social institutions with respect to virtue and moral worth, if this priority holds for distributive justice alone. This relatively minor confusion aside, the more basic question is how Rawls can admit desert in retributive justice without contradicting the theory of the self and related assumptions that ruled it out for purposes of distributive justice. If such notions as pre-institutional moral claims and intrinsic moral worth are excluded from a theory of distributive justice in virtue of an essentially unencumbered self too slender to support them, it is difficult to see how retributive justice could differ in any relevant way.[3]

Do not the same arguments from arbitrariness exclude desert as a basis for punishment as for distributive shares? Is the propensity to commit crimes, any less than the propensity to do good, the result of factors arbitrary from a moral point of view? And if not, why would the parties to the original position not agree to share one another's fate for the purpose of criminal liability as well as distributive arrangements? Since under the veil of ignorance, none can know whether he shall have the misfortune to be born into the unfavorable social and family circumstances that lead to a life of crime, why would the parties not adopt a kind of difference principle for punishments as well as distributive shares, and agree, in effect, to regard the distribution of natural and social liabilities as a common burden?

Rawls holds that 'those who are punished for violating just laws

3 In a footnote, Rawls (315) cites Feinberg in apparent support of this claim, but Feinberg allows a role for desert in both distributive and retributive justice. Feinberg's point is that retributive justice involves what he calls polar desert (where one either deserves good or deserves ill), whereas distributive justice involves nonpolar desert (where, as with a prize, some deserve and others do not). But both cases involve desert in the moral, pre-institutional sense (Feinberg 1970: 62).

have normally done something wrong', and so deserve their punishment (314). But suppose, by an act of vandalism, I deprive the community of a certain measure of well-being, say by throwing a brick through a window. Is there any reason why I deserve to bear the full costs of my destructiveness any more than the person who produced the window *deserves* to enjoy the full benefits of his productiveness? Rawls may reply that my 'propensity to commit such acts is a mark of bad character'. But if the worker's industriousness in making the window is not a mark of good character (in the moral, pre-institutional sense), why is my maliciousness in breaking the window a mark of bad character (in the moral, pre-institutional sense)? To be sure (following Rawls, p. 103), given a just system of criminal law, those who have done what the system announces it will punish are properly dealt with accordingly and in this sense are 'deserving' of their penalty. 'But this sense of desert presupposes the existence of the [retributive] scheme; it is irrelevant to the question whether in the first place the scheme is to be designed in accordance with the difference principle or some other criterion' (103).

Some may think that the criminal deserves his punishment in the strong moral sense because he deserves the low character his criminality reflects. Perhaps this is what Rawls has in mind when he writes that 'propensity to commit such acts is a mark of bad character', and punishments properly fall on those who display these faults. Because the transgressor is less worthy in this sense, he deserves the misfortune that befalls him. But again (following Rawls, p. 104), this view is surely incorrect. It seems to be one of the fixed points of our considered judgments that no one deserves his place in the distribution of native endowments or liabilities, any more than one deserves one's initial starting place in society. The assertion that a man deserves the inferior character that prevents him from overcoming his liabilities is equally problematic; for his character depends in large part upon unfortunate family and social circumstances for which he cannot be blamed. The notion of desert seems not to apply to these cases. None of which is to say that, generally speaking, a non-moral theory of distributive justice is incompatible with a moral, or desert-based theory of punishment, only that given Rawls' reasons for rejecting desert-based distributive arrangements, he seems clearly committed to rejecting desert-based retributive ones as well.

The apparent inconsistency between Rawls' retributive and distributive theories need not do serious damage to the theory as a whole. Given the method of reflective equilibrium, 'justification is a matter of the mutual support of many considerations, of everything fitting together into one coherent view' (21). From the standpoint of the overall theory, little hangs on Rawls' retributive theory, apart from the measure of plausibility it lends justice as fairness for those committed to a strong, desert-based notion of punishment. If Rawls' distinction succeeds, they need not choose between their retributive intuitions and the difference principle; if it does not, one or the other of those convictions must give way. If, on reflection, a non-moral theory of punishment appears unacceptable, even in the light of the arbitrariness of criminal characteristics and dispositions, then the difference principle – rejecting as it does the notion of desert – would be called into serious question. If, on the other hand, our intuition that criminals deserve punishment proves no more indispensable than our intuition that virtue deserves reward (an intuition of common sense Rawls explicitly rejects), then we may adjust our intuitions in a direction that affirms the difference principle rather than opposes it. Desert would be rejected as the basis for both distributive and retributive arrangements, and so the inconsistency resolved.

But such a resolution returns us to the larger difficulties of a theory of justice without desert and a notion of the self as essentially dispossessed, or barren of constituent traits. Nozick argues against Rawls that the foundations underlying desert need not themselves be deserved, all the way down. But as we have seen, Rawls' denial of desert does not depend on the thesis Nozick refutes, but instead on the notion of the self as a pure, unadulterated, 'essentially unencumbered' subject of possession. Rawls is not committed to the view that a person can only deserve a thing he produces if he deserves everything he used in producing it, but rather to the view that no one possesses anything in the strong, constitutive sense necessary to a desert base. No one can be said to deserve anything (in the strong, preinstitutional sense), because no one can be said to possess anything (in the strong, constitutive sense). This is the philosophical force of the argument from arbitrariness.

That the argument from arbitrariness works in this way can be seen by viewing the moves from natural liberty to fair opportunity to the democratic conception, as traced by Rawls, as stages in the dispossession of the person. With each transition, a substantive self, thick with particular traits, is progressively shorn of characteristics once taken to be essential to its identity; as more of its features are seen to be arbitrarily given, they are relegated from presumed constituents to mere attributes of the self. More becomes *mine*, and less remains *me*, to recall our earlier formulation, until ultimately the self is purged of empirical constituents altogether, and transformed into a condition of agency standing beyond the objects of its possession. The logic of Rawls' argument might be reconstructed as follows:

At the far end of the spectrum, even before natural liberty appears, are aristocratic and caste societies; in such societies, a person's life prospects are tied to a hierarchy into which he is born and from which his person is inseparable. Here, the self is most fully ascribed, merged almost indistinguishably with its condition, embedded in its situation. The system of natural liberty removes fixed status of birth as an assumed constituent of the person, and regards each as free, given his capacities and resources, to compete in the marketplace as best he can, and to reap his reward. By shifting the basis of expectations from status to contract, the system of natural liberty repairs the arbitrariness of hierarchical societies by taking the person more narrowly, so to speak, as distinct and separable from his surroundings. Still, some arbitrariness remains, most notably in the form of social and cultural contingencies. In the regime of natural liberty, a person's life prospects are governed by factors no more ascribable to the person (in the strong, constitutive sense) than his inherited status. Having relieved the person of his hierarchical baggage, the principle of natural liberty still conceives a thickly constituted self, burdened by the accidents of social and cultural contingency. And so the move to fair opportunity, which strips the self of social and cultural accidents as well as inherited status. In a 'fair meritocracy', the effects of class status and cultural disadvantage are understood to reflect more on the society and less on the person. Those with comparable talents and 'the same willingness to use them, should have the same prospects of success regardless of their initial place in the social system, that is, irrespective of the income class into which they are born' (73). In this way, the meritocratic conception extends the logic of natural liberty by ascribing less to the self and more to its situation.

But even the principle of fair opportunity, in rewarding individual effort, conceives the province of the self too expansively. For even

93

'the effort a person is willing to make is influenced by his natural abilities and skills and the alternatives open to him. The better endowed are more likely, other things equal, to strive conscientiously, and there seems to be no way to discount for their greater good fortune' (312). The self is still over-ascribed. Given its arbitrariness, even the character that determines a person's motivation cannot properly be regarded as an essential constituent of his identity. And so finally the move to the democratic conception, in which the self, shorn of all contingently given attributes, assumes a kind of supra-empirical status, essentially unencumbered, bounded in advance and given prior to its ends, a pure subject of agency and possession, ultimately thin. Not only my character but even my values and deepest convictions are relegated to the contingent, as features of my condition rather than as constituents of my person. 'That we have one conception of the good rather than another is not relevant from a moral standpoint. In acquiring it we are influenced by the same sort of contingencies that lead us to rule out a knowledge of our sex and class' (Rawls 1975: 537). Only in this way is it possible to install the self as invulnerable, to assure its sovereignty once and for all in a world threatening always to engulf it. Only if the fate of the self is thus detached from the fate of its attributes and aims, subject as they are to the vagaries of circumstance, can its priority be preserved and its agency guaranteed.

This is the vision of the person that Nozick and Bell, as defenders of natural liberty and meritocracy, respectively, emphatically reject, even if they do not spell out in any detail the conception of the self they rely on instead. Both object that the argument from arbitrariness, consistently applied, leads ineluctably to the dissolution of the person, and the abnegation of individual responsibility and moral choice. 'This line of argument can succeed in blocking the introduction of a person's autonomous choices and activities (and their results) only by attributing *everything* noteworthy about the person completely to certain sorts of "external" factors', writes Nozick. Echoing his argument against the notion of common assets, Nozick questions whether, on Rawls' account, any coherent conception of the person remains, and if so, whether it is any longer the kind of person worth the moral fuss deontological liberalism makes on its behalf.

So denigrating a person's autonomy and prime responsibility for his actions is a risky line to take for a theory that otherwise wishes to buttress the dignity and self-respect of autonomous beings; especially for a theory that founds so much (including a theory of the good) upon a person's choices. One doubts that the unexalted picture of human beings Rawls' theory presupposes and rests upon can be made to fit together with the view of human dignity it is designed to lead to and embody (1974: 214).

Bell summarizes the objection in an epigram: 'The person has disappeared. Only attributes remain' (1973: 419). Where Rawls seeks to assure the autonomy of the self by disengaging it from the world, his critics say he ends by dissolving the self in order to preserve it.

To recapitulate our reconstructed version of the argument between Rawls and Nozick on the issue of desert: Nozick first argues that the arbitrariness of assets does not undermine desert, because desert may depend not only on things I deserve, but also on things I just *have*, not illegitimately. Rawls' response is to invoke the distinction between the self and its possessions in the strongest version of that distinction, and so to claim that, strictly speaking, there *is* nothing that 'I', *qua* pure subject of possession, *have* – nothing that is attached, rather than related, to *me* – nothing at least in the strong, constitutive sense of possession necessary to a desert base. Nozick's rejoinder is that this defense cannot succeed for long, for it has the consequence of leaving us with a subject *so* shorn of empirically identifiable characteristics as to resemble once more the Kantian transcendent or disembodied subject Rawls resolved to avoid. It makes the individual inviolable only by making him invisible, and calls into question the dignity and autonomy this liberalism seeks above all to secure.

INDIVIDUAL AND SOCIAL CLAIMS: WHO OWNS WHAT?

But Nozick has a further objection, independent of the first, that goes something like this: even if Rawls is right that arbitrariness undermines individual possession and hence individual desert, the difference principle is not the inevitable result; something like the principle of natural liberty – and here Nozick prefers to speak in terms of his own version, which he calls the 'entitlement theory' – could still be true. For even if no one deserved any of his natural assets, it might still be that people were entitled to them, and to what flows from them.

At best, this argument maintains, Rawls' case for the difference principle is underdetermined by the argument from arbitrariness. To show that individuals, as individuals, do not deserve or possess 'their' assets is not necessarily to show that society as a whole *does* deserve or possess them. Simply because the attributes accidentally located in me are not *my* assets, why must it follow, as Rawls seems to think, that they are common assets, rather than nobody's assets? If they cannot properly be said to belong to me, why assume automatically that they belong to the community? Is their location in the *community's* province any less accidental, any less arbitrary from a moral point of view? And if not, why not regard them as free-floating assets, unattached in advance to *any* subject of possession, whether individual or social?

Here it is necessary to be more precise about the terms of relation between the person and the endowments he bears. Three descriptions seem to cover the possible cases; depending on the sense of possession intended, I may be described as the owner, the guardian, or the repository of the endowments I bear. In its strongest version, the notion of ownership implies that I have absolute, unqualified, exclusive rights with respect to my endowments, in its more moderate versions that I have certain privileged claims with respect to them, a bundle of rights, while not unlimited, at least more extensive with respect to my assets than any bundle of rights anyone else may have with respect to them. This is the sense of individual possession against which Rawls' argument from arbitrariness is addressed and which, if successful, it undermines.

If Rawls is right, and I cannot properly be described as the owner of my assets and attributes, two alternate accounts remain. One is the notion of guardianship, which denies individual ownership in favor of a more ultimate owner or subject of possession of which the individual person is the agent. To say that I am the guardian of the endowments I bear is to imply that they are owned by some other subject, on whose behalf, or in whose name, or by whose grace I cultivate and exercise them. This is a notion of possession reminiscent of the early Christian notion of property, in which man had what he had as the guardian of assets belonging truly to God, and it is a notion that fits with various communitarian notions of property as well.[4]

---

4 The Rev. Vernon Bartlet (1915: 97–8) writes that 'the essential Christian attitude' held the property rights of any individual to be 'purely relative, not only as compared with

In the third account, I am neither the owner nor the guardian but rather the repository of the assets and attributes accidentally located in my person. The notion of the individual as repository of endowments does not presuppose some other subject of possession whose endowments they ultimately are, but does without possession altogether. In so far as I am the repository of natural assets, there need be no further question to whom these assets ultimately *belong;* their residing in me has no consequence for claims I, or others, may have with respect to them.

Now in terms of these distinctions, Nozick claims in effect that Rawls' argument from arbitrariness, even if it succeeds in undermining individual possession and hence desert, warrants only the third description (that individuals are repositories of assets) and not the second. But if this is all the argument from arbitrariness establishes, then it does not lead to the difference principle. For the difference principle must presuppose the second description – that I am the guardian of assets to which the community as a whole has some prior title or claim. If all arbitrariness means is that I am the repository of assets which belong to no one in particular, then it cannot be assumed that the community owns them any more than I do. It would be as though assets, and the benefits that flow from them, fell like manna from heaven (the image is Nozick's), unmarked by prior claims and unattached to any subject of possession whether individual or social.

How then should they be distributed? On what basis should competing claims to such spontaneously generated bounty be assessed? From the standpoint of desert, there would seem to be no grounds on which to choose between letting the assets lie where they fall, and trying to distribute them in some other way. Unless distribution under such assumptions is to be regarded as a stand-off, a matter of

God's absolute rights as Producer and Owner both of all things and of all persons, but also as compared with the paramount human or derivative rights of Society as representing the common weal. Of this, the individual's weal is only a dependent part, and should be limited by the rights of all others to the conditions of personal well-being. . . . The resulting practical principles, viz. the stewardship of property on behalf both of God and Society, and the moral duty of fidelity in this relation as the condition of any correlative rights of private personal enjoyment, is too deeply embedded in Christ's teaching, notably in the parables, to need demonstration.' Bartlet quotes St. Paul, I *Corinthians* iv. 71: 'For who maketh thee to excel? And what hast thou that thou hast not received? But if thou didst receive it, why dost thou glory as if thou hadst not received it?'

moral indifference, people's entitlements must depend on considerations other than notions of possession or desert. On this, Rawls and
Nozick seem prepared to agree. But what could these considerations
be? On this, they part ways. Each thinks he can adduce considerations unrelated to desert to overcome the stand-off in favor of his own
conception.

For Nozick, the absence of desert creates a presumption in favor of
letting assets lie where they fall, at least once it is accepted that things
do not come into the world like manna from heaven but come into
being already held, attached to particular persons.

Since things come into being already held (or with agreements already
made about how they are to be held), there is no need to search for some
pattern for unheld holdings to fit. . . . The situation is not an appropriate one for wondering, 'After all, what is to become of these things; what
are we to do with them.' In the non-manna-from-heaven world in which
things have to be made or produced or transformed by people, there is
no separate process of distribution for a theory of distribution to be a theory of (1974: 219).

Nozick goes on to argue that if a person has an asset to which no
one else is entitled, then, although he may not *deserve* the asset, he is
nonetheless *entitled* to it, and to whatever flows from it by a process
that does not violate anyone else's entitlements. 'Whether or not people's natural assets are arbitrary from a moral point of view, they are
entitled to them, and to what flows from them' (1974: 226).

For Rawls, on the other hand, the absence of individual desert creates a presumption in favor of regarding the distribution of talents as
a common asset. The lack of desert or a pre-institutional concept of
virtue means that institutions are unconstrained by antecedent moral
claims in their pursuit of the primary virtue of social justice. In this
sense, the analogy of manna from heaven is apt. The array of assets
dealt by fortune is neither just nor unjust. 'These are simply natural
facts. What is just and unjust is the way that institutions deal with these
facts' (102). There is no reason to let assets and the benefits that flow
from them lie where they fall. This would be simply to incorporate
and affirm the arbitrariness of nature. The discovery that virtue and
entitlements await social institutions rather than constrain them is a
reason to pursue justice all the more insistently, not a reason to freeze
arbitrariness in place.

What, then, are we to make of these attempts to overcome the apparent moral stand-off created by the presumed absence of desert? Nozick is prepared to accept that people may not deserve their natural assets, but claims they are entitled to them nonetheless. 'If people have X, and their having X (whether or not they deserve to have it) does not violate anyone else's (Lockean) right or entitlement to X, and Y flows from (arises out of, and so on) X by a process that does not itself violate anyone's (Lockean) rights or entitlements, then the person is entitled to Y' (1974: 225). But he does not show why this is so, nor is he clear on what precisely the difference between desert and entitlement consists in. Rawls and Feinberg agree that 'desert is a *moral* concept in the sense that it is logically prior to and independent of public institutions and their rules' (Feinberg 1970: 87). Entitlements, by contrast, are claims that can only arise under the rules or qualifying conditions of institutions already established, what Rawls describes as legitimate expectations founded on social institutions. It is a consequence of this view that, for the purpose of designing or assessing social institutions, people's entitlements, being *derivative* from institutions, are without moral or critical force. Assessing the justice of an institution in the light of what people were entitled to would be like judging the validity of a rule in the light of claims arising under the rule; to recall our earlier discussion, it would be appealing to a standard of appraisal thoroughly implicated in the object of appraisal. It is for this reason that the concept of entitlement cannot provide a first principle of justice. As Rawls explains, it 'presupposes the existence of the co-operative scheme, and so is irrelevant to the question whether in the first place the scheme is to be designed in accordance with the difference principle or some other criterion' (103).

Nozick never comes to terms with this difficulty. In making his argument, he explicitly adopts the language of entitlement rather than desert, but does not acknowledge its lesser moral force. In Nozick's usage, the concept of entitlement does the same work as desert, but without its pre-institutional credentials ever being established. He begins with the premise that 'people are entitled to their natural assets', and proceeds to argue that they are entitled to the benefits that flow from them (1974: 225–6). But he never says why people are entitled to their assets in any sense of entitlement strong enough to get the argument going.

At one point, Nozick seems to claim that people are entitled to the things they 'just may *have*, not illegitimately', their natural assets presumably being among such things. But having something, not illegitimately, is not the same as being entitled to it; it is simply having it, in some unspecified sense of possession. While my intelligence, or physical strength, or good health may be among the things I have, not illegitimately, it does not follow that I am entitled to these things, for entitlements depend, as we have seen, on some scheme of co-operation already being in effect.

At other points, Nozick seems to argue instead that people are entitled to their natural assets and the benefits that flow from them in some sense of entitlement antecedent to social institutions, which is to say in some sense of entitlement equivalent to desert. ('It needn't be that the foundations underlying desert are themselves deserved, *all the way down.*') This would require that I possess the relevant assets in the strong sense of possession adequate to a desert base, and this in turn requires a theory of the person on which I possess some things, at least, as constituents and not merely as attributes of the self. But Nozick's theory of the person is not easy to discern. He complains that the 'purified' self implicit in Rawls' theory seems radically at odds with our more familiar notion of ourselves as beings 'thick with particular traits' (1974: 228), and further objects that so 'purified' a self, even if coherent, seems to threaten not only individual desert, but also such indispensable notions as individual autonomy, responsibility, and the very human dignity and self-respect deontological liberalism sets out to affirm (1974: 214). These, to be sure, are powerful objections. But they do little to articulate a substantive theory of the person that manages to leave the person 'thick with particular traits' while at the same time avoiding the moral and epistemological difficulties Rawls identifies with the self laden with contingencies. It is one thing simply to assert what is in some sense undeniable, that we are 'thick with particular traits', and quite another to show how this can be true in a way not subject to the rival incoherences associated with a radically situated self, indefinitely conditioned by its surroundings and constantly subject to transformation by experience. For this reason, Nozick's proposed solution to the stand-off can be of critical interest alone.

What, then, of Rawls' attempt? If Nozick fails to show that the absence of individual desert leads to a presumption in favor of letting natural assets lie where they fall, with what success does Rawls show a presumption in favor of a general social claim to such assets? According to Nozick, Rawls' view is that 'everyone has some entitlement or claim on the totality of natural assets (viewed as a pool), with no one having differential claims' (1974: 228), and indeed the notion of common assets seems to imply some such view. The question is what kind of 'entitlement or claim' is involved, and how it might be established. Two possibilities suggest themselves: the general social claim on the totality of natural assets might be a claim of desert, or it might be a claim to an entitlement, or legitimate expectation. If it is meant to be a claim of desert, then that claim is at best underdetermined by Rawls' theory, for as we have seen, the argument from arbitrariness works only to undermine individual desert, not necessarily to install a social one. Moreover, for the community as a whole to deserve the natural assets in its province and the benefits that flow from them, it is necessary to assume that society has some pre-institutional status that individuals lack, for only in this way could the community be said to possess its assets in the strong, constitutive sense of possession necessary to a desert base. But such a view would run counter to Rawls' individualistic assumptions, and in particular to his view that society is not 'an organic whole with a life of its own distinct from and superior to that of all its members in their relations with one another' (264).

The alternative would be to view society's claim on the distribution of assets as an entitlement given by legitimate expectations founded upon social institutions 'established for prior and independent social ends' (313), prior and independent, that is, to the entitlement itself. Rawls might argue along these lines that the difference principle does not assume that society has some pre-institutional status denied to individuals, only that the parties to the original position would agree to regard the distribution of natural talents as a common asset and to share in the benefits of this distribution. The notion of society as the owner of natural assets for which individuals are the guardians would then be seen as the result of the original position and not its premise.

But this still leaves us wondering about the 'prior and independent social ends', and the source of their priority and independence. Somehow the society's claim on the distribution of assets must make a difference before institutions get established. *Some* social claim on the distribution of assets would seem a necessary presupposition of the agreement in the original position, otherwise the parties would be deliberating about how to allocate shares that were not (yet) rightfully *theirs* to allocate. Nozick argues, along similar lines,

Do the people in the original position ever wonder whether *they* have the *right* to decide how everything is to be divided up? Perhaps they reason that since they are deciding this question, they must assume they are entitled to do so; and so particular people can't have particular entitlements to holdings (for then they wouldn't have the right to decide together on how all holdings are to be divided) (1974: 199n).

To this Rawls might reply that no antecedent social claim is involved, since the parties to the original position are not faced, strictly speaking, with the moral question of how they *ought* to allocate distributive shares (which would indeed imply their having an antecedent 'right' to decide), but only with the prudential question of how, given the relevant constraints on information, etc., they would, from the standpoint of individual self-interest, *prefer* that individual shares be allocated. The original position, Rawls might remind us, is not an actual site of allocation, but rather a way of thinking.

Still, we want to know why *this* way of thinking is appropriate to questions of distributive justice, and whether the appropriateness of this way of thinking does not itself depend on the parties to the original position having some antecedent claim on the totality of natural assets. For even if the parties to the original position would, as a matter of rational prudence, reason in the way Rawls says they would, it is not immediately clear, absent some prior social claim, why their collective choice should determine the just distribution of these assets. This leads us to the issue of justification and the question of how the argument from the original position serves to justify the principles that result. If society's claim to the distribution of natural assets can be shown to be a product of the original agreement rather than its premise, then Rawls will have resolved the stand-off in favor of the difference principle without having to attribute an antecedent claim of desert to society as a whole. If, on the other hand, the notion of common assets should turn out to be a presupposition of the original agreement, then Rawls will have overcome the stand-off only by implicit reliance on a claim of social desert, and hence reliance on a wider subject of possession, presumably the community, held to own the assets we individually bear. Once again an intersubjective dimension would intrude on Rawls' individualistic project. Although such a result would do considerable damage to the deontological ethic Rawls seeks to defend, I shall try to show that his version of contract theory cannot avoid it.

3

Contract Theory and Justification

In assessing the validity of the difference principle, we are led ulti-mately to the question of justification, and in particular to the ques-tion why the original position provides an appropriate way of think-ing about justice at all. Even assuming, for the sake of argument, that the parties to the original position really would choose the principles Rawls says they would, why does *this* give us reason to believe that these principles are just? Rawls writes that the principles of justice are those principles 'that free and rational persons concerned to further their own interests would accept in an initial position of equality' (11), and that the original position is 'the appropriate initial status quo which insures that the fundamental agreements reached in it are fair' (17). 'Understood in this way the question of justification is set-tled by working out a problem of deliberation: we have to ascertain which principles it would be rational to adopt given the contractual situation. This connects the theory of justice with the theory of ratio-nal choice' (17).

But it is not immediately clear how the original position confers moral status on the results of an exercise in rational choice, not obvi-ous what the justificatory force of the argument from the original position consists in. The question of justification is complicated by the fact that Rawls seems simultaneously to rely on two different sorts of justification, one appealing to the method of reflective equilib-rium, the other to the tradition of the social contract, and sorting out their respective roles poses certain difficulties (Lyons, *Reading Rawls:* 141–68).

For the moment, however, I shall put these difficulties aside in order to focus attention on the contractarian aspect of justice as fairness. In so far as the principles of justice depend for their justifi-cation on a contractarian appeal, what does the moral force of its appeal consist in? Exploring this question should provide us a further test of the internal coherence of Rawls' conception, and of the fit between the theory of justice and its correlative theory of the person. I shall try to show that the argument from the original position can be seen to justify its results only at considerable cost to certain volun-tarist and individualist assumptions central to the deontological project.

THE MORALITY OF CONTRACT

Rawls locates his theory of justice in the tradition of social contract the-ory going back to Locke, Rousseau, and Kant. The 'guiding idea' is that the principles of justice are the object of an original agreement. 'Thus we are to imagine that those who engage in social co-operation choose together, in one joint act, the principles which are to assign basic rights and duties and to determine the division of social benefits' (11). In designing the social contract, 'a group of persons must decide once and for all what is to count among them as just and unjust', and the principles they choose are 'to regulate all subsequent criticism and reform of institutions' (12–13). In this respect, the original contract would seem a kind of ordinary contract writ large.

But for Rawls, as for some of his contractarian predecessors, the original agreement is not an actual historical contract, only a hypo-thetical one (12). Its validity does not depend on its terms actually having been agreed to, but rather on the idea that they *would* have been agreed to under the requisite hypothetical conditions. In fact, Rawls' hypothetical social contract is even more imaginary than most. Not only did his contract never really happen; it is imagined to take place among the sorts of beings who never really existed, that is, beings struck with the kind of complicated amnesia necessary to the veil of ignorance. In this sense, Rawls' theory is doubly hypothetical. It imagines an event that never really happened, involving the sorts of beings who never really existed.

But this would seem to undermine the moral analogy that gives contract theory much of its intuitive appeal. Once the social contract turns hypothetical, the original agreement is no longer a contract writ large, only a contract that *might* have been writ large but never was. And as Ronald Dworkin has written, 'A hypothetical contract is not simply a pale form of an actual contract; it is no contract at all' (1997a: 17–18). How, then, can it serve to justify the principles it yields, to certify their status as principles of *justice*?

To answer this question, we might begin by taking up a simpler question, and inquire into the moral force of contracts and agreements generally. Once we can say something about how justification works with actual contracts, we may see more clearly how it works with hypothetical ones.

When two people make an agreement we may typically assess its justice from two points of view. We may ask about the conditions under which the agreement was made, whether the parties were free or coerced, or we may ask about the terms of the agreement, whether each party received a fair share. While these two considerations may well be related, they are by no means identical, and barring some special philosophical assumptions to be considered later, cannot normally be reduced the one to the other. Practically speaking, a contract freely agreed to may be more likely than others to yield terms that are fair, and a (substantively) fair exchange may well suggest a free contract rather than a coerced one, but there is no necessary connection either way.

Of any contractual agreement, however free, it is always intelligible and often reasonable to ask the further question, 'But is it *fair*, what they have agreed to?', where this question cannot be translated to the merely vacuous question, 'But is it what they have agreed to, what they have agreed to?' What *makes* it fair is not just that it was agreed to, but is a further question.

Similarly, any transaction or arrangement, however fair, is open in principle to the further question, 'But was it freely arrived at, this fair arrangement?', where this question cannot be reduced to the trivial question, 'But is it a fair arrangement, this fair arrangement?' What *makes* a transaction free is not that it ended fairly; being treated fairly neither makes us free nor entails that we are free. This, too, is a further question.

The distinction between these two sorts of questions suggests that we may think of the morality of contract as consisting of two related yet distinguishable ideals. One is the ideal of autonomy, which sees a contract as an act of will, whose morality consists in the voluntary character of the transaction. The other is the ideal of reciprocity, which sees a contract as an instrument of mutual benefit, whose morality depends on the underlying fairness of the exchange.[1]

---

1 Valuable discussions of the moral foundations of contract law, stressing the ideals of autonomy and reciprocity respectively, can be found in Fried (1981) and Atiyah (1979).

Each ideal suggests a different basis for contractual obligation. From the standpoint of autonomy, a contract's moral force derives from the fact of its voluntary agreement; when I enter freely into an agreement, I am bound by its terms, whatever they may be. Whether its provisions are fair or inequitable, favorable or harsh, I have 'brought them on myself', and the fact that they are self-imposed provides one reason at least why I am obligated to fulfill them.

The ideal of reciprocity, on the other hand, derives contractual obligation from the mutual benefits of co-operative arrangements. Where autonomy points to the contract itself as the source of obligation, reciprocity points *through* the contract to an antecedent moral requirement to abide by fair arrangements, and thus implies an independent moral principle by which the fairness of an exchange may be assessed. With reciprocity, the emphasis is less on the fact of my agreement than on the benefits I enjoy; contracts bind not because they are willingly incurred but because (or in so far as) they tend to produce results that are fair.

In its account of obligation, each ideal can be seen to highlight the moral incompleteness of the other. From the standpoint of autonomy, my obligations are limited to those I voluntarily incur, but these may include provisions onerous and harsh. From the standpoint of reciprocity, hard deals bind less, but on the other hand, the need for consent fades, and I may be obligated in virtue of benefits I do not want or dependencies beyond my control. In the first I may be bound to terms that are unfair; in the second I may be bound in ways I did not choose.

Finally, each account of contractual obligation relates contract to justification in a different way. On the ideal of autonomy, the contract *imparts* the justification; in so far as it is free, the process itself serves to justify the outcome, 'whatever it happens to be'. On the ideal of reciprocity, by contrast, the contract *approximates* justice rather than *confers* it; the process is instrumental to, rather than definitive of, a just result. On the first, a fair result is defined as the outcome of a process that is free; on the second, a free process is simply one means of arriving at a result which is (independently) fair.

Unlike obligations voluntarily incurred, obligations arising under the ideal of reciprocity must presuppose some criterion of fairness independent of contract, some way in which the objective fairness of an exchange may be assessed. Such obligations are thus not contractual in the strict sense that the contract creates the obligation, but rather in the limited epistemic or heuristic sense that the contract helps to identify or clarify an obligation that is already there (Atiyah 1979: 143–6). One consequence of this feature of benefit-based obligations is that the carrying out of a contract is not essential to the existence of the obligation. In principle at least, there may be ways of identifying such obligations without recourse to contract.

Those obligations arising on the ideal of autonomy, however, presume no quality of justice intrinsic to certain results which could, even in principle, be identified apart from or antecedent to the process that produced them. With obligations of this sort, no result can be identified as just without reference to a procedure actually having been carried out. What is just cannot be known directly because it is, by definition, the product of a process of a certain kind; it cannot be known directly because it must be created, and until it is created, it cannot be known.

The contrasting ways in which the two ideals relate contract to justification may be illuminated by Rawls' distinction between pure procedural justice and perfect (or imperfect) procedural justice. In pure procedural justice, 'there is no independent criterion for the right result: instead there is a correct or fair procedure such that the outcome is likewise correct or fair, whatever it is, provided that the procedure has been properly followed' (86). In perfect and imperfect procedural justice, on the other hand, 'there is an independent standard for deciding which outcome is just', and the question is simply whether or not a procedure can be found which is guaranteed to lead to it (85–6).

Now in so far as a contract realizes the ideal of autonomy, it approaches the case of pure procedural justice, in which the outcome is just, whatever it is, in virtue of the contract that produced it. On the ideal of reciprocity, a contract is a case of imperfect procedural justice, seeking as it does to approximate a standard of justice independently defined. As Rawls points out, 'A distinctive feature of pure procedural justice is that the procedure for determining the just result must actually be carried out; for in these cases there is no independent criterion by reference to which a definite outcome can be known to be just. . . . A fair procedure *translates its fairness* to the outcome only when it is actually carried out' [emphasis added] (86).

The answer, then, to our preliminary question how actual contracts justify seems 'incompletely'. As the non-trivial coherence of the 'further question' attests ('But is it *fair,* what they have agreed *to?*'), actual contracts are not self-sufficient moral instruments but presuppose a background morality in the light of which the obligations arising from them may be qualified and assessed. While it may be just, under certain circumstances, to hold a person to the terms of his prior agreement, it does not follow from his agreement that the terms themselves are just. Common sense suggests various reasons why, in practice, actual contracts may turn out unfairly; one or both of the parties may be coerced or otherwise disadvantaged by an unfavorable bargaining position, or deceived or otherwise mistaken about the value of the things being exchanged, or unclear about their own needs and interests. But even where an agreement turns out fairly (as when the effects of such factors are countervailing, for example), and where the fairness of the agreement provides a reason for its enforcement, it cannot be assumed that what *makes* it just is the fact that it was agreed to. Actual contracts are typically cases of imperfect procedural justice; pure procedural justice rarely, if ever, appears in the world.

CONTRACTS VERSUS CONTRACTARIAN ARGUMENTS

Rawls would not likely disagree with this formulation. Notwithstanding the contractarian basis of his theory, he does not suppose that the mere fact of an agreement is the test of its fairness, or that actual contracts are self-sufficient moral instruments that justify their own results, or that obligations voluntarily incurred are immune from criticism in the light of pre-existing principles of justice. Understanding the sense in which Rawls' theory does not rely on the notion of contract as an instrument of justification is essential to understanding the sense in which it does.

The first point to emphasize in this connection is that the agreement in the original position gives rise not to obligations (at least not directly), but to principles of justice. The principles of justice include principles of two sorts – 'principles for institutions', which apply to the basic structure of society, and 'principles for individuals', which set out the duties and obligations of persons with respect to institutions and each other. The first define what makes an institution or a social practice just, while the second specify the terms on which individuals are bound to abide by them.

The principles for individuals specify two different ways in which persons may be bound – as a matter of natural duty or of obligation. Natural duties are those moral claims that apply to persons irrespective of their consent, such as the duties to help others in distress, not be cruel, to do justice, and so on. Such duties are 'natural' in the sense that they are not tied to any particular institutions or social arrangements but are owed to persons generally (114–15).

Obligations, by contrast, describe those moral ties we voluntarily incur, whether by contract or promise or other expression of consent. The obligations of public office voluntarily sought are one such example. But even with obligations, consent is not sufficient to create the tie. A further condition is that the institution or practice agreed to be just (or nearly just), in accordance that is, with the two principles of justice. Rawls emphasizes that, notwithstanding their voluntary dimension, our actual obligations are never born of consent alone but inevitably presuppose an antecedent background morality, independently derived, in the light of which it is always possible to ask whether one *ought* to have consented or not.

Obligations arise only if certain background conditions are satisfied. Acquiescence in, or even consent to, clearly unjust institutions does not give rise to obligations. It is generally agreed that extorted promises are void *ab initio*. But similarly, unjust social arrangements are themselves a kind of extortion, even violence, and consent to them does not bind (343).

In particular, it is not possible to have an obligation to autocratic and arbitrary forms of government. The necessary background does not exist for obligations to arise from consensual or other acts, however expressed. Obligatory ties presuppose just institutions, or ones reasonably just in view of the circumstances (112).

Even promises cannot alone give rise to obligations. Rawls distinguishes here between the rule of promising and the principle of fidelity, and argues that the obligation to keep a promise is not a consequence of the promise, but of a moral principle antecedent to the promise, deriving from a theory of justice. 'It is essential to distinguish between the rule of promising and the principle of fidelity. The rule is simply a constitutive convention, whereas the principle of fidelity is a moral principle, a consequence of the principle of fairness. . . . The obligation to keep a promise is a consequence of the principle of fairness' (346). As a constitutive practice or convention, the rule of promising is analogous to legal rules, or the rules of a game; whether they are just or not is always a further question which cannot be answered without recourse to a moral standard independent of the practice. 'There are many variations of promising just as there are of the law of contract. Whether the particular practice . . . is just remains to be determined by the principles of justice' (345–6).

Strictly speaking, then, it is not *promises* that bind, but the principle of fidelity that binds us to (certain of) our promises, and this principle derives from the original position.

Even the rule of promising does not give rise to a moral obligation by itself. To account for fiduciary obligations we must take the principle of fairness as a premise. Thus along with most other ethical theories, justice as fairness holds that natural duties and obligations arise only in virtue of ethical principles. These principles are those that would be chosen in the original position (348).

But if Rawls does not take actual contracts or promises to be binding, at least not in themselves, in what sense is his theory contractarian? Here it is important to distinguish the role of consent in real life from its role in the original position. While consent is decisive in the original position, it plays less central a role in our actual duties and obligations. Notwithstanding their contractarian derivation, the natural duties apply without reference to our voluntary acts, and the consent obligations require is in any case distinct from the consent involved in the original position.

Even though the principles of natural duty are derived from a contractarian point of view, they do not presuppose an act of consent, express or tacit, or indeed any voluntary act, in order to apply. The principles that hold for individuals, just as the principles for institutions, are those that would be acknowledged in the original position. These principles are understood as the outcome of a hypothetical agreement. If their formulation shows that no binding action, consensual or otherwise, is a presupposition of their application, then they apply unconditionally. The reason why obligations depend upon voluntary acts is given by the second part of the principle of fairness which states this condition. It has nothing to do with the contractual nature of justice as fairness (115–16).

Real contracts issue in exchanges or arrangements whose justification must await a principle of justice; the hypothetical contract issues
in principles of justice capable of assessing those arrangements and
defining the moral consequences of contracts generally. As things
turn out, the role the parties decide to assign to (actual) agreements
is different from the role *their* (hypothetical) agreement plays in justification.

Nozick objects that it is somehow inconsistent for a contract theory
to produce principles of justice that do not give full justificatory force
to voluntary exchanges. If contracts are binding, Nozick suggests,
then Rawls' theory is wrong for yielding principles which would deny
their force in many cases, and if contracts cannot bind, then Rawls'
theory is undermined since it is founded on a contract.

Contract arguments embody the assumption that anything that emerges
from a certain process is just. Upon the force of this fundamental
assumption rests the force of a contract argument. Surely then no contract argument should be structured so as to preclude process principles
being the fundamental principles of distributive justice by which to judge
the institutions of a society; no contract argument should be structured
so as to make it impossible that its results be of the same sort as the
assumptions upon which it rests. If processes are good enough to found
a theory upon, they are good enough to be the possible result of the theory. One can't have it both ways (1974: 208–9).

But this objection overlooks the distinction between the imperfect
procedural justice that typically describes our actual agreements, and
the pure procedural justice that obtains, or at least is meant to obtain,
in the original position. Or to put the point another way, the objection confuses contracts with contract arguments. As Rawls observes,
real contracts are not arguments but social facts, whose moral consequences depend on some moral theory, contractarian or otherwise.
Some such distinction, between the fact of an agreement and the
grounds of its justification, is essential if we are to account for the
coherence of the 'further question' ('But is it fair, what they have
agreed to?'), or to make sense of the related question whether one
ought to have consented or not, or allow for the rival but correlative
claims of autonomy and reciprocity in arguments about justice.

Seen in this light, there is no contradiction in a contract argument
producing principles that limit the justificatory role of contracts. In

fact, there appears an important sense in which the results of a contract argument *cannot* be 'of the same sort' as the assumptions on which it rests. For if, as Nozick argues, 'contract arguments embody the assumption that anything that emerges from a *certain* process is just' [emphasis added] (1974: 208), it seems unlikely to suppose that just any agreement, arrived at under just any conditions, could produce results guaranteed to be just. And once the circumstances of an agreement are seen to be relevant to its justification, it cannot be claimed that the agreement itself does all the justifying. To acknowledge the relevance of circumstance is already to acknowledge a moral sanction independent of the agreement by which the morally necessary features of the situation are identified.

As Rawls shows in his analysis of promises, the source of *this* sanction cannot be a further promise or agreement (such as a promise to keep promises), since the credentials of this background promise would be equally open to question. The back-up of a promise (or a contract) must be more than just another promise (or contract). It must be a premise of a different sort. This premise, which on contract theory 'looks much like an agreement to keep agreements and yet which, strictly speaking, cannot be one' (349), is what the hypothetical agreement in the original position seeks to provide. Rawls believes this device can supply such a premise in a way that preserves the voluntarist appeal of contract theory without lapsing into the question-begging regress associated with a mere agreement to agree. Before assessing Rawls' solution, it may be helpful to summarize the problem of justification it seeks to address and briefly to consider two alternate solutions which Rawls rejects. In this way it may be possible to establish some connections between Rawls' account of justification and certain central features of his deontological project.

LIBERALISM AND THE PRIORITY OF PROCEDURE

To justify an exchange or institutional arrangement, it is not enough to show that it arose from a voluntary agreement between the parties involved, for at least two different sorts of reasons – one moral, the other epistemological. Although Rawls does not distinguish these arguments explicitly, both are implicit in his account, and each serves to reinforce the other. We might call the first the argument from contingency and the second the argument from conventionalism. The first recalls the argument from arbitrariness deployed in support of the difference principle against meritocratic, aristocratic, and other rival conceptions of equality falling short of Rawls' 'democratic conception'. In the case of justification, it begins with the observation that in practice, agreements turn out unfairly for a variety of reasons, as already suggested; one or the other party may be coerced or otherwise disadvantaged in his bargaining position, or misled or otherwise misinformed about the value of the objects being exchanged, or confused or mistaken about his own needs and interests, or, where uncertain future returns are involved, a bad judge of risk, and so on. In some of these cases, notably those involving outright coercion or deception, we may be tempted to say that the exchange was not truly a voluntary one, or that the 'contract' is invalid, and so attribute the unfairness of the result to an inadequacy of consent. Libertarians and others who argue that voluntary agreements are wholly self-justifying are anxious to rule out such cases by invoking distinctions between coercive and non-coercive influences, legitimate and illegitimate bargaining tactics, threats and inducements, and so on (Nozick 1972; Kronman 1980).

But Rawls would deny that any such distinction could succeed in marking out a range of self-justifying agreements as long as some morally arbitrary influences were allowed to remain. However strictly one defines the requirements of a voluntary agreement, the fact that different persons are situated differently will assure that some differences of power and knowledge persist, allowing agreements, even 'voluntary' ones, to be influenced by factors arbitrary from a moral point of view. 'Somehow we must nullify the effects of specific contingencies which put men at odds and tempt them to exploit social and natural circumstances to their own advantage' (136).

Even voluntary agreements are likely to fall short of the ideal of autonomy, in which the obligations incurred are self-imposed in the strict sense of 'self' defined as prior to its attributes and ends and thus free from heteronomous determinations. Only this sense of self, and the notion of autonomy it permits, rules out arbitrary influences completely. Ruling out coercion alone cannot justify a contract any more than ruling out, say, class privileges alone can justify a meritocracy. In both cases, too much is left subject to contingencies arbitrary from a moral point of view. Once we are bothered by the most conspicuous obstacles to individual autonomy, we are bound on reflection to reject heteronomous influences wherever they appear.[2]

Beyond the moral difficulty with the notion that contracts are self-justifying lies an epistemological difficulty. This concerns the status of contracts as 'constitutive conventions', in Rawls' phrase, and recalls the problem that arose in connection with the Archimedean point, the problem of distinguishing a standard of appraisal from the thing being assessed. In the case of contracts, the parallel distinction is between a moral principle on the one hand and a rule or a practice or convention on the other. Notwithstanding the normative import of, say, the practice of promising or the rules of a game or the law of contracts, practices and rules and laws as such cannot justify anything on their own, but must depend for their moral consequences on some principle independent of them. 'The contract doctrine holds that no moral requirements follow from the existence of institutions alone' (348). Given its status as a constitutive convention, an exchange can no more be justified by showing that it was voluntarily agreed to than a law can be justified by showing that it was duly enacted. The fact that a transaction is agreed to or a law enacted may be sufficient, given the relevant background norms, to establish a legal or institutional requirement to abide by it, but 'whether these requirements are connected with moral duties and obligations is a separate question' (349). We still need to know whether the parties ought to have given their consent or whether the legislators ought to have voted the way they did.

If actual contracts must presuppose an antecedent principle to justify their results, the question naturally arises how such a principle might be derived. We might be tempted to seek such a principle in a prior, more general agreement, setting out the terms on which particular agreements are just. But this solution is quickly undermined once it is seen that the problems of contingency and conventionalism would simply be deferred. Once the problems of contingency and conventionalism are acknowledged, there is no reason to think that second-order contracts can be made self-justifying in a way that particular contracts cannot. A contract can no more be sanctioned by a prior agreement to keep agreements than a law can be justified by a law about legislation. In each case, the 'further question' is not dis-

2 Compare Rawls on the difference principle (1971: 74–5).

solved but postponed. A convention about conventions does not make a moral principle, only a further social fact.

If no actual contract, however general, can justify contracts, owing to its implication in the practices and conventions of some particular society, the alternative would seem recourse to a principle of justice somehow prior to particular practices and conventions. This, in fact, is the solution sought by traditional contract theorists, who backed up the Social Contract by an appeal to Natural Law (Barker 1948:x–xi). Thus, for Locke, it is 'the law of God and Nature' that sanctions the original compact and sets bounds on the powers of the common-wealth the compact brings forth.

Thus the law of nature stands as an eternal rule to all men, legislators as well as others. The rules that they make for other men's actions must, as well as their own, and other men's actions, be conformable to the law of nature, i.e., to the will of God, of which that is a declaration, and the fundamental law of nature being the preservation of mankind, no human sanction can be good or valid against it (1690: 90).

But this traditional solution is unavailable to Rawls for at least two reasons. The most obvious is that reliance on 'the law of God and Nature' involves a more substantial theological and metaphysical commitment than Rawls is prepared to assume. So controversial an assumption would clash with his determination to argue from 'generally shared and preferably weak conditions' (20), and 'to insure that the principles of justice do not depend upon strong assumptions. At the basis of the theory, one tries to assume as little as possible' (129).

For Rawls' purpose, a further difficulty with the idea of founding justice on a premise of natural law such as Locke invokes is that it runs counter to the core assumptions of the deontological project. As we have seen, a central aspiration of deontological liberalism is to derive a set of regulative principles that do not presuppose any particular conception of the good, nor depend on any particular theory of human motivation. Connected with this aim are the views that conceptions of the good are diverse, that there is no single, dominant human end, that man is a being whose ends are chosen rather than given, and that the well-ordered society is therefore one in which people are free to pursue their various aims, whatever they may be, on terms that are just. 'Liberty in adopting a conception of the good is limited only by principles that are deduced from a doctrine which imposes no prior constraints on those conceptions' (253). To emphasize the voluntarist conception of human agency that underlies those principles, Rawls assumes that the parties to the original position are unbound by prior moral ties, and 'think of themselves as beings who can and do choose their final ends (always plural in number)' (563).

By appealing to the law of nature as a premise of the original compact, Locke founds justice on certain claims about human ends and motivations which a deontological ethic would be reluctant to admit. When he assumes that men join in society with others 'in order to unite for the mutual preservation of their lives, liberties, and estates, which I call by the general name, property', he attributes to human beings a certain dominant end and makes this end a premise of the principles that result. 'The great and chief end, therefore, of men's uniting into commonwealths, and putting themselves under government, is the preservation of their property; to which in the state of nature there are many things wanting' (1690: 90).

But for Rawls, to found principles of justice on ends or desires said to be given by nature, whether they be the pursuit of happiness or the preservation of property or of life itself, is to place the good prior to the right, to deny the essential plurality of human ends and to posit instead a single dominant end, to base justice on certain natural contingencies, and to reverse the priority of self and ends by conceiving man as a subject of ends given in advance rather than a willing subject of ends he has chosen.

Once a dominant end given by nature is admitted as a premise of the original compact, the parties can no longer 'think of themselves as beings who can and do choose their final ends', but instead are bound in advance. The voluntarist dimension of their enterprise fades, and the terms of the contract are no longer a matter of choice but are determined in advance, given by the requirements of the natural law that is their prerequisite (Pitkin 1965: 990–9).

That a deontological liberal would reject a Lockean solution on these grounds is strengthened by the fact that Kant mounts a similar objection to traditional contract views. Though Kant's critique is directed against Hobbes, his objections would seem equally applicable in this respect to Locke.

Kant distinguishes between those social agreements among men designed to further some common end they may happen to share, and those dedicated to the one end in itself which all ought to share, namely the principle of right. Only the second sort of contract constitutes a civil state, in which the freedom of each is made to harmonize with the freedom of everyone else under terms governed by right. But such an arrangement cannot be based on any particular view of human nature or motivated by any merely contingent human ends.

The whole concept of an external right is derived entirely from the concept of *freedom* in the mutual external relationships of human beings, and has nothing to do with the end which all men have by nature (i.e., the aim of achieving happiness) or with the recognized means of attaining this end. And thus the latter end must on no account interfere as a determinant with the laws governing external right (1793: 73).

For Kant, the principle that serves as sanction to the original contract is not 'the great and chief end of preserving property', or pursuing happiness, but the duty in itself which is 'the highest formal condition of all other external duties, the right of men under coercive public laws by which each can be given what is due to him and secured against attack from any others' (1793: 73). And this duty comes not from nature but 'is the requirement of pure reason, which legislates a priori, regardless of all empirical ends (which can all be summed up under the general heading of happiness)'. Since men have different views on the empirical end of happiness and what it consists of, happiness could not bring their will under any external law harmonizing with the freedom of everyone. The civil state can thus only be established in accordance with 'pure rational principles of external human right' given a priori. It must be based on a priori principles, for neither nature nor experience can provide knowledge of what is right (Kant 1793: 73–4, 86). The result is a liberalism that departs significantly from Locke's, and contains the essentials of the deontological ethic taken up by Rawls. As Kant writes,

We are not concerned here with any happiness which the subject might expect to derive from the institutions or administration of the commonwealth, but primarily with the rights which would thereby be secured for everyone. *And this is the highest principle from which all maxims relating to the commonwealth must begin, and which cannot be qualified by any other principles.*

No generally valid principle of legislation can be based on happiness. For both th e current circumstances and the highly conflicting and variable illusions as to what happiness is (and no-one can prescribe to others how they should attain it) make all fixed principles impossible, so that happiness alone can never be a suitable principle of legislation [emphasis added] (1793: 80).

Where Locke backs up the original contract with the law of God and Nature, Kant backs it up with a principle of right given not by nature but by pure reason. Of the two solutions, Kant's is the more congenial to Rawls' conception in that it avoids deriving the right from the good and so preserves deontological assumptions. But as we have seen, Rawls is resistant to Kant's solution in so far as it seems to depend on metaphysical assumptions he finds objectionable. He is dubious of the idealist metaphysics by which pure reason does its work, and is troubled by what seems to be the arbitrariness of the a priori derivation of the Kantian moral law. And so rather than adopt Kant's solution to the problem of justification directly, Rawls seeks instead to reformulate Kant's deontological teachings, 'to detach the underlying structure of Kant's doctrine from its metaphysical surroundings so that it can be seen more clearly and presented relatively free from objection' (264). Here we return to the mission of the original position in its bid to provide an Archimedean point: to find a middle way between conventionalism and arbitrariness, to seek a standard of appraisal neither compromised by its implication in the world nor dissociated and so disqualified by detachment.

With contract theory, the challenge posed by the Archimedean point takes more determinate form. Clearly, justification involves some sort of interplay between contracts and principles. Actual contracts presuppose principles of justice, which derive in turn from a hypothetical original contract. But how does justification work *there*? Is recourse to yet a further layer of antecedent principles required? Or is contract at that stage morally self-sufficient, and fully self-justifying? At times the search for the ultimate sanction appears an infinitely elusive dance of procedure and principle, each receding in turn behind the other. For given the assumptions of contract theory, neither seems to offer a stable resting point on which to found the other. If the parties to the original contract *choose* the principles of justice, what is to say that they have chosen *rightly*? And if they choose in the light of principles antecedently *given*, in what sense can it be said that they have *chosen* at all? The question of justification thus becomes a question of priority; which comes first – really, ultimately first – the contract or the principle?

With Kant, it is unclear whether the principle of right is the product of the original agreement or its premise, and his reliance on 'pure reason, which legislates a priori', (1793: 73), seems to suggest the latter. This, in any case, is the point at which Rawls seeks to reformulate the Kantian position, to assert the priority of contract and so to emphasize the connection of justice with the theory of rational choice. 'The merit of the contract terminology is that it conveys the idea that principles of justice may be conceived as principles that would be chosen by rational persons, and that in this way conceptions of justice may be explained and justified' (16).

By founding justice on an original contract, Rawls seeks to express what he takes to be the central Kantian insight, 'the idea that moral principles are the object of rational choice' (251). He describes the original position as 'a *procedural* interpretation of Kant's conception of autonomy and the categorical imperative . . . a natural *procedural* rendering of Kant's conception of the kingdom of ends, and of the notions of autonomy and the categorical imperative' [emphasis added] (256, 264).

Why a procedural rendering? Why is it necessary to amend Kant in order to give these principles an explicitly procedural or contractual derivation? Rawls' answer must be that by casting the moral law as the outcome of a certain process of rational choice, however hypothetical, it is possible to establish its claim on human experience in a way that might not otherwise be apparent. 'No longer are these notions purely transcendent and lacking explicable connections with human conduct, for the procedural conception of the original position allows us to make these ties' (256).

The priority of procedure in Rawls' account of justification recalls the parallel priorities of the right over the good, and of the self over its ends. It thus connects the account of justification with the theory of the person which justice as fairness was seen to entail, and suggests the importance of contract theory to the deontological project generally. As the self is prior to the ends it affirms, so the contract is prior to the principles it generates. Of course, not just any contract is prior to the principles of justice; as we have seen, actual contracts cannot justify precisely because they are typically situated in the practices and conventions which justice must assess. Similarly, real persons, ordinarily conceived as 'thick with particular traits', are not strictly prior with respect to their ends, but are embedded in and conditioned by the values and interests and desires from among which the 'sovereign' self, *qua* subject of possession, would take its purposes. To assert the priority of the self whose sovereign agency is assured, it was necessary to identify an 'essentially unencumbered' self, conceived as a pure subject of possession, distinct from its contingent aims and attributes, standing always behind them.

In the case of contract, the priority of procedure depends on distinguishing the special case of pure procedural justice, a sort of purified, pre-situated version of ordinary procedure in which no independent criteria of fairness are available. Only the purified self is guaranteed to be a sovereign agent, and only pure procedural justice is guaranteed to produce results that are fair. It is this notion of procedure that Rawls invokes in the original position.

The idea of the original position is to set up a fair procedure so that any principles agreed to will be just. The aim is to use the notion of pure procedural justice as a basis of theory (136).

Pure procedural justice obtains when there is no independent criterion for the right result: instead there is a correct or fair procedure such that the outcome is likewise correct or fair, whatever it is, provided that the procedure has been properly followed (86).

Two further parallels link Rawls' account of justification with his theory of the person. One highlights the role of choice in deontological ethics; the other emphasizes the assumption of plurality. In our discussion of the self, we considered two accounts of agency by which the self might come by its ends, a voluntarist account which related self to ends as willing subject to objects of choice, and a cognitive account which related self to ends as knowing subject to objects of understanding. The priority of the self over its ends was seen to require the voluntarist account.

Once we imagine the parties to the original position seeking principles of justice, we can similarly conceive two possible accounts of justification, a voluntarist account in which the parties arrive at the principles through an act of choice or agreement, and a cognitive account in which the parties arrive at the principles through an act of discovery or collective insight. As with agency, so with justification: for contract to be prior to principle, the parties must choose the principles of justice rather than find them. Both the priority of the self and the priority of procedure require the voluntarist notions of agency and justification respectively. For the self to be prior, its aims must be chosen rather than given; for contract to be prior, the principles of justice must be products of agreement rather than objects of discovery.

In addition to the emphasis on choice, the assumption of plurality is common to both the theory of the person and the account of justification on the contractarian view. Just as 'the plurality of distinct persons with separate systems of ends' (29) is essential to Rawls' notion of the subject, so the antecedent plurality of the parties to the original position is essential to the notion of their hypothetical agreement. For a contract to be a contract requires a plurality of persons. I cannot make a contract or an agreement with myself except in a metaphorical sense in which part of the metaphor involves speaking as though 'I' were two persons rather than one, a plurality of selves within a single human being. As Rawls notes, principles of justice 'apply to the relations among several persons or groups. The word "contract" suggests this plurality' (16).

Having reconstructed the problem of justification Rawls seeks to address and considered the form of solution he undertakes, it remains to be shown whether this solution succeeds in providing the foundation the deontological ethic requires. And so we turn at last to the hypothetical contract in the original position, in order to see what exactly goes on there, and how it justifies, if that is what it does. At the risk of belaboring the familiar, we must explore the text with some detail if the phenomenology of the original agreement is to become clear.

WHAT REALLY GOES ON BEHIND THE VEIL OF IGNORANCE

What goes on in the original position is first of all a choice, or more precisely, a choosing together, an agreement among parties. What the parties agree to are the principles of justice. Unlike most actual contracts, which cannot justify, the hypothetical contract the parties agree to does justify; the principles they choose are just in virtue of their choosing them. As the voluntarist account of justification would suggest, the principles of justice are the products of choice.

The guiding idea is that the principles of justice for the basic structure of society are the object of the original *agreement* [emphasis added] (11).

Thus we are to imagine that those who engage in social cooperation *choose together, in one joint act,* the principles which are to assign basic rights and duties and to determine the division of social benefits. Men are to *decide* in advance how they are to regulate their claims against one another [emphasis added] (11).

Just as each person must *decide* by rational reflection what constitutes his good, that is, the system of ends which it is rational for him to pursue, so *a group of persons must decide* once and for all what is to count among them as just and unjust. The *choice* which rational men would make in this hypothetical situation of equal liberty, assuming for the present that this *choice* problem has a solution, determines the principles of justice [emphasis added] (11–12).

Since all are similarly situated and no one is able to design principles to favor his particular condition, the principles of justice are the result of a fair *agreement or bargain* [emphasis added] (12).

Justice as fairness begins, as I have said, with one of the most general of all *choices* which persons might make together, namely with the *choice* of the first principles of a conception of justice [emphasis added] (13).

The principles of justice are those which would be *chosen* in the original position. They are the outcome of a certain *choice* situation [emphasis added] (41–2).

The principles of justice are not thought of as self-evident, but *have their justification in the fact that they would be chosen* [emphasis added] (42).

On a contract doctrine the moral facts are determined by the principles which would be *chosen* in the original position. . . . *[I]t is up to the persons* in the original position *to choose* these principles [emphasis added] (45).

Justice as fairness differs from traditional contract theories in that 'the relevant agreement is not to enter a given society or to adopt a given form of government, but to accept certain moral principles' (16). The result of the agreement is not a set of obligations applying to individuals, at least not directly, but principles of justice applying to the basic structure of society. Still, the voluntarist aspect of justification corresponds in some sense to the notion of society as a voluntary agreement. Rawls writes that living in a society governed by principles of justice derived from a voluntary account of justification is, in effect, the next best thing to living in a society we have actually chosen.

No society can, of course, be a scheme of co-operation which men enter voluntarily in a literal sense; each person finds himself placed at birth in some particular position in some particular society, and the nature of this position materially affects his life prospects. Yet a society satisfying the principles of justice as fairness comes as close as a society can to being a *voluntary scheme,* for it meets the principles which free and equal persons *would assent to* under circumstances which are fair. In this sense its members are autonomous and the obligations they recognize *self-imposed* [emphasis added] (13).

As our reconstruction suggests, the voluntarist nature of Rawls' contract view is bound up with the essential plurality of human subjects and the need to resolve conflicting claims. Without plurality, contracts, and for that matter principles of justice, would be neither possible nor necessary. 'Principles of justice deal with conflicting claims upon the advantages won by social co-operation; they apply to the relations among several persons or groups. The word "contract" suggests this plurality as well as the condition that the appropriate division of advantages must be in accordance with principles acceptable to all parties' (16).

As previously seen, justice as fairness differs from utilitarianism in its emphasis on the plurality and distinctiveness of individuals, and this difference is embodied in the role contract plays in justification.

Whereas the utilitarian extends to society the principles of choice for one man, justice as fairness, *being a contract view,* assumes that the principles of social choice, and so the principles of justice, are themselves the object of an original *agreement* [emphasis added] (28).

From the standpoint of *contract theory* one cannot arrive at a principle of social choice merely by extending the principle of rational prudence to the system of desires constructed by the impartial spectator. To do this is not to take seriously the *plurality and distinctness of individuals,* nor to recognize as the basis of justice that to which men would *consent* [emphasis added] (29).

In basing the principles of justice on an agreement among parties, Rawls emphasizes two characteristics that the hypothetical contract shares with actual ones, namely choice and plurality. But we have already seen that the ingredients of choice and plurality are not sufficient to make justice; actual contracts, which include both, cannot justify. This is due to the problems we have described as contingency and conventionalism. Actual agreements often turn out unfairly because of the various (coercive and non-coercive) contingencies associated with the inevitable differences of power and knowledge among persons differently situated. But in the original position, such contingencies are cured. Due to the veil of ignorance and other conditions of equality, all are similarly situated, and so none can take advantage, even inadvertently, of a more favorable bargaining position.

The original position is designed to overcome the problem of conventionalism as well. Where actual contracts are inescapably embedded in the practices and conventions of some particular society, the agreement in the original position is not implicated in the same way. It is not an actual contract, only a hypothetical one. Since it is imagined to occur before the principles of justice arrive on the scene, it may be thought of as 'pre-situated' in the relevant sense, a status quo antecedent to the arrival of justice such that no prior moral principles are available by which its results might be impugned. In this way it is able to realize the ideal of pure procedural justice. (Ironically, where the hypothetical nature of the original agreement at first appeared to weaken its justificatory force, it now appears as a positive, perhaps indispensable, advantage. Where Rawls emphasizes that 'nothing resembling [the original agreement] need ever have taken place' (120), it might be the case that no such agreement ever *could* take place and still overcome the problem of conventionalism.)

Since *all are similarly situated* and no one is able to design principles to favor his particular condition, the principles of justice are the result of a *fair* agreement or bargain [emphasis added] (12).

The original position is, one might say, the *appropriate initial status quo,* and thus the fundamental agreements reached in it are *fair.* This explains the propriety of the name 'justice as fairness': it conveys the idea that the principles of justice are agreed to in *an initial situation that is fair* [emphasis added] (12).

It is a state of affairs in which the parties are equally represented as moral persons and *the outcome is not conditioned by arbitrary contingencies* or the relative balance of social forces. Thus justice as fairness is able to use the idea of pure procedural justice from the beginning [emphasis added] (120).

By imposing the veil of ignorance it is possible to 'nullify the effects of specific contingencies which put men at odds and tempt them to exploit social and natural circumstances to their own advantage' (136).

If a knowledge of particulars is allowed, then the outcome is biased by *arbitrary contingencies*. As already observed, to each according to his threat advantage is not a principle of justice. If the original position is to yield agreements that are just, the parties must be *fairly situated* and treated equally as moral persons. The arbitrariness of the world must be corrected for by adjusting the circumstances of the initial contractual situation [emphasis added] (141).

Once the parties to an agreement are assumed to be similarly situated in all relevant respects, differences of power and knowledge disappear, and the possible sources of unfairness are thus eradicated. Since no one is able to choose on the basis of contingently given attributes, the ideal of autonomy, implicit but imperfect in actual contracts, is fulfilled, the ideal of reciprocity is realized as a matter of course, and the vulnerability of contract to the 'further question' ('But is it fair?') is eliminated. 'The veil of ignorance deprives the persons in the original position of the knowledge that would enable them to choose heteronomous principles. The parties arrive at their choice together as free and equal rational persons knowing only that those circumstances obtain which give rise to the need for principles of justice' (252).

Once the 'further question' of fairness loses its independent moral force, owing to the fact that the parties are situated in such a way that no unfairness conceivably could result, any agreement reached becomes a case of pure procedural justice; its outcome is fair, 'whatever it is', in virtue of its agreement alone. Under such conditions, a contract ceases to be a constitutive convention and becomes instead an instrument of justification.

The aim is to characterize this situation so that the principles that would be chosen, *whatever they turn out to be,* are acceptable from a moral point of view. The original position is defined in such a way that it is a status quo in which *any agreements reached are fair* [emphasis added] (120).

The idea of the original position is to set up a fair procedure so that *any principles agreed to will be just.* The aim is to use the notion of pure procedural justice as a basis of theory [emphasis added] (136).

But at this point a crucial ambiguity arises, for it is not clear what exactly it means 'to use the notion of pure procedural justice as a basis of theory'. Rawls claims that *once* the situation is appropriately characterized, *then* the principles chosen, *whatever they turn out to be,* are acceptable from a moral point of view; *once* the original position is properly defined, *then any agreements reached* in it are fair; *once* a fair procedure is established, *then any principles agreed to* will be just.

What is unclear is how generous these provisions are to the choosers. On one reading, the terms seem generous indeed, the very embodiment of the voluntarist provisions suggested above. Once the parties find themselves in a fair situation, anything goes; the scope for their choice is unlimited. The results of their deliberations will be morally acceptable 'whatever they turn out to be'. No matter what principles they choose, those principles will count as just.

But there is another, less expansive reading of their situation, which gives considerably less scope to their enterprise. On this interpretation, what it means to say that the principles chosen will be just 'whatever they turn out to be' is simply that, given their situation, the parties are guaranteed to choose the *right* principles. While it may be true that, strictly speaking, they can choose any principles they wish, their situation is designed in such a way that they are guaranteed to 'wish' to choose only certain principles. On this view, 'any agreements reached' in the original position are fair, not because the procedure sanctifies just any outcome, but because the situation guarantees a particular outcome. But if the principles agreed to are just because only (the) just principles can be agreed to, the voluntarist aspect of the enterprise is not as spacious as would first appear. The distinction between pure and perfect procedural justice fades, and it becomes unclear whether the procedure 'translates its fairness to the outcome', or whether the fairness of the procedure is given by the fact that it necessarily leads to the right result.

Rawls confirms the less voluntarist reading when he writes, 'The acceptance of these principles is not conjectured as a psychological law or probability. Ideally anyway, I should like to show that their acknowledgement is the only choice [sic] consistent with the full description of the original position. The argument aims eventually to be strictly deductive' (121). The notion that the full description of the original position determines a single 'choice' which the parties cannot but acknowledge seems to introduce a cognitive element to justification after all and to call into question the priority of procedure over principle which the contract view – and the deontological project generally – seemed to require. But a more immediate consequence of this reading is that it complicates our account of what goes on in the original position. Rawls maintains that what happens behind the veil of ignorance is that a plurality of persons come to a unanimous agreement on a particular conception of justice. It is worth examining his description closely.

To begin with, it is clear that since the differences among the parties are unknown to them, and everyone is equally rational and similarly situated, *each is convinced by the same arguments.* Therefore, we can view the choice in the original position from the standpoint of one person selected at random. *If anyone after due reflection prefers a conception of justice to another, then they all do, and a unanimous agreement can be reached* [emphasis added] (139).

Rawls suggests that, to make the circumstances more vivid, we might imagine that the parties communicate with each other through a referee, who transmits proposed alternatives, informs the parties when they have come to an understanding, and so on. 'But such a referee is actually superfluous, assuming that the deliberations of the parties must be similar' (139).

Thus there follows the very important consequence that the parties have no basis for bargaining in the usual sense. No one knows his situation in society nor his natural assets, and therefore no one is in a position to tailor principles to his advantage (139).

The veil of ignorance makes possible a unanimous choice of a particular conception of justice. Without these limitations on knowledge the bargaining problem of the original position would be hopelessly complicated (140).

Since the parties are 'similarly situated', they are guaranteed to reason in the same way, and have no basis for bargaining 'in the usual sense'. This would seem to imply that they have a basis for bargaining in some other sense ('The principles of justice are the result of a fair agreement or bargain.' (12)), but it is difficult to imagine what this sense could be. Bargaining in *any* sense requires some difference in the interests or preferences or power or knowledge of the bargainers, but in the original position, there are none. Under such conditions, it is difficult to imagine how any bargain, in any sense, could ever get going.

If no bargaining could take place, the question also arises whether any discussion could take place. Rawls suggests that various alternatives might be proposed before the final agreement is reached. But if the parties are assumed to reason in the same way and to be convinced by the same arguments, it seems unlikely that a certain idea could occur to one but not to another. Discussion, like bargaining, presupposes some differences in the perceptions or interests or knowledge or concerns of the discussants, but in the original position, there are no such differences. We must therefore assume that the 'deliberations' of the parties proceed in silence and issue in a single conception which is unanimously agreed to.

But this makes the account of the agreement in the original position more puzzling still. For if there is no basis for bargaining or discussion, it is doubtful that there can be any basis for agreement, even a unanimous agreement, either. Rawls states, 'If anyone after due reflection prefers a conception of justice to another, then they all do, *and* a unanimous agreement can be reached' [emphasis added] (139). But why 'and'? What does the agreement *add* once the discovery has been made? Suppose that everyone, after due reflection, found that he preferred a particular conception of justice, and suppose further that everyone knew that all preferred the same one. Would they then *go on* to agree to this conception? What would it mean for them to make this discovery first, and then *go on* to make an agreement about it? Even if we could imagine what it would mean to go on to make an agreement under such circumstances, what would the agreement *add* to the discovery that all preferred the same conception? Would the conception be justified after they 'went on to make the agreement' in a way that it was not justified when they *saw* that all preferred the conception but before they 'made the agreement'?

At this point it is important to distinguish two different senses of 'agreement'. The first involves agreement with a person (or persons) with respect to a proposition, the second agreement to a proposition. The first sort of agreement is a kind of 'choosing together', and requires a plurality of persons. (One will not do, except in the metaphorical sense in which I make an agreement with myself.) It is this sort of agreement that is typically engaged in making a contract, where part of the agreement involves forming an intention. Although we may speak of two persons agreeing *to* a contract, what we mean is that two persons agree *with* each other to abide by certain terms. The agreement and the terms, taken together, constitute the contract. Since agreement in this sense requires an intentional act, or an exercise of will, we might describe it as agreement in the voluntarist sense.

The second sort of agreement, an agreement to a proposition, does not require more than a single person, and does not involve an exercise of will. In this sense of agreement, to agree to a proposition amounts to acknowledging its validity, and this requires neither that others be involved nor that I take the validity of the proposition to be a matter of choice. It may be enough that I *see* it to be valid, as when I agree to (or accept, or acknowledge) the proposition that $2 + 2 = 4$. To agree in this sense is to grasp something already there. Although I may say I have 'decided' that the answer to this difficult problem in mathematics is 'x', it is not a decision that *decides* anything except whether I have got it right. Since agreement in this second sense is a question of knowing rather than willing, we might describe it as agreement in the cognitive sense.

Once this distinction is borne in mind, Rawls' account of the original agreement appears in a new light. Passages that first seemed to describe an agreement in the voluntarist sense can now be seen to admit a cognitive interpretation as well. Where at first Rawls writes as though 'the choice . . . *determines* the principles of justice' [emphasis added] (12), in other places he writes as though the parties have merely to *acknowledge* principles already there.

The relevant agreement is not to enter a given society or to adopt a given form of government, but to *accept* certain moral principles [emphasis added] (16).

I argue that the two principles would be *acknowledged* [in the original position] [emphasis added] (118).

They are the principles that free and rational persons concerned to further their own interests would *accept* in an initial position of equality [emphasis added] (11).

[The members of a well-ordered society] could all view their arrangements as meeting the stipulations which they would *acknowledge* in an initial situation that embodies widely accepted and reasonable constraints on the choice of principles [emphasis added] (13).

Thus men exhibit their freedom, their independence from the contingencies of nature and society, by acting in ways they would *acknowledge* in the original position [emphasis added] (256).

Ironically, the Kantian interpretation of justice as fairness highlights the shift from the voluntarist interpretation to the cognitive one. Although some reference to choice remains, the parties are described less as willing agents than as subjects who *perceive* the world in a certain way.

My suggestion is that we think of the original position as the *point of view* from which noumenal selves *see* the world. The parties qua noumenal selves have complete freedom to choose whatever principles they wish; but they also have a desire to express their nature as rational and equal members of the intelligible realm with precisely this liberty to choose, that is, as beings who can *look at the world in this way* and express this *perspective* in their life as members of society [emphasis added] (255).

In both Rawls' theory of the person and his account of justification, the assumptions of choice and of plurality have stood together as central features of the conception. As the voluntarist interpretation of the original position gives way to a cognitive one, the assumption of plurality is called into question as well. Rawls speaks throughout of the *parties* to the original position and in the Kantian interpretation even speaks of noumenal *selves*. But since the veil of ignorance has the effect of depriving the parties, *qua* parties to the original position, of all distinguishing characteristics, it becomes difficult to see what their plurality could possibly consist in.

Rawls acknowledges this condition in part when he writes that 'all are similarly situated' (12), and that in this way a unanimous agreement is guaranteed. But once *all* individuating characteristics are excluded, the parties are not merely *similarly* situated (as persons in real life with similar life circumstances and certain overlapping interests), but *identically* situated. And as we have seen, Rawls' own theory of the person acknowledges that no two subjects could ever be regarded as identically situated and still count as distinguishable persons. The notion that not persons but only a single subject is to be found behind the veil of ignorance would explain why no bargaining or discussion can take place there. It would also explain why there can be no contract or agreement in the voluntarist sense. For contracts, like discussions, require a plurality of persons, and when the veil of ignorance descends, this plurality dissolves.

At the beginning of the book, and again at the end, Rawls asks why, if the original position is merely hypothetical, we should take any interest in it, moral or otherwise. His answer in each case is that 'the conditions embodied in the description of the original position are ones that we do in fact accept. Or if we do not, then perhaps we can be persuaded to do so by philosophical reflection' (21, also 587). The philosophical considerations by which Rawls would persuade us set out from the contractarian tradition. The well-ordered society he recommends 'comes as close as a society can to being a voluntary scheme' (13). But what begins as an ethic of choice and consent ends, however unwittingly, as an ethic of insight and self-understanding. In the final passage of the book, the language of choosing and willing is displaced by the language of seeing and perceiving, as the voluntarist image of Kant gives way to the cognitive image of Spinoza.

Once we *grasp* this conception, we can at any time *look* at the social world from the required *point of view*. . . . Thus to *see* our place in society from the *perspective* of this position is to *see* it *sub specie aeternitatis*: it is to *regard* the human situation not only from all social but also from all temporal *points of view*. The *perspective of eternity* is not a *perspective* from a certain place beyond the world, nor the point of view of a transcendent being; rather it is a certain *form of thought* and feeling that rational persons can adopt within the world. . . . Purity of heart, if one could attain it, would be *to see clearly* and to act with grace and self-command from *this point of view* [emphasis added] (587).

The secret to the original position – and the key to its justificatory force – lies not in what they *do* there but rather in what they *apprehend* there. What matters is not what they choose but what they see, not what they decide but what they discover. What goes on in the original position is not a contract after all, but the coming to self-awareness of an intersubjective being.

4

Justice and the Good

We set out to assess Rawls' claim for the primacy of justice and found that it required a certain conception of the moral subject. We sought then to examine this conception in the light of Rawls' moral theory as a whole to check for its consistency with that theory and for its plausibility generally. We hoped eventually in this way to assess first Rawls' theory of the subject and finally the claim for the primacy of justice it must support.

Thus far we have considered Rawls' theory of the subject primarily in relation to his theory of justice, or conception of right. But as Rawls points out, a full moral theory must give some account of the good as well as the right, and the final third of his book seeks to provide one. Indeed the primacy of justice is itself a claim not only about justice but about the relation of justice to those virtues falling under the concept of the good. So before we can assess this ultimate claim, we must consider Rawls' theory of the subject in relation to this theory of the good as well.

THE UNITY OF THE SELF

We might begin by recalling the main points of correspondence between Rawls' moral theory on the one hand and his theory of the subject on the other. Where the morality of right corresponds to the bounds of the self and speaks to that which distinguishes us, the morality of good corresponds to the unity of persons and speaks to that which connects us. On a deontological ethic, where the right is prior to the good, this means that what separates us is in some important sense prior to what connects us – epistemologically prior as well as morally prior. We are distinct individuals first, and *then* we form relationships and engage in co-operative arrangements with others; hence the priority of plurality over unity. We are barren subjects of possession first, and *then* we choose the ends we would possess; hence the priority of the self over its ends.

These in brief are the interlocking claims of moral theory and philosophical anthropolgy on which deontological liberalism has been seen to depend. In considering Rawls' theory of the subject from the standpoint of the right, we have focused on the distinctness of the self and the constitution of its bounds. In considering Rawls' theory of the subject now from the standpoint of the good, our focus will shift to the unity of the self and the question how its bounds may be negotiated or traversed. This question comes in two parts. The first concerns Rawls' theory of community and its account of how antecedently individuated persons come to join together in social union. The second concerns his theory of agency and its account of how subjects of possession bounded in advance come to acquire their purposes and ends.

We have spoken of the two central features of the self – its distinctness and its unity – as though each were in some sense self-sufficient, as though each could be described independently of the other. But it is difficult in practice to observe the distinction between these two features of the self without also remarking their internal connection. Even as we have focused on the bounds of the self and the conception of right, we have already had occasion to seek a principle of unity and to anticipate a theory of community that might provide it. Even from the standpoint of right the bounds of the self as posited by Rawls have been seen to give way.

In so far as the difference principle has been seen to require a wider subject of possession, the principles of justice have spilled over the bounds of the antecedently individuated subject, so to speak, and relied in advance on a form of unity reserved by Rawls to the province of the good. Where Rawls would fix the identities of persons independently of their commonality and define the right without reference to the (full theory of the) good, the notion that the difference principle relies on a theory of community 'from the start' would deny these priorities in important ways. Where Rawls sees a theory of the good as a complement rather than a prerequisite of justice, designed to show its stability and its tendency to generate its own support, the wider notion of possession implicit in the difference principle would require certain theories of community and agency at the foundation of justice and not only at its perimeter.

We need therefore assess Rawls' theory of the good, and in particular his accounts of community and agency, not only for their plausibility generally, but also for their ability to provide the sort of account the theory of justice requires for its completion. I shall try to show that Rawls' conception fails in both respects, and for similar reasons. But before taking up his theory of the good directly, it may be helpful to consider a concrete illustration of what exactly is at stake for justice in a theory of community, and what goes wrong with the liberal position when it tries to do without one. For this purpose I propose to consider an argument by Ronald Dworkin in favor of affirmative action, or preferential treatment of minorities in university admissions. Although Dworkin's argument is not identical to the one Rawls might make, it has much in common with Rawls' general view of merit, desert, and the nature of the moral subject, and serves to highlight the deontological assumptions with which we are concerned.

THE CASE OF AFFIRMATIVE ACTION

Dworkin defends affirmative-action admissions policies for professional schools such as medicine and law on the grounds that they are an effective, or at least possibly effective means to a desirable social goal, namely to increase the presence of blacks and other minorities in these socially strategic professions, and so eventually 'to reduce the degree to which American society is over-all a racially conscious society' (1977b: 11). His basic argument is an argument of social utility. Affirmative action is justified, not because those who are given preference are entitled to an advantage, whether in compensation for past discrimination or for any other reason, but simply because 'helping them is now an effective way of attacking a national problem' (1977b: 12).

But Dworkin, like Rawls, believes that no social policy can be justified, however well it serves the general welfare, if it violates individual rights. He therefore considers the argument that affirmative action violates the rights of those whites it puts at a disadvantage and in some cases excludes. He concludes in the negative: the idea that preferential treatment 'presents a conflict between a desirable social goal and important individual rights is a piece of intellectual confusion' (1977b: 12).

One version of the argument Dworkin considers is a claim that taking race into account is unfair because it fixes on a quality beyond a person's control. Dworkin answers that this does not distinguish race as a criterion but applies equally to most standards typically used in college and university admissions, including intelligence. While it is true that persons do not choose their race,

it is also true that those who score low in aptitude or admissions tests do not choose their levels of intelligence. Nor do those denied admission because they are too old, or because they do not come from a part of the country underrepresented in the school, or because they cannot play basketball well, choose not to have the qualities that made the difference (1977b: 15).

Race may seem a different factor because exclusions based on race have historically expressed prejudice or contempt for the excluded race as such. But whites excluded as a result of affirmative action are excluded not out of contempt but only on the same sort of instrumental calculation that justifies the more familiar criteria. While it is true that a white with marginal test scores would have been accepted if he were black, 'it is also true, and in exactly the same sense, that he would have been accepted if he had been more intelligent, or made a better impression in his interview. . . . Race is not, in *his* case, a different matter from these other factors equally beyond his control' (1977b: 15).

Another version of the argument Dworkin considers is the claim that by admitting blacks with lower test scores than those achieved by some whites who are excluded, affirmative action violates the right of applicants to be judged on the basis of merit. Dworkin responds that what counts as merit cannot be determined in the abstract but depends on those qualities deemed relevant to the social purpose the institution serves. In the case of medical and law schools, intelligence as measured by standardized tests may well be among the relevant characteristics, but it is by no means the only appropriate consideration, as the long-standing practice of admissions committees attests. Other attributes of person and background are typically weighed in assessing the likely ability of the applicant to perform the needed function, and where being black is relevant to the social purpose at hand, being black must count as merit as well.

There is no combination of abilities and skills and traits that constitutes 'merit' in the abstract; if quick hands count as 'merit' in the case of a prospective surgeon, this is because quick hands will enable him to serve the public better and for no other reason. If a black skin will, as a matter of regrettable fact, enable another doctor to do a different medical job better, then that black skin is by the same token 'merit' as well (1977b: 13).

Dworkin acknowledges that some may find dangerous the argument counting race as a form of merit, but 'only because they confuse its conclusion – that black skin may be a socially useful trait in particular circumstances – with the very different and despicable idea that one race may be inherently more worthy than another' (1977b: 12).

Implicit in much of Dworkin's argument is the idea that no one can justly claim his rights are violated by affirmative action programs, because no one, white or black, *deserves* to go to medical school or law school to begin with; no one has an antecedent right to be admitted. To be sure, those who meet to the fullest extent the conditions established for admission are *entitled* to be admitted, and it would be wrong to exclude them. But it cannot be said that they or any others *deserve* to be admitted, for at least two reasons. First, their having the relevant characteristics is in most cases no doing of theirs; their native intelligence, family environment, social and cultural opportunities and so on are for the most part factors beyond their control, a matter of good fortune. And in any case, no one is entitled that medical schools or law schools undertake to reward any particular kind of qualifications in the first place. What counts as a qualification for any particular task depends on the qualities that task happens to require, nothing more. The benefits associated with the professions are thus not rewards for superior attainment but incentives to attract the relevant qualities. There can therefore be no antecedent right to be judged according to any particular set of criteria.

From this it seems clear that Dworkin's arguments coincide with Rawls' theory in several respects. The notion that traditional criteria of admission, as well as race, are no doing of the applicant recalls Rawls' argument that the advantages of the fortunate are arbitrary from a moral point of view. Dworkin's argument that there is no such thing as 'merit' in the abstract, without reference to the purposes institutions may define and pursue, parallels Rawls' argument against meritocracy that the concepts of merit and virtue and moral worth have no antecedent or pre-institutional moral status and so cannot provide an independent standpoint from which otherwise just institutions could be criticized. And the general implication of Dworkin's argument, that no one, black or white, deserves to go to medical or law school, that no one has an antecedent right to be admitted, corresponds to Rawls' distinction between moral desert and legitimate expectations.

Rawls' and Dworkin's positions are similar in a more general sense as well. Both are rights-based theories, defined in explicit opposition to utilitarian conceptions, and seek to defend certain individual claims against the calculus of social interests. But notwithstanding their individualist aspirations, both rely on a theory of the subject that has the paradoxical effect of confirming the ultimate frailty, perhaps even incoherence, of the individual whose rights they seek above all to secure. We have already seen how on Rawls' conception the self threatens at different points in the argument either to dissolve into a radically disembodied subject or to collapse into a radically situated subject. As we shall now see, Dworkin's argument for affirmative action illustrates how these perplexities, identified first in the abstract, find consequence in practice.

Central to any case for affirmative action is the ability to distinguish discrimination against blacks and other minorities, as in historic color bars and anti-Jewish quotas, from discrimination in favor of blacks and other minorities of the kind involved in affirmative action programs. Dworkin argues that justification for the first sort of discrimination typically depends in part on 'the despicable idea that one race may be inherently more worthy than another', while justification for the second depends instead on the utilitarian notion that society as a whole would gain by having more widely representative medical and legal professions.

With respect to the first justification, Rawls like Dworkin would clearly reject the idea that one race may be inherently more worthy than another. What is striking to recall is why, on Rawls' theory of the subject at least, this despicable idea must be wrong. For Rawls, the fallacy with the claim that whites are inherently more worthy than blacks is not that it denies the intrinsic worth of blacks but that it falsely attributes an intrinsic worth to whites, and so attributes to them an unfounded claim of desert. The reason is that for Rawls, the concept of moral worth, like the concept of the good, is 'secondary to those of right and justice, and it plays no role in the substantive definition of distributive shares' (312–13). Persons can no more have an intrinsic worth than they can have intrinsic merit or desert, that is, a worth or merit or desert that is theirs prior to or independent of what just institutions may attribute to them. And as we have seen, no one can strictly speaking be said to deserve anything because no one can be said to *have* anything, at least not in the undistanced, constitutive sense of possession necessary to a desert base. On Rawls' theory of the subject, no person or race can be inherently more worthy or deserving than another, not because all are intrinsically worthy and deserving – and equally so – but because none is intrinsically worthy or deserving, and so all claims must equally await the arrival of just institutions.

Some will object to Dworkin's argument for affirmative action – and to Rawls' theory of justice in so far as it supports it – on the standard meritocratic grounds that the individual possesses his attributes in some unproblematic sense and therefore deserves the benefits that flow from them, and that part of what it means for an institution or distributive scheme to be just is that it rewards individuals antecedently worthy of reward. But Rawls and Dworkin present powerful arguments against these assumptions which defenders of meritocracy would be hard-pressed to meet. The difficulty with Dworkin's argument, it seems to me, lies elsewhere; it concerns the possible alternative visions of the subject that remain once the meritocratic conception of the individual is rejected. And this returns us to the problem of the bounds of the self.

We have already considered the difficulties associated with the notion of a person essentially dispossessed, barren of constituent features, without intrinsic worth or desert, and wholly dependent for his life prospects on the rights and opportunities institutions of justice may dispense. We have remarked as well the irony that a person so morally disempowered should be the product of a liberal ethic designed to establish the rights of the individual as inviolable. But if the denial of individual desert and the insistence on the bounds between the self and its attributes lead in the direction of a radically disembodied subject, the notion of common assets poses a different threat to the integrity of the self in its implication that the bounds between the self and the other must somehow be relaxed. For unless some principle of individuation other than a merely empirical one can be found, the danger here is the drift into a radically situated subject.

On Dworkin's argument for affirmative action, this perplexity takes the following form: Once admission or exclusion cannot plausibly be seen to depend on a notion of 'merit' in the abstract or on an antecedent individual claim, the alternative is to assume that the collective ends of the society as a whole should automatically prevail. But the bounds of the relevant society are never established, its status as the appropriate subject of possession never confirmed. Once the self, *qua* individual self, is dispossessed, the claims of the individual fade to betray an underlying utilitarianism which is never justified. And as Rawls implies early on, utilitarianism is in a sense the ethic of the unbounded subject, the ethic that fails to take seriously the distinction between persons.

For Dworkin, however, utilitarian considerations are precisely the ones that distinguish the legitimate discrimination involved in affirmative action from the unjustifiable sort based on prejudice and contempt. If it cannot be said that some are inherently more *worthy* than others, it can at least be said that some are more *valuable* than others with respect to the social purposes at hand, and discrimination on this basis is justifiable. So long as a policy of preferential treatment *uses* people for the sake of worthy ends rather than *judges* people as more or less worthy in themselves, it is permissible. So long as an exclusion based on race is motivated not by prejudice but by an 'instrumental calculation', a 'rational calculation about the socially most beneficial use of limited resources', or an idea such as the one that 'black skin may be a socially useful trait' (1977: 12), the exclusion is consistent with utilitarian considerations and may be justifiable. A person's expectations, unless they are founded on rights in Dworkin's special sense of the term, must always give way in the face of a 'more general social concern', as when a small businessman must go under so that a new and superior road might be built (1977: 15). Although their disappointment is understandable, even worthy of our sympathy, rejected applicants can no more stand in the way of the medical profession society needs than the small businessman can stand in the way of the superhighway.

Although Dworkin's argument assumes that where no individual rights are at stake, social policy is properly decided on utilitarian grounds, he never says why this should be so. Apart from showing why utilitarian arguments cannot defeat individual rights, his theory does not offer an explicit defense of utilitarian ethics as such, and says little about why utilitarianism should prevail when individual rights are not involved. Dworkin may not feel the need to justify his underlying utilitarian assumptions because they seem on the surface to have a certain self-evident appeal. If no individual has an antecedent claim to the benefits of his accidentally given assets and endowments, it might seem natural to suppose that the society as a whole therefore does. But as we saw in the discussion of common assets and the difference principle, this assumption is without warrant. The arbitrariness of an individual's assets argues only against the proposition that the individual owns them or has a privileged claim to their benefits, not in favor of the proposition that some particular society owns them or has a privileged claim with respect to them. And unless this second proposition can be established, there would seem no grounds for favoring a utilitarian dispensation of such assets and endowments rather than just letting them lie where they fall.

Without some conception of a wider subject of possession, such as Rawls' notion of common assets seems also to require, there would seem no obvious reason why these assets should be made to serve general social ends rather than individual ones. To the contrary; in the absence of some wider subject of possession, to regard 'my' abilities and endowments as mere instruments of a wider social purpose is to use me as a means to others' ends, and thus to violate a central Rawlsian and Kantian moral injunction.

The moral oddness of basing university admissions on the assumption Rawls and Dworkin suggest, whether or not affirmative action is involved, might be illustrated by imagining the following letters of rejection and acceptance written to convey the moral basis of the policy they recommend:

Dear (Unsuccessful) Applicant,
We regret to inform you that your application for admission has been rejected. Please understand that we intend no offense by our decision. Your rejection indicates neither that we hold you in contempt nor even that we regard you as less deserving of admission than those who were accepted.

It is not your fault that when you came along society happened not to need the qualities you had to offer. Those admitted instead of you were not themselves deserving of a place, nor worthy of praise for the factors that led to their admission. We are in any case only using them – and you – as instruments of a wider social purpose.

You will likely find this news disappointing in the sense that your hopes of reaping the benefits given those whose qualities do coincide with society's needs at any given moment will not be realized. But this sort of disappointment occurs whenever an individual's preferences must give way to society's preferences, and should not be exaggerated by the thought that your rejection reflects in any way on your intrinsic moral worth; please be assured that those who were admitted are intrinsically as worthless as you.

You have our sympathy in the sense that it is too bad you did not happen to have the qualities society happened to want when you applied. Better luck next time. Sincerely yours . . .

Dear (Successful) Applicant,

We are pleased to inform you that your application for admission has been accepted. Through no doing of your own, it turns out that you happen to have the traits that society needs at the moment, so we propose to exploit your assets for society's advantage by admitting you to the study of medicine/law.

No praise is intended or to be inferred from this decision, as your having the relevant qualities is arbitrary from a moral point of view. You are to be congratulated, not in the sense that you deserve credit for having the qualities that led to your admission – you do not – but only in the sense that the winner of a lottery is to be congratulated. You are lucky to have come along with the right traits at the right moment, and if you choose to accept our offer you will ultimately be entitled to the benefits that attach to being used in this way. For this, you may properly celebrate.

You, or more likely your parents, may be tempted to celebrate in the further sense that you take this admission to reflect favorably, if not on your native endowments, at least on the conscientious effort you have made to cultivate your abilities and overcome the obstacles to your achievements. But the assumption that you deserve even the superior character necessary to your effort is equally problematic, for your character also depends on fortunate circumstances of various kinds for which you can claim no credit. The notion of desert seems not to apply to your case.

We look forward nonetheless to seeing you in the fall. Sincerely yours . . .

As these letters suggest, the policy Rawls and Dworkin defend can be troubling even for those who do not hold the meritocratic assumptions they effectively call into question. One can imagine, for example, a response along the following lines.

I do not claim that I, as an individual, either possess (in any exclusive sense) the assets with which I am endowed, or that I have any special moral claim on the fruits of their exercise. I acknowledge that I am indebted in a complex variety of ways for the constitution of my identity – to parents, family, city, tribe, class, nation, culture, historical epoch, possibly God, Nature, and maybe chance – and I can therefore claim little or no credit (or for that matter, blame) for having turned out the way I have. Sorting out just who or what is accountable for this or that part of me is a difficult if at times indispensable moral activity which after a certain point may become impossible to complete. But I agree in any case that I do not deserve to be admitted to any particular opportunity in any antecedent moral sense, first because I do not possess in my own right the qualities that would make me eligible, and second, because even if I did, I would not be entitled that the rules in force reward any particular set of attributes or qualifications rather than others.

From this it seems reasonable to suppose that what at first glance appear as 'my' assets are more properly described as common assets in some sense; since others made me, and in various ways continue to make me, the person I am, it seems appropriate to regard them, in so far as I can identify them, as participants in 'my' achievements and common beneficiaries of the rewards they bring. Where this sense of participation in the achievements and endeavors of (certain) others engages the reflective self-understandings of the participants, we may come to regard ourselves, over the range of our various activities, less as individuated subjects with certain things in common, and more as members of a wider (but still determinate) subjectivity, less as 'others' and more as participants in a common identity, be it a family or community or class or people or nation.

One consequence of an enlarged self-understanding such as this is that when 'my' assets or life prospects are enlisted in the service of a common endeavor, I am likely to experience this less as a case of being used for others' ends and more as a way of contributing to the purposes of a community I regard as my own. The justification of my sacrifice, if it can be called a sacrifice, is not the abstract assurance that unknown others will gain more than I will lose, but the rather more compelling notion that by my efforts I contribute to the realization of a way of life in which I take pride and with which my identity is bound. While it would of course remain true that I could not, as an individual, claim credit for possessing the qualities relevant to the common endeavor, I could none the less take pride in my fitness to contribute in this way, and this fitness, perhaps even more than the benefits I might glean, would be just cause for celebration.

This is not of course to say that a claim on 'my' resources from just any quarter can be described in this way. The scope of community ties, however expansive, is not without limit. Even an enlarged self, conceived as a community, has its bounds, however provisional its contours may be. The bounds between the self and (some) others are thus relaxed on the intersubjective account, but not so completely relaxed as to give way to a radically situated subject. The bounds that remain are not given by the physical, bodily differences between individual human beings, but by the capacity of the self through reflection to participate in the constitution of its identity, and where circumstances permit, to arrive at an expansive self-understanding.

A further feature of the intersubjective description of common assets is that it renders the dispossession of the person as it appears from the individualistic point of view less ultimately disempowering. While the argument from arbitrariness systematically deprives the subject, *qua* individual person, of its attributes and possessions, leaving a self so shorn of empirically identifiable features as to dissolve into abstraction ('The person has disappeared; only attributes remain'), the notion of a wider subject of possession goes some way toward reconstituting the person and restoring its powers. If I cannot be the owner I can at least be the guardian of the assets located 'here', and what is more, a guardian for a community of which I count myself a member.

None of this is an argument against affirmative action as such. But it does suggest a further moral issue that Dworkin must address before his argument for affirmative action can be complete, and that is the question of how to establish the relevant subject of possession, or how to identify those among whom the assets I accidentally bear are properly regarded as common. To put the point another way, utilitarianism is an ethic of sharing. (In this respect, it resembles the difference principle.) As such it must presuppose some antecedent bond or tie among those whose satisfactions it would maximize and whose efforts and expectations it would expend in the process. Otherwise it is simply a formula for using some as means to others' ends, a formula deontological liberals are committed to reject.

But Dworkin's position on this question is ambiguous at best. At times he speaks as though no account of a wider subject of possession

is required, as though it is enough for a utilitarian argument to succeed that an individual expectation come up against 'some more general social concern', where that expectation is not protected as a matter of right. On this interpretation, I must share 'my' assets wth
'society as a whole' not because this particular society has made me
what I am and so is responsible for these assets and endowments in a
way that I, individually, am not, but rather on the dubious assumption
that 'society' is the residuary beneficiary of the free-floating assets
that remain once the individual is dispossessed. This assumes without
argument that 'society' in some indeterminate sense (all of humankind?) has a prior claim on whatever assets the individual does not.
But simply because I, as an individual, do not have a privileged claim
on the assets accidentally residing 'here', it does not follow that everyone in the world collectively does. For there is no reason to think in
advance that their location in 'society's' province (or for that matter,
within the province of humankind) is any less arbitrary from a moral
point of view. And if their arbitrariness within *me* makes them ineligible to serve *my* ends, there seems no obvious reason why their arbitrariness within a particular society should not make them ineligible
to serve that society's ends as well.

Dworkin speaks at other times as though he does have a determinate subject of possession in mind after all, and that it is the nation-
state. He writes, for example, that '*American society* is currently a
racially conscious society', and that it is the goal of affirmative action
'to reduce the degree to which *American society* is over-all a racially
conscious society'. These programs are said to provide 'an effective
way of attacking a *national* problem' [emphasis added] (1977b:
11–12). But if Dworkin means to claim that, for the sake of determining university admissions and career prospects, the purposes of
the *national* community properly predominate, then he must say a
good deal more about why this should be so. And part of this argument would have to include some evidence of the nation's responsibility for having cultivated the qualities and endowments it would
now enlist, its capacity to engage the reflective self-understanding of
its members as the basis of their common identity, and its ability to
claim if not agreement at least allegiance to the purposes that would
arise from this identity. It would need to demonstrate, in short, that
of the various communities and forms of identity, the nation is the
one that is properly entitled to define the common purpose and to

deploy the common assets necessary to its pursuit, at least in so far as university education and the choice of certain professional careers are concerned. It may or may not be the case that the American nation today defines a community in the relevant sense;[1] but in so far as Dworkin means to invoke the nation as the relevant subject of possession, it remains for him to show that this is so.

Despite Dworkin's passing references to the nation, both he and Rawls seem generally to assume that once the rights of the individual are dealt with, an unspecified social claim predominates without any account of a determinate community or wider subject of possession being required. Thus Dworkin speaks of the need to serve the 'more general social concern', and to provide 'what the more general society most needs' (1977b: 15), and Rawls writes of the need to arrange distributive schemes so as to further 'the common interest' (311), and to serve 'prior and independent social ends' (313).

We might summarize the difficulties with this assumption as follows: first, there is no such thing as '*the* society as a whole', or '*the* more general society', taken in the abstract, no single 'ultimate' community whose pre-eminence just goes without argument or further description. Each of us moves in an indefinite number of communities, some more inclusive than others, each making different claims on our allegiance, and there is no saying in advance which is *the* society or community whose purposes should govern the disposition of any particular set of our attributes and endowments.

Second, if there is no such thing as '*the* society as a whole', taken in the abstract, then it would seem unlikely that any particular society, arbitrarily identified, could have any greater claim to some particular set of endowments than the individual in whom they accidentally reside, for surely their location within the province of such an arbitrarily identified community could be no less arbitrary from a moral point of view. In particular there would be no obvious reason why 'more general social concerns' as such should in all cases defeat more local or particular concerns merely in virtue of their generality.

---

1 An illuminating discussion of the nation as a community can be found in Beer (1966). He distinguishes between the centralization of government and the process of national integration and points out that the two tendencies, however interdependent, are not guaranteed to coincide. In national integration, the nation is 'made more of a community', and the sense in which its members share a common life deepens (1966: 80–2).

It is interesting to note in this connection that utilitarianism in its earlier, theological versions (as in Tucker and Paley) did offer an explicit account of the ultimate subject of possession – namely God – whose purposes necessarily predominated over more local concerns (MacIntyre 1967: 462–6). But once utilitarianism turns secular, the relevant subject of possession is no longer a settled matter, and the grounds for asserting the precedence of one range of concerns over another must await some further description of the relevant subject or community and the basis of its claims.

Finally, unless it is possible to identify the relevant community across which 'my' assets are properly shared and to establish its credentials, Dworkin's argument for affirmative action and Rawls' notion of common assets have the effect either of contradicting the central Kantian and Rawlsian injunction against using some as means to others' ends, or evading this contradiction by relaxing altogether the bounds between the self and the other, thus lapsing into a radically situated subject.

Having seen a practical illustration of how justice, on the deontological ethic, requires a notion of community for its very coherence and not simply to demonstrate its 'congruence and stability', we must now consider whether Rawls' conception can supply it. Rawls writes that 'justice as fairness has a central place for the value of community', and claims in this respect a resemblance to the idealist side of Kant he otherwise rejects (264). The question is whether the theory of community Rawls provides is capable of completing the principles of justice as required and also of accounting for the virtue of community generally.

THREE CONCEPTIONS OF COMMUNITY

In assessing Rawls' theory of community it may be helpful to recall that the individualism of his conception describes the subject and not the object of motivations. The interests pursued by the parties to the original position are not interests *in* the self but interests *of* a self, and more specifically the interests of an antecedently individuated self. By identifying the individualism of his theory with the subject rather than the object of desires, Rawls believes he can avoid relying on any particular theory of human motivations and especially the assumption, common to some traditional liberal theories, that man is by nature selfish or egoistic. Deriving a theory of justice without reference to any particular motivations or conceptions of the good is essential to the deontological project and has the further consequence, Rawls believes, of allowing a fuller theory of community than is available on traditional individualistic assumptions. Where the content of motivations is left open, it is possible to suppose that individuals may pursue social or communitarian aims as well as merely private ones, especially in a society governed by a scheme of reciprocity that works to affirm their sense of self-esteem.

There is no reason why a well-ordered society should encourage primarily individualistic values if this means ways of life that lead individuals to pursue their own way and to have no concern for the interests of others (although respecting their rights and liberties). Normally one would expect most people to belong to one or more associations and to have at least some collective ends in this sense (Rawls 1975: 550).

In his discussion of the 'idea of social union' (section 79), Rawls distinguishes two senses of the 'good of community'. The first is based on conventional individualist assumptions which take for granted the self-interested motivations of the agents. This account conceives community in wholly instrumental terms and evokes the image of a 'private society', where individuals regard social arrangements as a necessary burden and cooperate only for the sake of pursuing their private ends. From this instrumental conception Rawls distinguishes his own view of community in which the participants have certain 'shared final ends' and regard the scheme of co-operation as a good in itself. Their interests are not uniformly antagonistic but in some cases complementary and overlapping. Since Rawls does not assume in advance that all are given to selfish motivations alone, he does not foreclose the possibility that some may take account of others' welfare and seek to promote it. 'We need not suppose . . . that persons never make substantial sacrifices for one another, since moved by affection and ties of sentiment they often do. But such actions are not demanded as a matter of justice by the basic structure of society' (178).

Of the two accounts of community Rawls presents, both are individualistic, although the way they are individualistic differs in each case. The instrumental account is individualistic in that the subjects of co-operation are assumed to be governed by self-interested motivations alone, and the good of community consists solely in the advantages individuals derive from co-operating in pursuit of their egoistic ends. Rawls' account is individualistic in the sense of assuming the antecedent individuation of the subjects of co-operation, whose actual motivations may include benevolent aims as well as selfish ones. As a result, the good of community for Rawls consists not only in the direct benefits of social co-operation but also in the quality of motivations and ties of sentiment that may attend this co-operation and be enhanced in the process. Where community on the first account is wholly *external* to the aims and interests of the individuals who comprise it, community on Rawls' view is partly *internal* to the subjects, in that it reaches the feelings and sentiments of those engaged in a co-operative scheme. In contrast to the instrumental conception of a community, we might therefore describe Rawls' account as the sentimental conception.

But neither the instrumental nor the sentimental account seems capable of generating the strong theory of community which Rawls' and Dworkin's arguments seem to require – Rawls' to redeem the notion of common assets involved in the difference principle, Dworkin's to define the relevant community of sharing in his argument for affirmative action. As we have seen, both arguments seem to require for their completion a wider subject of possession capable of laying legitimate claim to the assets necessary to its purposes without using some as means to others' ends and without collapsing into a radically situated subject. But neither the instrumental nor the sentimental account of community, presupposing as they do the antecedent individuation of the subject, can offer a way in which the bounds of the subject might be redrawn; neither seems capable of relaxing the bounds between the self and the other without producing a radically situated subject.

For this, one would have to imagine a conception of community that could penetrate the self more profoundly than even the sentimental view permits. For while Rawls allows that the good of community can be internal to the extent of engaging the aims and values of the self, it cannot be so thoroughgoing as to reach beyond the motivations to the subject of motivations. The good of community cannot reach *that* far, for to do so would be to violate the priority of the self over its ends, to deny its antecedent individuation, to reverse the priority of plurality over unity, and to allow the good a hand in the constitution of the self, which on Rawls' view is reserved to the concept of right. ('The essential unity of the self is already given by the concept of right' (563).)

A theory of community whose province extended to the subject as well as the object of motivations would be individualistic in neither the conventional sense nor in Rawls'. It would resemble Rawls' conception in that the sense of community would be manifest in the aims and values of the participants – as fraternal sentiments and fellow-feeling, for example – but would differ from Rawls' conception in that community would describe not just a *feeling* but a mode of self-understanding partly constitutive of the agent's identity. On this strong view, to say that the members of a society are bound by a sense of community is not simply to say that a great many of them profess communitarian sentiments and pursue communitarian aims, but rather that they conceive their identity – the subject and not just the object of their feelings and aspirations – as defined to some extent by the community of which they are a part. For them, community describes not just what they *have* as fellow citizens but also what they *are*, not a relationship they choose (as in a voluntary association) but an attachment they discover, not merely an attribute but a constituent of their identity. In contrast to the instrumental and sentimental conceptions of community, we might describe this strong view as the constitutive conception.

Despite Rawls' resistance to the constitutive conception of community and the theory of the subject it requires, we have already seen how his language seems at times to carry him beyond the sentimental conception, as if implicitly to acknowledge what we have argued is the case, that his theory of justice depends ultimately for its coherence on precisely the intersubjective dimension he officially rejects. In the account of the difference principle we are told that the distribution of natural talents is best described as a 'common asset', and that in justice as fairness men agree to 'share one another's fate'. In the account of social union, the bounds between empirical, bodily persons seem more attenuated still. Human beings are said to have 'shared final ends', and to participate through community 'in the total sum of the realized natural assets of the others'. We are thus led 'to the notion of the community of humankind', whose boundaries can be imagined to extend even across time and space, 'for those widely separated by history and circumstance can nevertheless co-operate in realizing their common nature' (527). 'Only in social union is the individual complete', for it is here that 'we cease to be mere fragments' (529). The members of community 'participate in one another's nature', and 'the self is realized in the activities of many selves' (565).

It is difficult to know how seriously to take these 'intersubjective-sounding' passages, for much is couched in metaphor, and often the metaphor is mixed. Intersubjective and individualistic images appear in uneasy, sometimes infelicitous combinations, as if to betray the incompatible commitments contending within. Assets described as 'common' in one passage turn 'collective' in another. A conception in which men 'share one another's fate' is later re-described as a principle of 'reciprocity' and 'mutual benefit'. Those who 'participate in one another's nature' at one point are said elsewhere more distantly to engage in 'associative activities'. And those who at one moment can overcome their partiality and realize their nature only in community later find their communitarian imperative reduced to the mere likelihood that they will join one or more associations and 'have at least some collective ends in this sense'. In perhaps the most conspicuously unsettled imagery of all, community is said at one point to consist in the fact that 'different persons with *similar* or *complementary* capacities may *co-operate so to speak* in *realizing* their *common* or *matching* nature' [emphasis added] (523).

But as the distinction between the sentimental and constitutive conceptions of community suggests, the moral vocabulary of community in the strong sense cannot in all cases be captured by a conception that 'in its theoretical basis is individualistic'. Thus a 'community' cannot always be translated without loss to an 'association', nor an 'attachment' to a 'relationship', nor 'sharing' to 'reciprocating', nor 'participation' to 'co-operation', nor what is 'common' to what is 'collective'. Though Rawls' argument for the priority of plurality over unity may normally apply to the second of each of these pairs, it does not necessarily hold for the first. Where 'collective' assets imply endowments once separately held, now ceded to society as a whole, 'common' assets do not necessarily; they need not logically presuppose a prior individuation. And while 'reciprocity' implies a principle of exchange and hence a plurality of agents, the notion of 'sharing' may suggest a solidarity such that no exchange need be involved, as in sharing a joke, or an aspiration, or an understanding. And while 'association' and 'co-operation' typically presuppose the antecedent plurality of those who join together to associate or co-operate, 'community' and 'participation' may describe a form of life in which the members find themselves commonly situated 'to begin with', their commonality consisting less in relationships they have entered than in attachments they have found.

So it would appear that community in the strong, constitutive sense required by both Rawls and Dworkin cannot be accounted for by a conception that is individualistic even in Rawls' special sense of the term. For the individualistic account takes the bounds of the subject as antecedently given and finally fixed, but Rawls and Dworkin require a conception capable of marking out a wider subject of possession, a conception in which the subject is empowered to participate in the constitution of its identity. That such a conception is unavailable on deontological assumptions can be seen as follows.

For a subject to play a role in shaping the contours of its identity requires a certain faculty of reflection. Will alone is not enough. What is required is a certain capacity for self-knowledge, a capacity for what we have called agency in the cognitive sense. This can be seen by recalling the two accounts of agency and possession we considered in our initial reconstruction of Rawls' theory of the subject. The first account, corresponding to Rawls' conception, took the bounds of the self as given and related self to ends by agency in its voluntarist sense, as willing subject to objects of choice. This sort of agency depended on the faculty of will, for it is the will that allows the self to reach beyond itself, to transcend the bounds that are fixed in advance, to grasp the ends it would possess and hold them as it always must, external to itself.

The second account, by contrast, took the bounds of the self as open and conceived the identity of the subject as the product rather than the premise of its agency. The relevant agency here was not voluntarist but cognitive; the self came by its ends not by choice but by reflection, as knowing (or inquiring) subject to object of (self-) understanding. The problem here was not the distance of the self from its ends, but rather the fact that the self, being unbounded in advance, was awash with possible purposes and ends, all impinging indiscriminately on its identity, threatening always to engulf it. The challenge to the agent was to sort out the limits or the boundaries of the self, to distinguish the subject from its situation, and so to forge its identity.

For the subject whose identity is constituted in the light of ends already before it, agency consists less in summoning the will than in seeking self-understanding. Unlike the capacity for choice, which enables the self to reach beyond itself, the capacity for reflection enables the self to turn its lights inward upon itself, to inquire into its constituent nature, to survey its various attachments and acknowledge their respective claims, to sort out the bounds – now expansive, now constrained – between the self and the other, to arrive at a self-understanding less opaque if never perfectly transparent, a subjectivity less fluid if never finally fixed, and so gradually, throughout a lifetime, to participate in the constitution of its identity.

Now the capacity for reflection suggested by the cognitive account would seem precisely the feature Rawls' 'wider subject of possession' requires if it is not to dissolve into a radically situated subject, for this capacity holds out the possibility of arriving at the bounds of the self without taking them to be given in advance. Indeed, once the presumed antecedent individuation of the subject is called into question, the predicament of the self would seem to approach the dispossession described on the *cognitive* account, in which the greater threat to agency is not the distance of the self from its purposes and ends but rather the surfeit of seemingly indispensable aims which only sober self-examination can hope to sort out.

But on Rawls' moral epistemology, the scope for reflection would appear seriously limited. Self-knowledge seems not to be a possibility in the relevant sense, for the bounds it would define are taken as given in advance, unreflectively, once and for all, by a principle of antecedent individuation. But once these bounds are seen to fall away, there is nothing to take their place. For a subject such as Rawls' the paradigmatic moral question is not 'Who am I?', for the answer to this question is regarded as self-evident, but rather 'What ends shall I choose?', and this is a question addressed to the will. Rawls' subject would thus appear epistemologically impoverished where the self is concerned, conceptually ill-equipped to engage in the sort of self-reflection capable of going beyond an attention to its preferences and desires to contemplate, and so to re-describe, the subject that contains them.

It seems clear at least that the question of community leads naturally to the question of reflection, and that in order to assess the role of reflection in Rawls' scheme, we need to examine in greater detail

Rawls' theory of agency, his account of how the self arrives at its ends. We have seen that for Rawls the self comes by its ends by choosing them, or more elaborately, that the self is related to its ends as willing subject to objects of choice, and we have described this ability to choose as agency in the voluntarist sense. But what exactly goes on in this moment of choice, and what role, if any, does reflection play in arriving at it?

AGENCY AND THE ROLE OF REFLECTION

For Rawls, the account of agency and ends falls under the conception of good. Like the right, the good is conceived voluntaristically; it is founded in choice. As the principles of right are the product of a collective choice in the original position, conceptions of the good are the products of individual choices in the real world.

But here there arises an important difference. For while both the right and the good are founded in choice, the special (i.e. hypothetical) conditions under which the right is 'chosen' mean that actual persons do not have a hand in it. What counts as right or just is not something we are free to choose, because the principles of justice are in force from the moment the veil of ignorance disappears, that is, before any *actual* choosing can begin. The principles of justice, being antecedently derived, are not subject to our agency; they apply whether we like them or not.

With the good it is different. Here, each person is free to choose for himself, free to adopt whatever conception of the good he desires. Different things are good for different people, and subject only to the constraints of justice, each is 'free to plan his life as he pleases' (447). While there is assumed to be a single 'correct conception of justice from a philosophical point of view' (446), which everyone must adhere to, there is no comparably correct conception of the good from a philosophical point of view, and so each is free to launch out on his own.

Here then is further illustration of the priority of the right over the good, in both its moral and epistemological dimensions. The moral priority consists in the fact that the principles of justice limit the conceptions of the good individuals may choose to pursue; where a person's values clash with justice, it is justice that prevails. As Rawls repeatedly acknowledges, the principles of justice are not compatible with all conceivable plans of life, and plans that do not conform must be rejected.

In justice as fairness the concept of right is prior to that of the good. In contrast with teleological theories, something is good only if it fits into ways of life consistent with the principles of right already on hand (396).

Indeed, even rational plans of life which determine what things are good for human beings, the values of human life so to speak, are themselves constrained by the principles of justice (398).

Our way of life, whatever our particular circumstances, must always conform to the principles of justice that are arrived at independently (449).

These principles are then given absolute precedence so that they regulate social institutions without question and each frames his plan in conformity with them. Plans that happen to be out of line must be revised (565).

[Men's] desires and aspirations are restricted from the outset by the principles of justice which specify the boundaries that men's systems of ends must respect. . . . The priority of justice is accounted for, in part, by holding that the interests requiring the violation of justice have no value. Having no merit in the first place, they cannot override its claims (31).

The priority of right over good provides a meta-ethical background to the familiar liberal notion that the preferences and convictions of the majority, however intensely held, cannot defeat a legitimate claim of individual rights. On a deontological ethic, the convictions of the majority merely reflect particular conceptions of the good. As such, they cannot claim to be 'correct from a philosophical point of view', only preferred from a majoritarian point of view, and no mere preference can override the requirements of justice.

The intense convictions of the majority, if they are indeed mere preferences without any foundation in the principles of justice antecedently established, have no weight to begin with. The satisfaction of these feelings has no value that can be put in the scales against the claims of equal liberty. . . . Against these principles neither the intensity of feeling nor its being shared by the majority counts for anything (450).

Another way of viewing the contrast between the right and the good is to recall that the good, whether individual or collective, includes as ingredients various contingencies which are arbitrary from a moral point of view, while the right is free of such arbitrariness. The need, stressed by Rawls, to regulate the distribution of opportunities and benefits in a way that is not arbitrary from a moral point of view suggests one reason at least why the right must be prior. Once the precedence of right is secured, however, there is no objection to the pursuit of conceptions of the good tinged with contingency and arbitrariness. The principles of justice effectively domesticate such conceptions and keep them safely within bounds.

There is no objection to fitting rational plans to these contingencies, since the principles of justice have already been chosen and constrain the content of these plans, the ends that they encourage and the means they use (449).

Thus the arbitrary features of plans of life do not affect these principles, or how the basic structure is to be arranged. The indeterminacy in the notion of rationality does not translate itself into legitimate claims that men can impose on one another. . . . Since men's claims on one another are not affected, the indeterminacy is relatively innocuous (449, 564).

The priority of right might finally be viewed in terms of its antecedent derivation, and the need for some ultimately 'unchosen' background as a precondition of choice in conceptions of the good. If the principles of justice were themselves up for grabs, then 'the freedom of choice that justice as fairness assures to individuals and groups within the framework of justice' (447) would no longer be assured. Something must remain beyond choice (and so constrain it) if choice itself is to be secured. This is the epistemological priority that deontological ethics carries over into a moral priority.[2] Thus the morality of right, which assures freedom of choice within its bounds, cannot *itself* be vulnerable to any choice that would challenge or restrict it, for the moral force of such a challenge would in all cases fall short of the moral force of the framework within which it was conceived. For as we saw in our discussion of contract theory, the sanction of this framework, unlike the sanction for the aims and values

2 Compare Kant's argument in the transcendental deduction that concepts of objects in general must underlie all empirical knowledge as its *a priori* conditions. 'The objective validity of the categories as *a priori* rests, therefore, on the fact that, so far as the form of thought is concerned, through them alone does experience become possible' (1781: 126).

arising within it, is not simply a choice or even a contract but a hypothetical agreement conceived under special conditions whose fairness is independently established.

The epistemological aspect of the priority of right recalls the parallel priority of the self over its ends. In both cases, an 'unchosen' framework, antecedently given, is seen as a prerequisite of choice. As the principles of justice must be antecedently given (and hence beyond choice) in order to assure the possibility of choice in conceptions of the good, so the bounds of the self must be antecedently given (and hence beyond choice) in order to assure the agency of the subject, its capacity to choose its ends. While the bounds imposed by justice may seem an undue restriction on choice in that persons cannot participate in their constitution but can only choose within them, in fact these bounds secure the equal liberty of each to choose his ends for himself against the vagaries of a public opinion that might one day prefer otherwise. Similarly, while the bounds of the self may seem an undue restriction on agency in that the self cannot participate in their constitution, they are in fact a prerequisite of agency. For these are the bounds that hold the world off, so to speak, and provide the subject the detachment it needs to choose for itself. They secure for the self the capacity to choose against the vagaries of circumstances that would otherwise engulf it. The notion that the principles of justice, like the bounds of the self, provide a basis for choice that is not itself chosen is not a contradiction but a necessary presupposition of a subject capable of choice. In this it can be compared with parallel notions running throughout the deontological conception, including a subject of possession not itself possessed, a basis of desert not itself deserved, and a foundation of contract not itself contractual.

We have seen that the choice of ends is constrained from the start by the principles of justice antecedently defined. But in order to describe Rawls' account of choice and to assess the role of reflection, if any, we need to know in greater detail how the constraint of justice makes itself felt, how exactly it enters the deliberation of the agent. Are the constraints of right somehow built into the activity of deliberation such that only just desires or conceptions of the good can arise in the first place, or does the agent form values and aims based on certain unjust desires only to suppress them in practice or set them aside once it becomes clear that they violate justice?

At times Rawls writes as though the principles of justice shape a person's conception of the good from the start, even as the conception is formulated. 'In drawing up plans and in deciding on aspirations men are to take these constraints into account . . . [T]heir desires and aspirations are restricted from the outset by the principles of justice which specify the boundaries that men's systems of ends must respect' (31). At other times Rawls seems to favor the second account, as when he writes that in justice as fairness, persons 'implicitly agree. . . . to conform their conceptions of the good to what the principles of justice require, *or at least not to press claims* which directly violate them' [emphasis added] (31).

If it is unclear whether justice intervenes at the point I choose my life plans or only later, at the point I would pursue them, it seems clear at least that neither account introduces an element of self-reflection of the sort we are concerned with; both allow that the right does not wholly determine my good, that my conception of the good, however constrained within a certain range, still remains for me to choose. At this point Rawls introduces another set of considerations to narrow our choice, certain 'counting principles', as he describes them, which amount roughly to the basic tenets of instrumental rationality. These recommend, for example, that I choose more rather than less effective means to given ends, a more inclusive plan over a less inclusive one, the plan offering a greater rather than a lesser probability of success, and so on. Rawls acknowledges, however, that the counting principles, even when supplemented with various other principles of rational choice, 'do not suffice to order plans' (416), and that the constraints of right and of instrumental rationality taken together are not enough to lead us to a single determinate choice. Once these principles run out, we must simply choose. 'We may narrow the scope of purely preferential choice, but we cannot eliminate it altogether. . . . We eventually reach a point where we just have to decide which plan we most prefer without further guidance from principle' (552, 551).

It is at this point, according to Rawls, that our reflection must be engaged in order to determine as best we can what things we want and how much we want them, and to ascertain in the light of all the relevant facts the plan most likely to realize these desires most completely.

I shall suppose that while rational principles can focus our judgments and set up guidelines for reflection, we must finally choose for ourselves in the sense that the choice often rests on our direct self-knowledge not only of what things we want but also of how much we want them. Sometimes there is no way to avoid having to assess the relative intensity of our desires (416). We can say that the rational plan for a person is the one (among those consistent with the counting principles and other principles of rational choice once these are established) which he would choose with deliberative rationality. It is the plan that would be decided upon as the outcome of careful reflection in which the agent reviewed, in the light of all the relevant facts, what it would be like to carry out these plans and thereby ascertained the course of action that would best realize his more fundamental desires (417).

Rawls' account of how we choose would seem to confirm the limited scope for reflection on his conception. While the plan of life or conception of the good most appropriate to a particular person is said to be 'the outcome of careful reflection', it is clear that the objects of this reflection are restricted to (1) the various alternative plans and their likely consequences for the realization of the agent's desires, and (2) the agent's wants and desires themselves, and their relative intensities. In neither case does reflection take as its object the self *qua* subject of desires. The reflection involved in (1), sizing up the alternatives and estimating their likely consequences, is scarcely a form of *self*-reflection at all; it looks outward rather than inward, and amounts to a kind of prudential reasoning that could in principle be carried out with equal or greater success by an outside expert who knew relatively little about the agent but a good deal about the alternatives involved and the sorts of interests and desires they typically satisfy.

The reflection involved in (2), assessing the relative intensity of desires, looks inward in a sense but not *all the way* in. It takes as its objects the contingent wants and desires and preferences of the self, but not the self *itself*. It does not extend its lights to the self standing behind the wants and desires it surveys; it cannot reach the self *qua* subject of desires. Since for Rawls the faculty of self-reflection is limited to weighing the relative intensity of existing wants and desires, the deliberation it entails cannot inquire into the identity of the agent, ('Who *am* I, really?') only into the feelings and sentiments of the agent ('What do I really *feel* like or most *prefer?*'). Because this sort of deliberation is restricted to assessing the desires of a subject whose identity is given (unreflectively) in advance, it cannot lead to self-

understanding in the strong sense which enables the agent to participate in the constitution of its identity.

Although Rawls does speak briefly of 'our direct self-knowledge' of
what things we want and how much we want them, 'self-knowledge' in
this sense seems little more than an awareness of our immediate
wants and desires. And in so far as this self-knowledge is 'direct' in the
strict sense that it is given transparently to our awareness, it is difficult
to imagine how anything resembling reflection or deliberation in the
ordinary sense could ever take place, since we would likely know all
we would need to know 'in an instant', before anything recognizably
deliberative could begin. But even if 'our direct self-knowledge' permits some uncertainty for reflection to sort out, the self that is known
once the uncertainty is resolved is not really the self in the strict sense
distinguished throughout but merely the contingent accidents and
attributes of the self.

The difference between the sort of reflection that attends to the
desires of the agent alone and the sort that extends to the subject of
desires and explores its identity corresponds in part to a distinction
made by Charles Taylor in his account of human agency between the
'simple weigher' and the 'strong evaluator'. Central to both distinctions are the images of superficiality and depth. For Taylor, the 'simple weigher' is reflective in the minimal sense that he is capable of
evaluating courses of action and acting out of his evaluations. But the
reflection of the simple weigher lacks depth in that his evaluations
are limited to the inarticulate 'feel' of the alternatives.

Whereas for the simple weigher what is at stake is the desirability of different consummations, those defined by his *de facto* desires, for the
strong evaluator reflection also examines the different possible modes of
being of the agent. Whereas a reflection about what we feel like more,
which is all a simple weigher can do in assessing motivations, keeps us as
it were at the periphery; a reflection on the kind of beings we are takes
us to the center of our existence as agents. . . . It is in this sense deeper
(1977: 114–15).

For Rawls, reflection 'on the kind of beings we *are*' rather than on
the kind of desires we *have* is not a possibility, first because the kind
of beings we are is antecedently given and not subject to revision in
the light of reflection or any other form of agency, and second,
because Rawls' self is conceived as barren of constituent traits, pos-

sessed only of contingent attributes held always at a certain distance, and so there is nothing *in* the self for reflection to survey or apprehend. For Rawls, the identity of the subject can never be at stake in moments of choice or deliberation (although its future aims and attributes may of course be affected), for the bounds that define it are beyond the reach of the agency – whether voluntarist or cognitive – that would contribute to its transformation.

The distinction between a notion of reflection such as Rawls', which is limited to the objects of desire, and one such as Taylor's, which penetrates further to reach the subject of desire, corresponds to the distinction between the sentimental and the constitutive conceptions of community we identified earlier. For on the sentimental conception, the good of community was limited to the communitarian aims and sentiments of antecedently individuated subjects, while on the constitutive conception, the good of community was seen to penetrate the person more profoundly so as to describe not just his *feeling* but a mode of self-understanding partly constitutive of his identity, partly definitive of who he was.

We have seen that Rawls' theory of justice requires for its coherence a conception of community in the constitutive sense, which requires in turn a notion of agency in the cognitive sense, and we have found that Rawls' theory of the good can allow for neither. This calls into question the theory of justice, or the theory of the good, or both. But beyond the difficulties they raise for Rawls' conception as a whole, Rawls' limited accounts of agency and reflection are implausible in themselves, incapable of making sense of what choice and deliberation could possibly consist in. Or so at least I shall try to show, by considering the picture of choice that remains once reflection in the strong, thoroughgoing sense has been ruled out.

AGENCY AND THE ROLE OF CHOICE

As we have seen, Rawls' theory of the good is voluntaristic; our fundamental aims, values, and conceptions of the good are for us to choose, and in choosing them, we exercise our agency. As Rawls describes it, once the principles of rational (i.e. instrumental) choice run out, '*We must finally choose for ourselves* in the sense that the choice often rests on our direct self-knowledge not only of what things we want but also of how much we want them. . . . *It is clearly left to the* agent himself to decide what it is that he most wants' [emphasis added] (416). Since the principles of rational choice do not specify a single best plan of life, 'a great deal remains to be *decided*. . . . We eventually reach a point where *we just have to decide* which plan we most prefer without further guidance from principle. . . . [W]e may narrow the scope of *purely preferential choice*, but we cannot eliminate it altogether. . . . *The person himself must make this decision,* taking into account the full range of his inclinations and desires, present and future' [emphasis added] (449, 551, 552, 557).

If it is clear that Rawls would describe my values and conceptions of the good as the products of choice or decision, it remains to be seen what exactly this choice consists in and how I come to make it. According to Rawls, we 'choose for ourselves *in the sense that* the choice *often rests on* our direct self-knowledge' of what we want and how much we want it. But a choice that is a choice 'in the sense that' it 'often rests on' (is determined by?) my existing wants and desires is a choice only in a peculiar sense of the word. For assuming with Rawls that the wants and desires on which my choice 'rests' are not themselves chosen but are the products of circumstance ('We do not choose now what to desire now' (415)), such a 'choice' would involve less a voluntary act than a factual accounting of what these wants and desires really are. And once I succeed in ascertaining, by 'direct self-knowledge', this piece of psychological information, there would seem nothing left for me to *choose*. I would have still to match my wants and desires, thus ascertained, to the best available means of satisfying them, but this is a prudential question which involves no volition or exercise of will.

When Rawls writes that it is 'left to the agent himself to *decide* what it is he most wants' (416), and that 'we just have to *decide* which plans we most prefer' (551), the 'dicision' the agent must make amounts to nothing more than an estimate or psychic inventory of the wants and preferences he already has, not a choice of the values he would profess or the aims he would pursue. As with the collective 'choice' or 'agreement' in the original position, such a 'decision' decides nothing except how accurately the agent has perceived something already *there*, in this case the shape and intensity of his pre-existing desires. But if this is so, then the voluntarist aspect of agency would seem to fade altogether.

To arrive at a plan of life or a conception of the good simply by heeding my existing wants and desires is to choose neither the plan nor the desires; it is simply to match the ends I already have with the best available means of satisfying them. Under such a description, my aims, values, and conceptions of the good are not the products of choice but the objects of a certain superficial introspection, just 'inward' enough to survey uncritically the motives and desires with which the accidents of my circumstance have left me; I simply know them as I feel them and seek my way as best I can to their consummation.

It might be suggested that Rawls could escape the apparent collapse of this account of agency and choice in one of two ways. The first would be to introduce the idea that persons are capable of reflecting on their desires not only in the sense of assessing their intensity but also in the sense of assessing their desirability; capable, that is, of forming second-order desires, desires whose objects are certain first-order desires (Frankfurt 1971). I may thus want to have certain desires and not others, or regard certain sorts of desires as desirable and others less so. The fact that something was desired (and not unjust) would no longer be enough to make it good, for this would depend on the further question whether it was a desirable sort of desire or not. Once I ascertained what I (really) wanted as a matter of first-order desire, it would remain for me to assess the desirability of my desire and in this sense to affirm or reject it.

Indeed, Rawls seems vaguely to admit such a possibility when he writes that although 'we do not choose now what to desire now', we can at least 'choose now which desires we shall have at a later time. . . . We can certainly decide now to do something that we know will affect the desires we shall have in the future. . . . Thus we choose between future desires in the light of our existing desires' (415).

But even if a Rawlsian agent were capable of forming desires for certain other desires, his agency would not in any meaningful sense be restored. For he would have no grounds, apart from the mere fact of his second-order desire, on which to justify or defend the desirability of one sort of desire over another. He would still have only the psychological fact of his (now, second-order) preference to appeal to and only its relative intensity to assess. Neither the intrinsic worth of a desire nor its essential connection with the identity of the agent could provide a basis for affirming it, since on Rawls' account, the worth of a desire only appears in the light of a person's good, and the identity of the agent is barren of constituent traits so that no aim or desire can be essential to it. The affirmation or rejection of desires suggested by the formation of second-order desires would on Rawls' assumptions introduce no further element of reflection or volition, for such an assessment could only reflect a slightly more complicated estimate of the relative intensity of pre-existing desires, first- and second-order desires included. The resulting conception of the good could no more be said to be chosen than one arising from first-order desires alone.

A second possible attempt to restore the coherence of choice on Rawls' conception might be to imagine a case in which the various desires of the agent, properly weighed for their respective intensities, led to a tie, and where deliberation had already taken account of all relevant preferences such that no further preferences could be introduced to break the tie. In such a case, this account might continue, the agent would have no alternative but to plump, just arbitrarily, one way or the other, without relying on any preference or desire at all. It might be suggested that a 'choice' thus independent from the influence of pre-existing wants and desires – a 'radically free choice', as it is sometimes described – would allow for the voluntarist aspect of agency seemingly unavailable when the agent is bound to 'choose' in conformity with his pre-existing wants and desires.

But Rawls rejects a wholly arbitrary form of agency that would escape the influence of pre-existing wants and desires altogether. 'The notion of radical choice . . . finds no place in justice as fairness' (Rawls 1980: 568). Unlike the principles of right, which express the autonomy of the agent and must be free from contingencies, conceptions of the good are understood to be heteronomous throughout. Where incompatible aims arise, Rawls speaks not of radically free or arbitrary choice, but instead of 'purely preferential choice', suggesting the form of (non-)agency we first considered. In any case, the notion of a purely arbitrary 'choice' governed by no considerations at all is hardly more plausible an account of voluntarist agency than a 'choice' governed wholly by predetermined preferences and desires. Neither 'purely preferential choice' nor 'purely arbitrary choice' can redeem Rawls' notion of agency in the voluntarist sense; the first confuses choice with necessity, the second with caprice. Together they reflect the limited scope for reflection on Rawls' account, and the implausible account of human agency that results.

THE STATUS OF THE GOOD

The difficulty with Rawls' theory of the good is epistemological as well as moral, and in this it recalls a problem that arose in connection with the concept of right – that of distinguishing a standard of assessment from the thing being assessed. If my fundamental values and final ends are to enable me, as surely they must, to evaluate and regulate my immediate wants and desires, these values and ends must have a sanction independent of the mere fact that I happen to hold them with a certain intensity. But if my conception of the good is simply the product of my immediate wants and desires, there is no reason to suppose that the critical standpoint it provides is any more worthy or valid than the desires it seeks to assess; as the product of those desires, it would be governed by the same contingencies.

Rawls responds to this difficulty in the case of the right by seeking in justice as fairness an Archimedean point that 'is not at the mercy, so to speak, of existing wants and interests' (261). But as we have seen, Rawls' concept of right does not extend to private morality, nor does any other instrument of detachment save the good from thoroughgoing implication in the agent's existing wants and desires. 'Purely preferential choice' is thoroughly heteronomous choice, and no person's values or conception of the good can possibly reach beyond it. As Rawls strikingly concedes, 'That we have one conception of the good rather than another is not relevant from a moral standpoint. In acquiring it we are influenced by the same sort of contingencies that lead us to rule out a knowledge of our sex and class' (1975: 537).

The limited scope for reflection on Rawls' account, and the problematic, even impoverished theory of the good that results reveal the extent to which deontological liberalism accepts an essentially utilitarian account of the good, however its theory of right may differ. This utilitarian background first appeared in our discussion of Dworkin's defense of affirmative action; once no individual rights were seen to be at stake, utilitarian considerations automatically prevailed. Although Dworkin defends what he calls an 'anti-utilitarian concept of right', the scope of this right is strictly (if elusively) circumscribed, such that 'the vast bulk of the laws that diminish my liberty are justified on utilitarian grounds as being in the general interest or for the general welfare' (1977a: 269).[3]

3 For a compelling critique of Dworkin's view in this respect, see H. L. A. Hart (1979: 86–9).

The utilitarian background to Rawls' conception most clearly appears in his references to individual moral life. Where justice as fairness rejects utilitarianism as the basis of social, or public, morality, it has no apparent argument with utilitarianism as the basis of individual, or private, morality – the Kantian notion of 'duty to oneself' to the contrary. Rawls describes the utilitarian account of private morality, without discernible objection, as follows:

> A person quite properly acts, at least when others are not affected, to achieve his own greatest good, to advance his rational ends as far as possible. . . . [T]he principle for an individual is to advance as far as possible his own welfare, his own system of desires (23).

> To be sure, there is one formal principle that seems to provide a general answer [to an individual's choice of life plan]. This is the principle to adopt that plan which maximizes the expected net balance of satisfaction (416).

For Rawls, utilitarianism goes wrong not in conceiving the good as the satisfaction of arbitrarily given desires undifferentiated as to worth – for justice as fairness shares in this – but only in being indifferent to the way these consummations are spread across individuals. Its mistake as he sees it is to adopt 'for society as a whole the principle of rational choice for one man', to combine 'the desires of all persons into one coherent system of desire', and to seek its overall satisfaction (26–7). In so doing, it 'fuses' or 'conflates' all persons into one, it reduces social choice to 'essentially a question of efficient administration' (as, presumably, individual choice can properly be reduced), and so fails to take seriously the distinction between persons (27, 33).

Justice as fairness seeks to remedy these shortcomings by emphasizing the distinction between persons and by insisting on the separateness of those diverse 'systems of desires' that utilitarianism conflates. But the grounds for Rawls' departure from utilitarianism in this respect are not immediately apparent. Although he seems firm in his view that to each individual human being there corresponds exactly one 'system of desires', he never says why this must be so, or what exactly a 'system of desires' consists in, or why it is wrong to conflate them. Is a 'system of desires' a set of desires *ordered* in a certain way, arranged in a hierarchy of relative worth or essential connection with the identity of the agent, or is it simply a concatenation of desires arbitrarily arrayed, distinguishable only by their relative intensity and accidental location? If it is the second, if a *system* of desires means nothing more than an arbitrary collection of desires accidentally embodied in some particular human being, then it is unclear why the integrity of such a 'system' should be taken so morally and metaphysically seriously. If desires can properly be conflated within persons, why not between persons as well?

If, on the other hand, what makes a *system* of desires is a hierarchical ordering of qualitatively distinguishable desires, then it would be no more justifiable to 'conflate' desires within a person than between persons, and what is wrong with utilitarianism would also be wrong, in this respect at least, with justice as fairness. The tendency to conflate desires, whether within persons or between them, would reflect the failure to *order* them, or to acknowledge the qualitative distinctions between them. But this failure cuts across the distinction between individual and social choice, for there is no reason to suppose that a 'system of desires' in *this* sense corresponds in all cases to the empirically-individuated person. Communities of various sorts could count as distinct 'systems of desires' in this sense, so long as they were identifiable in part by an order or structure of shared values partly constitutive of a common identity or form of life. From this point of view, the utilitarian failure to take seriously the distinction between persons would appear a mere symptom of its larger failure to take seriously the qualitative distinctions of worth between different orders of desires, a failure rooted in an impoverished account of the good which justice as fairness has been seen to share.

For a deontological doctrine such as Rawls' it might be thought that viewing the good as wholly mired in contingency, despite its implausibility generally, would have at least the redeeming advantage of making the primacy of right all the more compelling. If the good is nothing more than the indiscriminate satisfaction of arbitrarily given preferences, regardless of worth, it is not difficult to imagine that the right (and for that matter a good many other sorts of claims) must outweigh it. But in fact the morally diminished status of the good must inevitably call into question the status of justice as well. For once it is conceded that our conceptions of the good are morally arbitrary, it becomes difficult to see why the highest of all (social) virtues should be the one that enables us to pursue these arbitrary conceptions 'as fully as circumstances permit'.

THE MORAL EPISTEMOLOGY OF JUSTICE

Our discussion of the good thus brings us back to the question of justice and the claim for its priority, and with this we return to the circumstances of justice in the original position. Here, the distinctness or separateness of persons on which Rawls insists as a corrective to utilitarianism is installed as the key assumption of mutual disinterest, the notion that individuals take no interest in one another's interests (218). When first we surveyed the conditions in the original position, this assumption in particular and the empiricist rendering of the circumstances of justice in general seemed to undermine the primacy of justice in various ways: Where justice depended for its virtue on the existence of certain empirical pre-conditions, the virtue of justice was no longer absolute, as truth to theories, but only conditional, as physical courage to a war zone; it presupposed a rival virtue or set of virtues of at least correlative status; it assumed in certain circumstances a remedial dimension; finally, where inappropriately displayed, justice appeared as a vice rather than a virtue. In sum, a Humean account of the circumstances of justice – such as Rawls explicitly adopts – seemed incompatible with the privileged status of justice required by Rawls and defended by Kant only by recourse to a moral metaphysic Rawls found unacceptable.

Hume's own view of justice confirms its partiality, at least in so far as it is derived from premises which Hume and Rawls seem to share. For Hume, the circumstances of justice describe certain unfortunate if unavoidable material and motivational conditions of actual human societies, most notably moderate scarcity and 'limited generosity'. Together, these circumstances demonstrate the sense in which the arrival of justice signifies the absence of certain nobler but rarer virtues.

'If every man had a tender regard for another, or if nature supplied abundantly all our wants and desires . . . the jealousy of interest, which justice supposes, could no longer have place'; nor, says Hume, would there be any occasion for distinctions of property and possession. 'Encrease to a sufficient degree the benevolence of men, or the bounty of nature, and you render justice useless, by supplying its place with much nobler virtues, and more valuable blessings'. If material scarcity were replaced with abundance, 'or if everyone had the same affection and tender regard for everyone as for himself; justice and injustice would be equally unknown among mankind'. And so, Hume concludes, "tis only from the scanty provision nature has made for his wants, that justice derives its origin' (1739: 494–5).

For Hume, justice cannot be the first virtue of social institutions (at least not in any categorical sense), and in some cases is doubtfully a virtue at all. In the institution of the family, for example, affections may be enlarged to such an extent that justice is scarcely engaged, much less as 'the first virtue'. And even in the wider society, where generosity is more limited and justice more extensively engaged, its virtue can only be accounted for against a background of higher or nobler virtues whose absence calls justice into being. In so far as mutual benevolence and enlarged affections could be cultivated more widely, the need for 'the cautious, jealous virtue of justice' would diminish in proportion, and mankind would be the better for it. Were scarcity or selfishness overcome altogether, then 'justice, being totally useless . . . could never possibly have place in the catalogue of virtue' (1777: 16), much less the first place to which Rawls would assign it.

But despite the parallel Rawls himself invites between Hume's account and his own, the assumption of mutual disinterest has a different meaning for Rawls. It does not imply that human beings are typically governed by 'selfishness and confined generosity'; indeed it is not meant as a claim about human motivations at all. It is rather a claim about the subject of motivations. It assumes interests *of* a self, not necessarily *in* a self, a subject of possession individuated in advance and given prior to its ends.

From this there follow important consequences for the status of justice. No longer is benevolence prior to justice and in some cases able to supplant it. Since, for Rawls, the virtue of justice does not presuppose egoistic motivations to begin with, it need not await the fading of benevolence to find its occasion, and even the full flowering of 'enlarged affections' cannot displace it. Justice ceases to be merely remedial with respect to the 'nobler virtues', for its virtue no longer depends on their absence. To the contrary, where persons are individuated in Rawls' sense, justice not only wins its independence from prevailing sentiments and motivations, but comes to stand above them as primary. For given the nature of the subject as Rawls conceives it, justice is not merely a sentiment or a feeling like other, lesser virtues, but above all a framework that constrains these virtues and is 'regulative' with respect to them.

Therefore in order to realize our nature we have no alternative but to plan to preserve our sense of justice as governing our other aims. This sentiment cannot be fulfilled if it is compromised and balanced against other ends as but one desire among the rest. . . . To the contrary, how far we succeed in expressing our nature depends on how consistently we act from our sense of justice as finally regulative. What we cannot do is express our nature by following a plan that views the sense of justice as but one desire to be weighed against others. For this sentiment reveals what the person is, and to compromise it is not to achieve for the self free rein but to give way to the contingencies and accidents of the world (574–5).

We have seen how the priority of justice, like the priority of the self, derives in large part from its freedom from the contingencies and accidents of the world. This much emerged in our discussion of right and the bounds of the self. In the light of our discussion of the good, we can now also see why on Rawls' theory of the subject, such virtues as benevolence and even love are not self-sufficient moral ideals but must await justice for their completion.

Given the limited role for reflection on Rawls' account, the virtues of benevolence and love, as features of the good, are forms of sentiment rather than insight, ways of feeling rather than knowing. Unlike personal or first-order sentiments and feelings, whose objects are given more or less directly to my awareness, benevolence and love are desires whose object is the good of another. But given the separateness of persons and the intractability of the bounds between them, the content of *this* good (that is, the good I wish another) must be largely opaque to me. On Rawls' view, love is blind, not for its intensity but rather for the opacity of the good that is the object of its concern. 'The reason why the situation remains obscure is that love and benevolence are second-order notions: they seek to further the good of beloved individuals that is already given' (191).

If arriving at one's own good is primarily a matter of surveying existing preferences and assessing their relative intensities, it is not the sort of inquiry in which another, even an intimate other, can readily participate. Only the person himself can 'know' what he really wants or 'decide' what he most prefers. 'Even when we take up another's point of view and attempt to estimate what would be to his advantage, we do so as an adviser, so to speak' (448), and given the limited cognitive access Rawls' conception allows, a rather unprivileged adviser at that.

Although we may at times overcome the difficulty of knowing the good of a beloved individual whose interests we would advance, the problem becomes hopelessly compounded when we would extend our love or benevolence to a plurality of persons whose interests may conflict. For we could not hope to know their respective goods well enough to sort them out and assess their relative claims. Even if benevolence could be as widely cultivated as Hume in his hypothetical vision suggests, its virtue would still not be self-sufficient, for it would remain unclear, without more, what the love of mankind would enjoin. 'It is quite pointless to say that one is to judge the situation as benevolence dictates. This assumes that we are wrongly swayed by self-concern. Our problem lies elsewhere. Benevolence is at sea as long as its many loves are in opposition in the persons of its many objects' (190). Not surprisingly, the anchor this benevolence requires is supplied by the virtue of justice; benevolence, even at its most expansive, depends on justice for its completion. 'A love of mankind that wishes to preserve the distinction of persons, to recognize the separateness of life and experience, will use the two principles of justice to determine its aims when the many goods it cherishes are in opposition' (191). Even in the face of so noble a virtue as the love of mankind, the primacy of justice prevails, although the love that remains is of an oddly judicial spirit.

This love is guided by what individuals themselves would consent to in a fair initial situation which gives them equal representation as moral persons (191).

Thus we see that the assumption of the mutual disinterestedness of the parties does not prevent a reasonable interpretation of benevolence and of the love of mankind *within the framework of justice as fairness* [emphasis added] (192).

For Rawls, the consequences of taking seriously the distinction between persons are not directly moral but more decisively epistemological. What the bounds between persons confine is less the reach of our sentiments – this they do not prejudge – than the reach of our understanding, of our cognitive access to others. And it is this *epistemic* deficit (which derives from the nature of the subject) more than any shortage of benevolence (which is in any case variable and contingent) that requires justice for its remedy and so accounts for its pre-eminence. Where for Hume we need justice because we do not *love* each other well enough, for Rawls we need justice because we cannot *know* each other well enough for even love to serve alone.

But as our discussion of agency and reflection suggests, we are neither as transparent to ourselves nor as opaque to others as Rawls' moral epistemology requires. If our agency is to consist in something more than the exercise in 'efficient administration' which Rawls' account implies, we must be capable of a deeper introspection than a 'direct self-knowledge' of our immediate wants and desires allows. But to be capable of a more thoroughgoing reflection, we cannot be wholly unencumbered subjects of possession, individuated in advance and given prior to our ends, but must be subjects constituted in part by our central aspirations and attachments, always open, indeed vulnerable, to growth and transformation in the light of revised self-understandings. And in so far as our constitutive self-understandings comprehend a wider subject than the individual alone, whether a family or tribe or city or class or nation or people, to this extent they define a community in the constitutive sense. And what marks such a community is not merely a spirit of benevolence, or the prevalence of communitarian values, or even certain 'shared final ends' alone, but a common vocabulary of discourse and a background of implicit practices and understandings within which the opacity of the participants is reduced if never finally dissolved. In so far as justice depends for its pre-eminence on the separateness or boundedness of persons in the cognitive sense, its priority would diminish as that opacity faded and this community deepened.

JUSTICE AND COMMUNITY

Of any society it can always be asked to what extent it is just, or 'well-ordered' in Rawls' sense, and to what extent it is a community, and the answer can in neither case fully be given by reference to the sentiments and desires of the participants alone. As Rawls observes, to ask whether a particular society is just is not simply to ask whether a large number of its members happen to have among their various desires the desire to act justly – although this may be one feature of a just society – but whether the society is itself a society of a certain kind, ordered in a certain way, such that justice describes its 'basic structure' and not merely the dispositions of persons within the structure. Thus Rawls writes that although we call the attitudes and dispositions of persons just and unjust, for justice as fairness the 'primary subject of justice is the basic structure of society' (7). For a society to be just in this strong sense, justice must be constitutive of its framework and not simply an attribute of certain of the participants' plans of life.

Similarly, to ask whether a particular society is a community is not simply to ask whether a large number of its members happen to have among their various desires the desire to associate with others or to promote communitarian aims – although this may be one feature of a community – but whether the society is itself a society of a certain kind, ordered in a certain way, such that community describes its basic structure and not merely the dispositions of persons within the structure. For a society to be a community in this strong sense, community must be constitutive of the shared self-understandings of the participants and embodied in their institutional arrangements, not simply an attribute of certain of the participants' plans of life.

Rawls might object that a constitutive conception of community such as this should be rejected 'for reasons of clarity among others', or on the grounds that it supposes society to be 'an organic whole with a life of its own distinct from and superior to that of all its members in their relations with one another' (264). But a constitutive conception of community is no more metaphysically problematic than a constitutive conception of justice such as Rawls defends. For if this notion of community describes a framework of self-understandings that is distinguishable from and in some sense prior to the sentiments and dispositions of individuals within the framework, it is only in the same sense that justice as fairness describes a 'basic structure' or framework that is likewise distinguishable from and prior to the sentiments and dispositions of individuals within it.

If utilitarianism fails to take seriously our distinctness, justice as fairness fails to take seriously our commonality. In regarding the bounds of the self as prior, fixed once and for all, it relegates our commonality to an aspect of the good, and relegates the good to a mere contingency, a product of indiscriminate wants and desires 'not relevant from a moral standpoint'. Given a conception of the good that is diminished in this way, the priority of right would seem an unexceptionable claim indeed. But utilitarianism gave the good a bad name, and in adopting it uncritically, justice as fairness wins for deontology a false victory.

Conclusion
Liberalism and the Limits of Justice

For justice to be the first virtue, certain things must be true of us. We must be creatures of a certain kind, related to human circumstance in a certain way. We must stand at a certain distance from our circumstance, whether as transcendental subject in the case of Kant, or as essentially unencumbered subject of possession in the case of Rawls. Either way, we must regard ourselves as independent: independent from the interests and attachments we may have at any moment, never identified by our aims but always capable of standing back to survey and assess and possibly to revise them (Rawls 1979: 7; 1980: 544–5).

DEONTOLOGY'S LIBERATING PROJECT

Bound up with the notion of an independent self is a vision of the moral universe this self must inhabit. Unlike classical Greek and medieval Christian conceptions, the universe of the deontological ethic is a place devoid of inherent meaning, a world 'disenchanted' in Max Weber's phrase, a world without an objective moral order. Only in a universe empty of *telos,* such as seventeenth-century science and philosophy affirmed,[1] is it possible to conceive a subject apart from and prior to its purposes and ends. Only a world ungoverned by a purposive order leaves principles of justice open to human construction and conceptions of the good to individual choice. In this the depth of opposition between deontological liberalism and teleological world views most fully appears.

Where neither nature nor cosmos supplies a meaningful order to be grasped or apprehended, it falls to human subjects to constitute meaning on their own. This would explain the prominence of contract theory from Hobbes onward, and the corresponding emphasis

---

1 For discussion of the moral, political, and epistemological consequences of the seventeenth-century scientific revolution and world view, see Strauss 1953; Arendt 1958: 248–325; Wolin 1960: 239–85; and Taylor 1975: 3–50.

on voluntarist as against cognitive ethics culminating in Kant. What can no longer be found remains somehow to be created.[2] Rawls describes his own view in this connection as a version of Kantian 'constructivism'.

The parties to the original position do not agree on what the moral facts are, as if there were already such facts. It is not that, being situated impartially, they have a clear and undistorted view of a prior and independent moral order. Rather (for constructivism), *there is no such order,* and therefore no such facts apart from the procedure as a whole [emphasis added] (1980: 568).

Similarly for Kant, the moral law is not a discovery of theoretical reason but a deliverance of practical reason, the product of pure will. 'The elementary practical concepts have as their foundation the form of a pure will given in reason', and what makes this will authoritative is that it legislates in a world where meaning has yet to arrive. Practical reason finds its advantage over theoretical reason precisely in this voluntarist faculty, in its capacity to generate practical precepts directly, without recourse to cognition. 'Since in all precepts of the pure will it is only a question of the determination of will,' there is no need for these precepts 'to wait upon intuitions in order to acquire a meaning. This occurs for the noteworthy reason that *they themselves produce the reality of that to which they refer*' [emphasis added] (1788: 67–8).

It is important to recall that, on the deontological view, the notion of a self barren of essential aims and attachments does not imply that we are beings wholly without purpose or incapable of moral ties, but rather that the values and relations we have are the products of choice, the possessions of a self given prior to its ends. It is similar with deontology's universe. Though it rejects the possibility of an objective moral order, this liberalism does not hold that just anything goes. It affirms justice, not nihilism. The notion of a universe empty of intrinsic meaning does not, on the deontological view, imply a world wholly ungoverned by regulative principles, but rather a moral

---

2 As one liberal writer boldly asserts, 'The hard truth is this: There is no moral meaning hidden in the bowels of the universe. . . . Yet there is no need to be overwhelmed by the void. We may create our own meanings, you and I' (Ackerman 1980: 368). Oddly enough, he insists nonetheless that liberalism is committed to no particular metaphysic or epistemology, nor any 'Big Questions of a highly controversial character' (356–7, 361).

universe inhabited by subjects capable of constituting meaning on their own – as agents of *construction* in case of the right, as agents of *choice* in the case of the good. *Qua* noumenal selves, or parties to the original position, we arrive at principles of justice; *qua* actual, individual selves, we arrive at conceptions of the good. And the principles we construct as noumenal selves constrain (but do not determine) the purposes we choose as individual selves. This reflects the priority of the right over the good. The deontological universe and the independent self that moves within it, taken together, hold out a liberating vision. Freed from the dictates of nature and the sanction of social roles, the deontological subject is installed as sovereign, cast as the author of the only moral meanings there are. As inhabitants of a world without *telos,* we are free to construct principles of justice unconstrained by an order of value antecedently given. Although the principles of justice are not strictly speaking a matter of choice, the society they define 'comes as close as a society can to being a voluntary scheme' (13), for they arise from a pure will or act of construction not answerable to a prior moral order. And as independent selves, we are free to choose our purposes and ends unconstrained by such an order, or by custom or tradition or inherited status. So long as they are not unjust, our conceptions of the good carry weight, whatever they are, simply in virtue of our having chosen them. We are 'self-originating sources of valid claims' (Rawls 1980: 543).

Now justice is the virtue that embodies deontology's liberating vision and allows it to unfold. It embodies this vision by describing those principles the sovereign subject is said to construct while situated prior to the constitution of all value. It allows the vision to unfold in that, equipped with these principles, the just society regulates each person's choice of ends in a way compatible with a similar liberty for all. Citizens governed by justice are thus enabled to realize deontology's liberating project – to exercise their capacity as 'self-originating sources of valid claims' – as fully as circumstances permit. So the primacy of justice at once expresses and advances the liberating aspirations of the deontological world view and conception of the self.

But the deontological vision is flawed, both within its own terms and more generally as an account of our moral experience. Within its own terms, the deontological self, stripped of all possible constitutive attachments, is less liberated than disempowered. As we have seen, neither the right nor the good admits of the voluntarist derivation deontology requires. As agents of construction we do not really construct (chapter 3), and as agents of choice we do not really choose (chapter 4). What goes on behind the veil of ignorance is not a contract or an agreement but if anything a kind of discovery; and what goes on in 'purely preferential choice' is less a choosing of ends than a matching of pre-existing desires, undifferentiated as to worth, with the best available means of satisfying them. For the parties to the original position, as for the parties to ordinary deliberative rationality, the liberating moment fades before it arrives; the sovereign subject is left at sea in the circumstances it was thought to command.

The moral frailty of the deontological self also appears at the level of first-order principles. Here we found that the independent self, being essentially dispossessed, was too thin to be capable of desert in the ordinary sense (chapter 2). For claims of desert presuppose thickly constituted selves, beings capable of possession in the constitutive sense, but the deontological self is wholly without possessions of this kind. Acknowledging this lack, Rawls would found entitlements on legitimate expectations instead. If we are incapable of desert, at least we are entitled that institutions honor the expectations to which they give rise.

But the difference principle requires more. It begins with the thought, congenial to the deontological view, that the assets I have are only accidentally mine. But it ends by assuming that these assets are therefore common assets and that society has a prior claim on the fruits of their exercise. This either disempowers the deontological self or denies its independence. Either my prospects are left at the mercy of institutions established for 'prior and independent social ends' (313), ends which may or may not coincide with my own, or I must count myself a member of a community defined in part by those ends, in which case I cease to be unencumbered by constitutive attachments. Either way, the difference principle contradicts the liberating aspiration of the deontological project. We cannot be persons for whom justice is primary and also be persons for whom the difference principle is a principle of justice.

CHARACTER, SELF-KNOWLEDGE, AND FRIENDSHIP

If the deontological ethic fails to redeem its own liberating promise, it also fails plausibly to account for certain indispensable aspects of our moral experience. For deontology insists that we view ourselves as independent selves, independent in the sense that our identity is never tied to our aims and attachments. Given our 'moral power to form, to revise, and rationally to pursue a conception of the good' (Rawls 1980: 544), the continuity of our identity is unproblematically assured. No transformation of my aims and attachments could call into question the person I am, for no such allegiances, however deeply held, could possibly engage my identity to begin with.

But we cannot regard ourselves as independent in this way without great cost to those loyalties and convictions whose moral force consists partly in the fact that living by them is inseparable from understanding ourselves as the particular persons we are – as members of this family or community or nation or people, as bearers of this history, as sons and daughters of that revolution, as citizens of this republic. Allegiances such as these are more than values I happen to have or aims I 'espouse at any given time'. They go beyond the obligations I voluntarily incur and the 'natural duties' I owe to human beings as such. They allow that to some I owe more than justice requires or even permits, not by reason of agreements I have made but instead in virtue of those more or less enduring attachments and commitments which taken together partly define the person I am.

To imagine a person incapable of constitutive attachments such as these is not to conceive an ideally free and rational agent, but to imagine a person wholly without character, without moral depth. For to have character is to know that I move in a history I neither summon nor command, which carries consequences none the less for my choices and conduct. It draws me closer to some and more distant from others; it makes some aims more appropriate, others less so. As a self-interpreting being, I am able to reflect on my history and in this sense to distance myself from it, but the distance is always precarious and provisional, the point of reflection never finally secured outside the history itself. A person with character thus knows that he is implicated in various ways even as he reflects, and feels the moral weight of what he knows.

This makes a difference for agency and self-knowledge. For, as we have seen, the deontological self, being wholly without character, is incapable of self-knowledge in any morally serious sense. Where the self is unencumbered and essentially dispossessed, no person is left for *self*-reflection to reflect upon. This is why, on the deontological view, deliberation about ends can only be an exercise in arbitrariness. In the absence of constitutive attachments, deliberation issues in 'purely preferential choice', which means the ends we seek, being mired in contingency, 'are not relevant from a moral standpoint' (Rawls 1975: 537).

When I act out of more or less enduring qualities of character, by contrast, my choice of ends is not arbitrary in the same way. In consulting my preferences, I have not only to weigh their intensity but also to assess their suitability to the person I (already) am. I ask, as I deliberate, not only what I really want but who I really am, and this last question takes me beyond an attention to my desires alone to reflect on my identity itself. While the contours of my identity will in some ways be open and subject to revision, they are not wholly without shape. And the fact that they are not enables me to discriminate among my more immediate wants and desires; some now appear essential, others merely incidental to my defining projects and commitments. Although there may be a certain ultimate contingency in my having wound up the person I am – only theology can say for sure – it makes a moral difference none the less that, being the person I am, I affirm these ends rather than those, turn this way rather than that. While the notion of constitutive attachments may at first seem an obstacle to agency – the self, now encumbered, is no longer strictly prior – some relative fixity of character appears essential to prevent the lapse into arbitrariness which the deontological self is unable to avoid.

The possibility of character in the constitutive sense is also indispensable to a certain kind of friendship, a friendship marked by mutual insight as well as sentiment. By any account, friendship is bound up with certain feelings. We like our friends; we have affection for them, and wish them well. We hope that their desires find satisfaction, that their plans meet with success, and we commit ourselves in various ways to advancing their ends.

But for persons presumed incapable of constitutive attachments, acts of friendship such as these face a powerful constraint. However much I might hope for the good of a friend and stand ready to advance it, only the friend himself can know what that good is. This restricted access to the good of others follows from the limited scope for self-reflection, which betrays in turn the thinness of the deontological self to begin with. Where deliberating about my good means no more than attending to wants and desires given directly to my awareness, I must do it on my own; it neither requires nor admits the participation of others. Every act of friendship thus becomes parasitic on a good identifiable in advance. 'Benevolence and love are second-order notions: they seek to further the good of beloved individuals that is already given' (191). Even the friendliest sentiments must await a moment of introspection itself inaccessible to friendship. To expect more of any friend, or to offer more, can only be a presumption against the ultimate privacy of self-knowledge.

For persons encumbered in part by a history they share with others, by contrast, knowing oneself is a more complicated thing. It is also a less strictly private thing. Where seeking my good is bound up with exploring my identity and interpreting my life history, the knowledge I seek is less transparent to me and less opaque to others. Friendship becomes a way of knowing as well as liking. Uncertain which path to take, I consult a friend who knows me well, and together we deliberate, offering and assessing by turns competing descriptions of the person I am, and of the alternatives I face as they bear on my identity. To take seriously such deliberation is to allow that my friend may grasp something I have missed, may offer a more adequate account of the way my identity is engaged in the alternatives before me. To adopt this new description is to see myself in a new way; my old self-image now seems partial or occluded, and I may say in retrospect that my friend knew me better than I knew myself. To deliberate with friends is to admit this possibility, which presupposes in turn a more richly-constituted self than deontology allows. While there will of course remain times when friendship requires deference to the self-image of a friend, however flawed, this too requires insight; here the need to defer implies the ability to know.

So to see ourselves as deontology would see us is to deprive us of those qualities of character, reflectiveness, and friendship that depend on the possibility of constitutive projects and attachments. And to see ourselves as given to commitments such as these is to admit a deeper commonality than benevolence describes, a commonality of shared self-understanding as well as 'enlarged affections'. As the independent self finds its limits in those aims and attachments from which it cannot stand apart, so justice finds its limits in those forms of community that engage the identity as well as the interests of the participants.

To all of this, deontology might finally reply with a concession and a distinction: it is one thing to allow that 'citizens in their personal affairs . . . have attachments and loves that they believe they would not, or could not, stand apart from', that they 'regard it as unthinkable . . . to view themselves without certain religious and philosophical convictions and commitments' (Rawls 1980: 545). But with public life it is different. There, no loyalty or allegiance could be similarly essential to our sense of who we are. Unlike our ties to family and friends, no devotion to city or nation, to party or cause, could possibly run deep enough to be defining. By contrast with our private identity, our 'public identity' as moral persons 'is not affected by changes over time' in our conceptions of the good (Rawls 1980: 544–5). While we may be thickly constituted selves in private, we must be wholly unencumbered selves in public, and it is there that the primacy of justice prevails.

But once we recall the special status of the deontological claim, it is unclear what the grounds for this distinction could be. It might seem at first glance a psychological distinction; detachment comes more easily in public life, where the ties we have are typically less compelling; I can more easily step back from, say, my partisan allegiances than certain personal loyalties and affections. But as we have seen from the start, deontology's claim for the independence of the self must be more than a claim of psychology or sociology. Otherwise, the primacy of justice would hang on the degree of benevolence and fellow-feeling any particular society managed to inspire. The independence of the self does not mean that I can, as a psychological matter, summon in this or that circumstance the detachment required to stand outside my values and ends, rather that I must regard myself as the bearer of a self distinct from my values and ends, whatever they may be. It is above all an epistemological claim, and has little to do with the relative intensity of feeling associated with public or private relations.

Understood as an epistemological claim, however, the deontological conception of the self cannot admit the distinction required. Allowing constitutive possibilities where 'private' ends are at stake would seem unavoidably to allow at least the possibility that 'public' ends could be constitutive as well. Once the bounds of the self are no longer fixed, individuated in advance and given prior to experience, there is no saying in principle what sorts of experiences could shape or reshape them, no guarantee that only 'private' and never 'public' events could conceivably be decisive.

Not egoists but strangers, sometimes benevolent, make for citizens of the deontological republic; justice finds its occasion because we cannot know each other, or our ends, well enough to govern by the common good alone. This condition is not likely to fade altogether, and so long as it does not, justice will be necessary. But neither is it guaranteed always to predominate, and in so far as it does not, community will be possible, and an unsettling presence for justice.

Liberalism teaches respect for the distance of self and ends, and when this distance is lost, we are submerged in a circumstance that ceases to be ours. But by seeking to secure this distance too completely, liberalism undermines its own insight. By putting the self beyond the reach of politics, it makes human agency an article of faith rather than an object of continuing attention and concern, a premise of politics rather than its precarious achievement. This misses the pathos of politics and also its most inspiring possibilities. It overlooks the danger that when politics goes badly, not only disappointments but also dislocations are likely to result. And it forgets the possibility that when politics goes well, we can know a good in common that we cannot know alone.

A Response to Rawls'
Political Liberalism

In this new closing chapter,[1] I reply to the revised version of liberalism that John Rawls presents in *Political Liberalism*.[2] Before doing so, however, I would like to set Rawls' recent book in context by describing the different strands of argument his remarkable work has inspired.

It is a measure of its greatness that Rawls' earlier work *A Theory of Justice*[3] provoked not one debate but three. The first, by now a starting point for students of moral and political philosophy, is the argument between utilitarians and rights-oriented liberals. Should justice be founded on utility, as Jeremy Bentham and John Stuart Mill argue, or does respect for individual rights require a basis for justice independent of utilitarian considerations, as Kant and Rawls maintain? Before Rawls wrote, utilitarianism was the dominant view within Anglo-American moral and political philosophy. Since *A Theory of Justice*, rights-oriented liberalism has come to predominate.[4]

The second debate inspired by Rawls' work is an argument within the terms of rights-oriented liberalism. If certain individual rights are so important that even considerations of the general welfare cannot override them, it remains to ask what rights these are. Libertarian liberals such as Robert Nozick and Friedrich Hayek argue that government should respect basic civil and political liberties, and also the right to the fruits of our labor as conferred by the market economy; redistributive policies that tax the rich to help the poor thus violate our rights.[5] Egalitarian liberals like Rawls disagree. They argue that we cannot meaningfully exercise our civil and political liberties with-

---

1 An earlier version of this chapter appeared in the *Harvard Law Review*, vol. 107, no. 7, May 1994, pp. 1765–94. I am grateful to Yochai Benkler, Joshua Cohen, Stephen Macedo, and J. Russell Muirhead for helpful comments and criticisms.

2 John Rawls, *Political Liberalism* (1993).   3 John Rawls, *A Theory of Justice* (1971).

4 See H. L. A. Hart, 'Between Utility and Rights', in Alan Ryan, ed., *The Idea of Freedom*, pp. 77–98 (1979).

5 Robert Nozick, *Anarchy, State, and Utopia* (1974); Friedrich A. Hayek, *The Constitution of Liberty* (1960).

out the provision of basic social and economic needs; government should therefore assure each person, as a matter of right, a decent level of such goods as education, income, housing, health care, and the like. The debate between the libertarian and egalitarian versions of rights-oriented liberalism, which flourished in the academy in the 1970s, corresponds roughly to the debate in American politics, familiar since the New Deal, between defenders of the market economy and advocates of the welfare state.

The third debate prompted by Rawls' work centers on an assumption shared by libertarian and egalitarian liberals alike. This is the idea that government should be neutral among competing conceptions of the good life. Despite their various accounts of what rights we have, rights-oriented liberals agree that the principles of justice that specify our rights should not depend for their justification on any particular conception of the good life.[6] This idea, central to the liberalism of Kant,[7] Rawls,[8] and many present-day liberals, is summed up in the claim that the right is prior to the good.

CONTESTING THE PRIORITY OF THE RIGHT
OVER THE GOOD

For Rawls, as for Kant, the right is prior to the good in two senses, and it is important to distinguish them. First, the right is prior to the good in the sense that certain individual rights "trump," or outweigh, considerations of the common good. Second, the right is prior to the good in that the principles of justice that specify our rights do not depend for their justification on any particular conception of the good life. It is this second claim for the priority of the right that prompted the most recent wave of debate about Rawlsian liberalism,

---

6 See Rawls, *A Theory of Justice;* Nozick, *Anarchy, State, and Utopia,* p. 33; Ronald Dworkin, 'Liberalism,' in Stuart Hampshire, ed., *Public and Private Morality,* p. 127 (1978); Ronald Dworkin, *Taking Rights Seriously* (1977); Bruce Ackerman, *Social Justice in the Liberal State* (1980); Charles Fried, *Right and Wrong* (1978); Thomas Nagel, 'Moral Conflict and Political Legitimacy,' 17 *Philosophy and Public Affairs,* 227–37 (1987); Charles Larmore, *Patterns of Moral Complexity* (1987).

7 Immanuel Kant, *Groundwork of the Metaphysics of Morals* (1785); Kant, *Critique of Pure Reason* (1788); Kant, 'On the Common Saying: "This May Be True in Theory, But It Does Not Apply in Practice"' (1793), in Hans Reiss, ed., *Kant's Political Writings,* pp. 61–92 (1970).

8 Rawls, *A Theory of Justice,* pp. 30–2, 446–51, 560.

an argument that has flourished in the 1980s and 1990s under the somewhat misleading label of the liberal-communitarian debate.

A number of political philosophers writing in the 1980s took issue with the notion that justice can be detached from considerations of the good. Challenges to contemporary rights-oriented liberalism found in the writings of Alasdair MacIntyre,[9] Charles Taylor,[10] Michael Walzer,[11] and also in my own work,[12] are sometimes described as the 'communitarian' critique of liberalism. The term 'communitarian' is misleading, however, insofar as it implies that rights should rest on the values or preferences that prevail in any given community at any given time. Few if any of those who have challenged the priority of the right are communitarians in this sense. The question is not whether rights should be respected but whether rights can be identified and justified in a way that does not presuppose any particular conception of the good. At issue in the third wave of debate about Rawls' liberalism is not the relative weight of individual and communal claims but the terms of relation between the right and the good.[13]

Those who dispute the priority of the right argue that justice is relative to the good, not independent of it. As a philosophical matter, our reflections about justice cannot reasonably be detached from our reflections about the nature of the good life and the highest human ends. As a political matter, our deliberations about justice and rights cannot proceed without reference to the conceptions of the good that find expression in the many cultures and traditions within which those deliberations take place.

Much of the debate about the priority of the right has focused on competing conceptions of the person, of how we should understand our relation to our ends. Are we as moral agents bound only by the ends and roles we choose for ourselves, or can we sometimes be obli-

---

9 Alasdair MacIntyre, *After Virtue* (1981); MacIntyre, *Is Patriotism a Virtue?* (1984); MacIntyre, *Whose Justice? Which Rationality?* (1988).

10 Charles Taylor, 'The Nature and Scope of Distributive Justice', in Charles Taylor, *Philosophy and the Human Sciences*, 2 *Philosophical Papers* 289–317 (1985); Taylor, *Sources of the Self* (1989).

11 Michael Walzer, *Spheres of Justice* (1983).

12 Michael J. Sandel, *Liberalism and the Limits of Justice* (1982); Sandel, 'The Procedural Republic and the Unencumbered Self,' 12 *Political Theory*, pp. 81–96 (1984).

13 This debate is carried on in the works cited in Part II of this book's bibliography, which date from the 1980s and 1990s.

gated to fulfill certain ends we have not chosen – ends given by nature or God, for example, or by our identity as a member of a family or people, culture or tradition? In various ways, those who have criticized the priority of right have resisted the notion that we can make sense of our moral and political obligations in wholly voluntarist or contractual terms.

In *A Theory of Justice*, Rawls links the priority of the right to a voluntarist or broadly Kantian conception of the person. According to this conception, we are not simply defined as the sum of our desires, as utilitarians assume, nor are we beings whose perfection consists in realizing certain purposes or ends given by nature, as Aristotle held. Rather, we are free and independent selves, unbound by antecedent moral ties, capable of choosing our ends for ourselves. This is the conception of the person that finds expression in the ideal of the state as a neutral framework. It is precisely because we are free and independent selves, capable of choosing our own ends, that we need a framework of rights that is neutral among ends. To base rights on some conception of the good would impose on some the values of others and so fail to respect each person's capacity to choose his or her own ends.

This conception of the person, and its link to the case for the priority of the right, finds expression throughout *A Theory of Justice*. Its most explicit statement comes toward the end of the book, in Rawls' account of the 'good of justice'. There Rawls argues, following Kant, that teleological doctrines are 'radically misconceived' because they relate the right and the good in the wrong way.

We should not attempt to give form to our life by first looking to the good independently defined. It is not our aims that primarily reveal our nature but rather the principles that we would acknowledge to govern the background conditions under which these aims are to be formed and the manner in which they are to be pursued. For the self is prior to the ends which are affirmed by it; even a dominant end must be chosen from among numerous possibilities. . . . We should therefore reverse the relation between the right and the good proposed by teleological doctrines and view the right as prior.[14]

In *A Theory of Justice*, the priority of the self to its ends supports the priority of the right to the good: 'A moral person is a subject with

14 Rawls, *A Theory of Justice*, p. 560.

ends he has chosen, and his fundamental preference is for conditions that enable him to frame a mode of life that expresses his nature as a free and equal rational being as fully as circumstances permit.'[15] The notion that we are free and independent selves, unclaimed by prior moral ties, assures that considerations of justice will always outweigh other, more particular aims. In an eloquent expression of Kantian liberalism, Rawls explains the moral importance of the priority of the right in the following terms:

The desire to express our nature as a free and equal rational being can be fulfilled only by acting on the principles of right and justice as having first priority. . . . It is acting from this precedence that expresses our freedom from contingency and happenstance. Therefore in order to realize our nature we have no alternative but to plan to preserve our sense of justice as governing our other aims. This sentiment cannot be fulfilled if it is compromised and balanced against other ends as but one desire among the rest. . . . [H]ow far we succeed in expressing our nature depends upon how consistently we act from our sense of justice as finally regulative. What we cannot do is express our nature by following a plan that views the sense of justice as but one desire to be weighed against others. For this sentiment reveals what the person is, and to compromise it is not to achieve for the self free rein but to give way to the contingencies and accidents of the world.[16]

In different ways, those who disputed the priority of the right took issue with Rawls' conception of the person as a free and independent self, unencumbered by prior moral ties.[17] They argued that a conception of the self given prior to its aims and attachments could not make sense of certain important aspects of our moral and political experience. Certain moral and political obligations that we commonly recognize – obligations of solidarity, for example, or religious duties – may claim us for reasons unrelated to a choice. Such obligations are difficult to dismiss as merely confused, and yet difficult to account for if we understand ourselves as free and independent selves, unbound by moral ties we have not chosen.[18]

---

15 Ibid., p. 561.   16 Ibid., pp. 574–5.

17 See, for example, Larmore, *Patterns of Moral Complexity*, pp. 118–30 (1987).

18 See MacIntyre, *After Virtue*, pp. 190–209 (1981); MacIntyre, *Is Patriotism a Virtue? The Lindley Lecture* (1984); Sandel, *Liberalism and the Limits of Justice*, pp. 175–183 (1982); Taylor, *Sources of the Self* (1989).

DEFENDING THE PRIORITY OF THE RIGHT OVER THE GOOD

In *Political Liberalism*, Rawls defends the claim for the priority of the right over the good. He sets aside, for the most part, issues raised in the first two waves of debate, about utility versus rights and libertarian versus egalitarian notions of distributive justice. *Political Liberalism* focuses instead on issues posed by the third wave of debate, about the priority of the right.

Given the controversy over the Kantian conception of the person that supports the priority of the right, at least two lines of reply are possible. One is to defend liberalism by defending the Kantian conception of the person; the other is to defend liberalism by detaching it from the Kantian conception. In *Political Liberalism*, Rawls adopts the second course. Rather than defend the Kantian conception of the person as a moral ideal, he argues that liberalism as he conceives it does not depend on that conception of the person after all. The priority of the right over the good does not presuppose any particular conception of the person – not even the one advanced in Part III of *A Theory of Justice*.

Political versus Comprehensive Liberalism. The case for liberalism, Rawls now argues, is political, not philosophical or metaphysical, and so does not depend on controversial claims about the nature of the self. The priority of the right over the good is not the application to politics of Kantian moral philosophy, but a practical response to the familiar fact that people in modern democratic societies typically disagree about the good. Since people's moral and religious convictions are unlikely to converge, it is more reasonable to seek agreement on principles of justice that are neutral with respect to those controversies.

Central to Rawls' revised view is the distinction between political liberalism and liberalism as part of a comprehensive moral doctrine. Comprehensive liberalism affirms liberal political arrangements in the name of certain moral ideals, such as autonomy, individuality, or self-reliance. Examples of liberalism as a comprehensive moral doctrine include the liberal visions of Kant and John Stuart Mill.[19] As

---

19 For recent examples of comprehensive liberalism, see George Kateb, *The Inner Ocean: Individualism and Democratic Culture* (1992), and Joseph Raz, *The Morality of Freedom* (1986). Ronald Dworkin describes his view as a version of comprehensive liberalism in

Rawls acknowledges, the version of liberalism presented in *A Theory of Justice* is also an instance of comprehensive liberalism: 'An essential feature of a well-ordered society associated with justice as fairness is that all its citizens endorse this conception on the basis of what I now call a comprehensive philosophical doctrine.'[20] Rawls now revises this feature by recasting his theory as a 'political conception of justice'.

Unlike comprehensive liberalism, political liberalism refuses to take sides in the moral and religious controversies that arise from comprehensive doctrines, including controversies about conceptions of the self: 'Which moral judgments are true, all things considered, is not a matter for political liberalism. . . . To maintain impartiality between comprehensive doctrines, it does not specifically address the moral topics on which those doctrines divide.'[21] Given the difficulty of securing agreement on any comprehensive conception, it is unreasonable to expect that, even in a well-ordered society, people will support liberal institutions for the same reason, as expressing the priority of the self to its ends, for example. Political liberalism abandons this hope as unrealistic and contrary to the aim of basing justice on principles that adherents of various moral and religious conceptions can accept. Rather than seek a philosophical foundation for principles of justice, political liberalism seeks the support of an 'overlapping consensus'. This means that different people can be persuaded to endorse liberal political arrangements, such as equal basic liberties, for different reasons, reflecting the various comprehensive moral and religious conceptions they espouse. Since political liberalism does not depend for its justification on any one of those moral or religious conceptions, it is presented as a 'freestanding' view; it 'applies the principle of toleration to philosophy itself'.[22]

Although political liberalism renounces reliance on the Kantian conception of the person, it does not do without a conception of the person altogether. As Rawls acknowledges, some such conception is necessary to the idea of the original position, the hypothetical social contract that gives rise to the principles of justice. The way to think about justice, Rawls argued in *A Theory of Justice*, is to ask what princi-

'Foundations of Liberal Equality,' *XI The Tanner Lectures on Human Values*, pp. 1–119 (1990).
20 Rawls, *Political Liberalism*, p. xvi.
21 Ibid., pp. xx, xxviii.   22 Ibid., p. 10.

ples would be agreed to by persons who found themselves gathered in an initial situation of equality, each in temporary ignorance of his or her race and class, religion and gender, aims and attachments. But in order for this way of thinking about justice to carry weight, the design of the original position must reflect something about the sort of persons we actually are, or would be in a just society.

One way of justifying the design of the original position would be to appeal to the Kantian conception of the person that Rawls advanced in Part III of *A Theory of Justice*. If our capacity to choose our ends is more fundamental to our nature as moral persons than the particular ends we choose, if 'it is not our aims that primarily reveal our nature but rather the principles that we would acknowledge to govern the background conditions under which these aims are to be formed', [23] if 'the self is prior to the ends which are affirmed by it', [24] then it makes sense to think about justice from the standpoint of persons deliberating prior to any knowledge of the ends they will pursue. If 'a moral person is a subject with ends he has chosen, and his fundamental preference is for conditions that enable him to frame a mode of life that expresses his nature as a free and equal rational being as fully as circumstances permit', [25] then the original position can be justified as an expression of our moral personality and the 'fundamental preference' that flows from it.

Once Rawls disavows reliance on the Kantian conception of the person, however, this way of justifying the original position is no longer available. But this raises a difficult question: What reason remains for insisting that our reflections about justice should proceed without reference to our purposes and ends? Why must we 'bracket,' or set aside, our moral and religious convictions, our conceptions of the good life? Why should not the principles of justice that govern the basic structure of society be based on our best understanding of the highest human ends?

The Political Conception of the Person. Political liberalism replies as follows: The reason we should think about justice from the standpoint of persons who abstract from their ends is not that this procedure expresses our nature as free and independent selves given prior to

---

23 Rawls, *A Theory of Justice*, p. 560.   24 Ibid., p. 560.
25 Ibid., p. 561.

our ends. Rather, this way of thinking about justice is warranted by the fact that, for *political* purposes, though not necessarily for all moral purposes, we should think of ourselves as free and independent citizens, unclaimed by prior duties or obligations. For political liberalism, what justifies the design of the original position is a 'political conception of the person'. The political conception of the person embodied in the original position closely parallels the Kantian conception of the person, with the important difference that its scope is limited to our public identity, our identity as citizens. Thus, for example, our freedom as citizens means that our public identity is not claimed or defined by the ends we espouse at any given time. As free persons, citizens view themselves 'as independent from and not identified with any particular such conception with its scheme of final ends'.[26] Our public identity is not affected by changes over time in our conceptions of the good.

In our personal, nonpublic identity, Rawls allows, we may regard our 'ends and attachments very differently from the way the political conception supposes'. There, persons may find themselves claimed by loyalties and commitments 'they believe they would not, indeed could and should not, stand apart from and evaluate objectively. They may regard it as simply unthinkable to view themselves apart from certain religious, philosophical, and moral convictions, or from certain enduring attachments and loyalties.'[27] But however encumbered we may be in our personal identities, however claimed by moral or religious convictions, we must bracket our encumbrances in public, and regard ourselves, qua public selves, as independent of any particular loyalties or attachments or conceptions of the good.

A related feature of the political conception of the person is that we are 'self-authenticating sources of valid claims'.[28] The claims we make as citizens carry weight, whatever they are, simply in virtue of our making them (provided they are not unjust). That some claims may reflect high moral or religious ideals, or notions of patriotism and the common good, while others express mere interests or preferences is not relevant from the standpoint of political liberalism. From a political point of view, claims founded on duties and obligations of citizenship, solidarity, or religious faith are merely things peo-

26 Rawls, *Political Liberalism*, p. 30. 27 Ibid., p. 31.
28 Ibid., p. 32.

ple want – nothing more, nothing less. Their validity as political claims has nothing to do with the moral importance of the goods they affirm, but consists solely in the fact that someone asserts them. Even divine commandments and imperatives of conscience count as 'self-authenticating' claims, politically speaking.[29] This ensures that even those who regard themselves as claimed by moral or religious or communal obligations are nonetheless, for political purposes, unencumbered selves.

This political conception of the person explains why, according to political liberalism, we should reflect about justice as the original position invites us to do, in abstraction from our ends. But this raises a further question: Why should we adopt the standpoint of the political conception of the person in the first place? Why should our political identities not express the moral and religious and communal convictions we affirm in our personal lives? Why insist on the separation between our identity as citizens and our identity as moral persons more broadly conceived? Why, in deliberating about justice, should we set aside the moral judgments that inform the rest of our lives?

Rawls' answer is that this separation or 'dualism' between our identity as citizens and our identity as persons 'originates in the special nature of modern democratic societies'.[30] In traditional societies, people sought to shape political life in the image of their comprehensive moral and religious ideals. But in a modern democratic society like our own, marked as it is by a plurality of moral and religious views, we typically distinguish between our public and personal identities. Confident though I may be of the truth of the moral and religious ideals I espouse, I do not insist that these ideals be reflected in the basic structure of society. Like other aspects of political liberalism, the political conception of the person as a free and independent self is 'implicit in the public political culture of a democratic society'.[31]

But suppose Rawls is right, and the liberal self-image he attributes to us is implicit in our political culture. Would this provide sufficient

---

29 The notion that we should regard our moral and religious duties as 'self-authenticating from a political point of view' (ibid., p. 33) accords with Rawls' statement, in *A Theory of Justice,* that 'from the standpoint of justice as fairness, these [moral and religious] obligations are self-imposed' (206). But it is not clear what the justification can be, on such a view, for according religious beliefs or claims of conscience a special respect not accorded other preferences people may hold with equal or greater intensity (205–11).

30 Ibid., p. xxi.   31 Ibid., p. 13.

grounds for affirming it, and for adopting the conception of justice it supports? Some have read Rawls' recent writings as suggesting that justice as fairness, being a political conception of justice, requires no moral or philosophical justification apart from an appeal to the shared understandings implicit in our political culture. Rawls seemed to invite this interpretation when he wrote, in an article published after *A Theory of Justice* but before *Political Liberalism*, as follows:

What justifies a conception of justice is not its being true to an order antecedent to and given to us, but its congruence with our deeper understanding of ourselves and our aspirations, and our realization that, given our history and the traditions embedded in our public life, it is the most reasonable doctrine for us.[32]

Richard Rorty, in an insightful article, interprets (and welcomes) Rawls' revised view as 'thoroughly historicist and antiuniversalist'.[33] Whereas *A Theory of Justice* seemed to base justice on a Kantian conception of the person, Rorty writes, Rawls' liberalism 'no longer seems committed to a philosophical account of the human self, but only to a historic-sociological description of the way we live now'.[34] On this view, Rawls is not 'supplying philosophical foundations for democratic institutions, but simply trying to systematize the principles and intuitions typical of American liberals'.[35] Rorty endorses what he takes to be Rawls' pragmatic turn, a turn away from the notion that liberal political arrangements require a philosophical justification, or 'extra-political grounding' in a theory of the human subject.

Insofar as justice becomes the first virtue of a society, [Rorty writes,] the need for such legitimation may gradually cease to be felt. Such a society will become accustomed to the thought that social policy needs no more authority than successful accommodation among individuals, individuals who find themselves heir to the same historical traditions and faced with the same problems.[36]

In *Political Liberalism*, Rawls pulls back from this purely pragmatic account. Although justice as fairness begins 'by looking to the public

32 Rawls, 'Kantian Constructivism in Moral Theory', 77 *Journal of Philosophy*, 519 (1980).
33 Richard Rorty, 'The Priority of Democracy to Philosophy,' in Merrill D. Peterson and Robert C. Vaughan, eds., *The Virginia Statute for Religious Freedom*, p. 262 (1988).
34 Ibid., p. 265.   35 Ibid., p. 268.
36 Ibid., p. 264.

culture itself as the shared fund of implicitly recognized basic ideas and principles',[37] it does not affirm these principles simply on the grounds that they are widely shared. While Rawls argues that his principles of justice could gain the support of an overlapping consensus, the overlapping consensus he seeks 'is not a mere modus vivendi',[38] or compromise among conflicting views. Adherents of different moral and religious conceptions begin by endorsing the principles of justice for reasons drawn from within their conceptions. But if all goes well, they come to support those principles as expressing important political values. As people learn to live in a pluralist society governed by liberal institutions, they acquire virtues that strengthen their commitment to liberal principles.

The virtues of political cooperation that make a constitutional regime possible are . . . very great virtues. I mean, for example, the virtues of tolerance and being ready to meet others halfway, and the virtue of reasonableness and the sense of fairness. When these virtues are widespread in society and sustain its political conception of justice, they constitute a very great public good.[39]

Rawls emphasizes that affirming liberal virtues as a great public good and encouraging their cultivation is not the same as endorsing a perfectionist state based on a comprehensive moral conception. It does not contradict the priority of the right over the good. The reason is that political liberalism affirms liberal virtues for political purposes only – for their role in supporting a constitutional regime that protects people's rights. Whether and to what extent these virtues should figure in people's moral lives generally is a question political liberalism does not claim to answer.[40]

ASSESSING POLITICAL LIBERALISM

If *Political Liberalism* defends the priority of right by detaching it from the Kantian conception of the person, how convincing is its defense? As I shall try to argue, *Political Liberalism* rescues the priority of the right from controversies about the nature of the self, but only at the

---

37 Rawls, *Political Liberalism*, p. 8.   38 Ibid., p. 147.
39 Ibid., p. 157.   40 Ibid., pp. 194–5.

cost of rendering it vulnerable on other grounds. Specifically, I shall try to show that liberalism conceived as a political conception of justice is open to three objections.

First, notwithstanding the importance of the 'political values' Rawls appeals to, it is not always reasonable to bracket, or set aside for political purposes, claims arising from within comprehensive moral and religious doctrines. Where grave moral questions are concerned, whether it is reasonable to bracket moral and religious controversies for the sake of political agreement partly depends on which of the contending moral or religious doctrines is true.

Second, for political liberalism, the case for the priority of the right over the good depends on the claim that modern democratic societies are characterized by a 'fact of reasonable pluralism' about the good. While it is certainly true that people in modern democratic societies hold a variety of conflicting moral and religious views, it cannot be said that there is a 'fact of reasonable pluralism' about morality and religion that does not also apply to questions of justice.

Third, according to the ideal of public reason advanced by political liberalism, citizens may not legitimately discuss fundamental political and constitutional questions with reference to their moral and religious ideals. But this is an unduly severe restriction that would impoverish political discourse and rule out important dimensions of public deliberation.

Bracketing Grave Moral Questions. Political liberalism insists on bracketing our comprehensive moral and religious ideals for political purposes, and on separating our political from our personal identities. The reason is this: In modern democratic societies like ours, where people typically disagree about the good life, bracketing our moral and religious convictions is necessary if we are to secure social cooperation on the basis of mutual respect. But this raises a question that political liberalism cannot answer within its own terms. Even granting the importance of securing social cooperation on the basis of mutual respect, what is to ensure that this interest is always so important as to outweigh any competing interest that could arise from within a comprehensive moral or religious view?

One way of ensuring the priority of the political conception of justice (and hence the priority of the right) is to deny that any of the moral or religious conceptions it brackets could be true.[41] But this would implicate political liberalism in precisely the sort of philosophical claim it seeks to avoid. Time and again Rawls emphasizes that political liberalism does not depend on skepticism about the claims of comprehensive moral and religious doctrines. If political liberalism therefore allows that some such doctrines might be true, then what is to ensure that none can generate values sufficiently compelling to burst the brackets, so to speak, and morally outweigh the political values of toleration, fairness, and social cooperation based on mutual respect?

It might be replied that political values and values arising from within comprehensive moral and religious doctrines address different subjects. Political values, it might be said, apply to the basic structure of society and constitutional essentials, while moral and religious values apply to the conduct of personal life and voluntary associations. But if it were simply a difference of subject matter, no conflict between political values and moral and religious values could ever arise, and there would be no need to assert, as Rawls repeatedly does, that in a constitutional democracy governed by political liberalism, 'political values normally outweigh whatever nonpolitical values conflict with them'.[42]

The difficulty of asserting the priority of 'political values' without reference to the claims of morality and religion can best be seen by considering two political controversies that bear on grave moral and religious questions. One is the contemporary debate over abortion rights. The other is the famous debate between Abraham Lincoln and Stephen Douglas over popular sovereignty and slavery.

Given the intense disagreement over the moral permissibility of abortion, the case for seeking a political solution that brackets the contending moral and religious issues – that is neutral with respect to them – would seem especially strong. But whether it is reasonable to bracket, for political purposes, the comprehensive moral and reli-

---

41 Thomas Hobbes, who can be interpreted as advancing a political conception of justice, ensured the priority of his political conception with respect to claims arising from contending moral and religious conceptions by denying their truth. See Hobbes, *Leviathan* (1651).
42 Rawls, *Political Liberalism*, p. 146, also p. 155.

gious doctrines at stake largely depends on which of those doctrines is true. If the doctrine of the Catholic Church is true, if human life in the relevant moral sense does begin at conception, then bracketing the moral-theological question of when human life begins is far less reasonable than it would be on rival moral and religious assumptions. The more confident we are that fetuses are, in the relevant moral sense, different from babies, the more confident we can be in affirming a political conception of justice that sets aside the controversy about the moral status of fetuses.

The political liberal might reply that the political values of toleration and equal citizenship for women are sufficient grounds for concluding that women should be free to choose for themselves whether to have an abortion; government should not take sides in the moral and religious controversy over when human life begins.[43] But if the Catholic Church is right about the moral status of the fetus, if abortion is morally tantamount to murder, then it is not clear why the political values of toleration and women's equality, important though they are, should prevail. If the Catholic doctrine is true, the political liberal's case for the priority of political values must become an instance of just-war theory; he or she would have to show why these values should prevail even at the cost of some 1.5 million civilian deaths each year.

Of course, to suggest the impossibility of bracketing the moral-theological question of when human life begins is not to argue against a right to abortion. It is simply to show that the case for abortion rights cannot be neutral with respect to that moral and religious controversy. It must engage rather than avoid the comprehensive moral and religious doctrines at stake. Liberals often resist this engagement, since it violates the priority of the right over the good. But the abortion debate shows that this priority cannot be sustained. The case for respecting a woman's right to decide for herself whether to have an abortion depends on showing, as I believe can be shown, that there is a relevant moral difference between aborting a fetus at a relatively early stage of development and killing a child.

A second illustration of the difficulty with a political conception of

---

43 Rawls seems to take this view in a footnote on abortion, but he does not explain why political values should prevail even if the Catholic doctrine is true. See *Political Liberalism*, pp. 243–4.

justice that tries to bracket controversial moral questions is offered by the 1858 debates between Abraham Lincoln and Stephen Douglas. Douglas' argument for the doctrine of popular sovereignty is perhaps the most famous case in American history for bracketing a controversial moral question for the sake of political agreement. Since people were bound to disagree about the morality of slavery, Douglas argued, national policy should be neutral on that question. The doctrine of popular sovereignty he defended did not judge slavery right or wrong, but left the people of each territory free to make their own judgments. 'To throw the weight of federal power into the scale, either in favor of the free or the slave states,' would violate the fundamental principles of the Constitution and run the risk of civil war. The only hope of holding the country together, he argued, was to agree to disagree, to bracket the moral controversy over slavery and respect 'the right of each state and each territory to decide these questions for themselves.'[44]

Lincoln argued against Douglas' case for a political conception of justice. Policy should express rather than avoid a substantive moral judgment about slavery. Although Lincoln was not an abolitionist, he believed government should treat slavery as the moral wrong it was, and prohibit its extension to the territories. 'The real issue in this controversy – the one pressing upon every mind – is the sentiment on the part of one class that looks upon the institution of slavery as a wrong, and of another class that does not look upon it as a wrong.' Lincoln and the Republican party viewed slavery as a wrong and insisted that it 'be treated as a wrong, and one of the methods of treating it as a wrong is to make provision that it shall grow no larger.'[45]

Whatever his personal moral views, Douglas claimed that, for political purposes at least, he was agnostic on the question of slavery; he did not care whether slavery was 'voted up or down'. Lincoln replied that it was reasonable to bracket the question of the morality of slavery only on the assumption that it was not the moral evil he considered it to be. Any man can advocate political neutrality

who does not see anything wrong in slavery, but no man can logically say it who does see a wrong in it; because no man can logically say he don't

44 Paul M. Angle, ed., *Created Equal? The Complete Lincoln-Douglas Debates of 1858*, pp. 369, 374 (1958).
45 Ibid., p. 390.

care whether a wrong is voted up or voted down. He may say he don't care whether an indifferent thing is voted up or down, but he must logically have a choice between a right thing and a wrong thing. He contends that whatever community wants slaves has a right to have them. So they have it if it is not a wrong. But if it is a wrong, he cannot say people have a right to do wrong.[46]

The debate between Lincoln and Douglas was primarily not about the morality of slavery, but about whether to bracket a moral controversy for the sake of political agreement. In this respect, their debate over popular sovereignty is analogous to the current debate over abortion rights. As some contemporary liberals argue that government should not take a stand one way or the other on the morality of abortion, but should let each woman decide the question for herself, so Douglas argued that national policy should not take a stand one way or the other on the morality of slavery, but should let each territory decide the question for itself. There is, of course, the difference that, in the case of abortion rights, those who would bracket the substantive moral question typically leave the choice to the individual, whereas in the case of slavery, Douglas' way of bracketing was to leave the choice to the territories.

But Lincoln's argument against Douglas was an argument against bracketing as such, at least where grave moral questions are at stake. Lincoln's point was that the political conception of justice defended by Douglas depended for its plausibility on a particular answer to the substantive moral question it claimed to bracket. This point applies with equal force to those arguments for abortion rights that claim to take no side in the controversy over the moral status of the fetus. Even in the face of so dire a threat to social cooperation as the prospect of civil war, Lincoln argued that it made neither moral nor political sense to bracket the most divisive moral controversy of the day:

I say, where is the philosophy or the statesmanship based on the assumption that we are to quit talking about it, and that the public mind is all at once to cease being agitated by it? Yet this is the policy . . . that Douglas is advocating – that we are to care nothing about it! I ask you if it is not a false philosophy? Is it not a false statesmanship that undertakes to build

46 Ibid., p. 392.

up a system of policy upon the basis of caring nothing about the very thing that every body does care the most about?[47]

Present-day liberals will surely resist the company of Douglas and want national policy to oppose slavery, presumably on the grounds that slavery violates people's rights. The question is whether liberalism conceived as a political conception of justice can do so consistent with its own strictures against appeals to comprehensive moral ideals. For example, a Kantian liberal can oppose slavery as a failure to treat people as ends in themselves, worthy of respect. But this argument, resting as it does on a Kantian conception of the person, is unavailable to political liberalism. Other historically important arguments against slavery are unavailable to political liberalism for similar reasons. American abolitionists of the 1830s and 1840s, for example, typically cast their arguments in religious terms that political liberalism cannot invoke.

How, then, can political liberalism escape the company of Douglas and oppose slavery without presupposing some comprehensive moral view? It might be replied that Douglas was wrong to seek social peace at any price; not just any political agreement will do. Even conceived as a political conception, justice as fairness is not merely a modus vivendi. Given the principles and self-understandings implicit in our political culture, only an agreement on terms that treat people fairly, as free and equal citizens, can provide a reasonable basis for social cooperation. For twentieth-century Americans, at least, the rejection of slavery is a settled matter. The historic demise of Douglas' position is by now a fact of our political tradition that any political agreement must take as given.

This appeal to the conception of citizenship implicit in our political culture might explain how political liberalism can oppose slavery today; our present political culture was importantly shaped, after all, by the Civil War, Reconstruction, the adoption of the Thirteenth, Fourteenth, and Fifteenth Amendments, *Brown v. Board of Education,* the civil rights movement, the Voting Rights Act, and so on. These experiences, and the shared understanding of racial equality and equal citizenship they formed, provide ample grounds for holding

47 Ibid., p. 388–9.

that slavery is at odds with American political and constitutional practice as it has developed over the past century.

But this does not explain how political liberalism could oppose slavery in 1858. The notions of equal citizenship implicit in American political culture of the mid-nineteenth century were arguably hospitable to the institution of slavery. The Declaration of Independence proclaimed that 'all Men are created equal, . . . endowed by their Creator with certain unalienable rights', but Douglas argued, not implausibly, that the signers of the Declaration were asserting the right of the colonists to be free of British rule, not the right of their black slaves to equal citizenship.[48] The Constitution itself did not prohibit slavery but, on the contrary, accommodated it by allowing states to count three-fifths of their slave population for apportionment purposes,[49] providing that Congress could not prohibit the slave trade until 1808,[50] and requiring the return of fugitive slaves.[51] And in the notorious *Dred Scott* case, the Supreme Court upheld the property rights of slaveholders in their slaves and ruled that African-Americans were not citizens of the United States.[52] To the extent that political liberalism refuses to invoke comprehensive moral ideals and relies instead on notions of citizenship implicit in the political culture, it would have had a hard time explaining in 1858 why Lincoln was right and Douglas was wrong.

The Fact of Reasonable Pluralism. The abortion debate today and the Lincoln-Douglas debate of 1858 illustrate the way a political conception of justice must presuppose some answer to the moral questions it purports to bracket, at least where grave moral questions are concerned. In cases such as these, the priority of the right over the good cannot be sustained. Another difficulty with political liberalism concerns the reason it gives for asserting the priority of the right over the good in the first place. For Kantian liberalism, the asymmetry between the right and the good arises from a certain conception of the person. Since we must think of ourselves as moral subjects given prior to our aims and attachments, we must regard the right as regulative with

---

48 Ibid., p. 374.
50 Article I, sec. 9, cl. 1.
52 *Dred Scott v. Sandford*, 60 U.S. (19 Howard) 393 (1857).

49 Article I, sec. 2, cl. 3.
51 Article IV, sec. 2, cl. 3.

respect to the particular ends we affirm; the right is prior to the good because the self is prior to its ends.

For political liberalism, the asymmetry between the right and the good is based not on a Kantian conception of the person but instead on a certain feature of modern democratic societies. Rawls describes this feature as the 'fact of reasonable pluralism': 'A modern democratic society is characterized not simply by a pluralism of comprehensive religious, philosophical, and moral doctrines but by a pluralism of incompatible yet reasonable comprehensive doctrines. No one of these doctrines is affirmed by citizens generally.'[53] Nor is it likely that sometime in the foreseeable future this pluralism will cease to hold. Disagreement about moral and religious questions is not a temporary condition but 'the normal result of the exercise of human reason' under free institutions.[54]

Given the 'fact of reasonable pluralism', the problem is to find principles of justice that free and equal citizens can affirm despite their moral, philosophic, and religious differences. 'This is a problem of political justice, not a problem about the highest good'.[55] Whatever principles it generates, the solution to this problem must uphold the priority of the right over the good. Otherwise it will fail to provide a basis for social cooperation among adherents of incompatible but reasonable moral and religious convictions.

For political liberalism, then, the priority of the right is based on the 'fact of reasonable pluralism' about the good. But here arises a difficulty. For even if true, this fact is not sufficient to establish the priority of the right; the asymmetry between the right and the good depends on a further assumption. This is the assumption that, despite our disagreements about morality and religion, we do not have, or on due reflection would not have, similar disagreements about justice. Political liberalism must assume not only that the exercise of human reason under conditions of freedom will produce disagreements about the good life but also that the exercise of human reason under conditions of freedom will *not* produce disagreements about justice. The 'fact of reasonable pluralism' about morality and religion creates an asymmetry between the right and the good only when coupled

---

53 Rawls, *Political Liberalism*, p. xvi. 54 Ibid. 55 Ibid., p. xxv.

with the assumption that there is no comparable 'fact of reasonable pluralism' about justice.

It is not clear that this further assumption is justified. We need only look around us to see that modern democratic societies are teeming with disagreements about justice. Consider, for example, contemporary debates about affirmative action, income distribution and tax fairness, health care, immigration, gay rights, free speech versus hate speech, and capital punishment, to name just a few. Or consider the divided votes and conflicting opinions of Supreme Court justices in cases involving religious liberty, freedom of speech, privacy rights, voting rights, the rights of the accused, and so on. Do not these debates display a 'fact of reasonable pluralism' about justice? If so, how does the pluralism about justice that prevails in modern democratic societies differ from the pluralism about morality and religion? Is there reason to think that, sometime in the foreseeable future, our disagreements about justice will dissolve even as our disagreements about morality and religion persist?

The political liberal might reply by distinguishing two different kinds of disagreement about justice. There are disagreements about what the principles of justice should be and disagreements about how these principles should be applied. Many of our disagreements about justice, it might be argued, are of the second kind. While we generally agree, for example, that freedom of speech is one of the basic rights and liberties, we disagree about whether the right to free speech should protect racial epithets, or violent pornographic depictions, or commercial advertising, or unlimited contributions to political campaigns. These disagreements, vigorous and even intractable though they may be, are consistent with our agreeing at the level of principle that a just society includes a basic right to free speech.

Our disagreements about morality and religion, by contrast, might be seen as more fundamental. They reflect incompatible conceptions of the good life, it might be argued, not disagreements about how to put into practice a conception of the good life that commands, or on reflection would command, widespread agreement. If our controversies about justice concern the application of principles we share or would share on due reflection, while our controversies about morality and religion run deeper, then the asymmetry between the right and the good advanced by political liberalism would be vindicated.

But with what confidence can this contrast be asserted? Do all of our disagreements about justice concern the application of principles we share or would share on due reflection, rather than the principles themselves? What of our debates about distributive justice? Here it would seem that our disagreements are at the level of principle not application. Some maintain, consistent with Rawls' difference principle, that only those social and economic inequalities are just that improve the condition of the least advantaged members of society. They argue, for example, that government must ensure the provision of certain basic needs, such as income, education, health care, housing, and the like, so that all citizens will be able to exercise their basic liberties meaningfully.

Others reject the difference principle. Libertarians argue, for example, that it may be a good thing for people to help those less fortunate than themselves, but that this should be a matter of charity, not entitlement. Government should not use its coercive power to redistribute income and wealth, but should respect people's rights to exercise their talents as they choose, and to reap their rewards as defined by the market economy.[56]

The debate between liberal egalitarians like Rawls and libertarians like Nozick and Milton Friedman is a prominent feature of political argument in modern democratic societies. This debate reflects disagreement about what the correct principle of distributive justice is, not disagreement about how to apply the difference principle. But this would suggest that there exists in democratic societies a 'fact of reasonable pluralism' about justice as well as about morality and religion. And if this is the case, the asymmetry between the right and the good does not hold.

Political liberalism is not without a reply to this objection, but the reply it must make departs to some extent from the spirit of toleration it otherwise evokes. Rawls' reply must be that, while there is a fact of pluralism about distributive justice, there is no fact of *reasonable* pluralism.[57] Unlike disagreements about morality and religion, dis-

---

56 See Robert Nozick, *Anarchy, State, and Utopia* (1974); Milton Friedman, *Capitalism and Freedom* (1962); Milton and Rose Friedman, *Free to Choose* (1980); Friedrich A. Hayek, *The Constitution of Liberty* (1960).

57 Although Rawls does not state this view explicitly, it is necessary for making sense of the 'fact of reasonable pluralism' and the role it plays in supporting the priority of the right. He notes that reasonable disagreements may arise over what policies fulfill the difference principle, but adds, 'This is not a difference about what are the correct principles

agreements about the validity of the difference principle are not reasonable; libertarian theories of distributive justice would not be sustained on due reflection. Our differences about distributive justice, unlike our differences of morality and religion, are not the natural outcome of the exercise of human reason under conditions of freedom.

At first glance, the claim that disagreements about distributive justice are not reasonable may seem arbitrary, even harsh, at odds with political liberalism's promise to apply 'the principle of toleration to philosophy itself'.[58] It contrasts sharply with Rawls' apparent generosity toward differences of morality and religion. These differences, Rawls repeatedly writes, are a normal, indeed desirable feature of modern life, an expression of human diversity that only the oppressive use of state power can overcome.[59] Where comprehensive moralities are concerned, 'it is not to be expected that conscientious persons with full powers of reason, even after free discussion, will all arrive at the same conclusion'.[60] Since the exercise of human reason produces a pluralism of reasonable moral and religious doctrines, 'it is unreasonable or worse to want to use the sanctions of state power to correct, or to punish, those who disagree with us'.[61] But this spirit of toleration does not extend to our disagreements about justice. Since disagreements between, say, libertarians and advocates of the difference principle do not reflect a reasonable pluralism, there is no objection to using state power to implement the difference principle.

Intolerant though it may seem at first glance, the notion that theories of distributive justice at odds with the difference principle are not reasonable, or that libertarian theories of justice would not survive due reflection, is no arbitrary claim. On the contrary, in *A Theory of Justice* Rawls offers a rich array of compelling arguments on behalf of the difference principle and against libertarian conceptions: The distribution of talents and assets that enables some to earn more and others less in the market economy is arbitrary from a moral point of view; so is the fact that the market happens to prize and reward, at any given moment, the talents you or I may have in abundance; libertari-

but simply a difference in the difficulty of seeing whether the principles are achieved' (*Political Liberalism*, pp. 229–30).
58 Ibid., p. 10.   59 Ibid., p. 304.
60 Ibid., p. 58.   61 Ibid., p. 138.

ans would agree that distributive shares should not be based on social status or accident of birth (as in aristocratic or caste societies), but the distribution of talents given by nature is no less arbitrary; the notion of freedom that libertarians invoke can be meaningfully exercised only if people are assured satisfaction of certain basic social and economic needs; if people deliberated about distributive justice without reference to their own interests, or without prior knowledge of their talents and the value of those talents in the market economy, they would agree that the natural distribution of talents should not be the basis of distributive shares; and so on.[62]

My point is not to rehearse Rawls' argument for the difference principle, but only to recall the kinds of reasons he offers. Viewing justification as a process of mutual adjustment between principles and considered judgments that aims at a 'reflective equilibrium',[63] Rawls tries to show that the difference principle is more reasonable than the alternative offered by libertarians. To the extent that his arguments are convincing, as I believe they are, and to the extent that they can be convincing to citizens of a democratic society, the principles they support are properly embodied in public policy and law. Disagreement will doubtless remain. Libertarians will not fall silent or disappear. But their disagreement need not be regarded as a 'fact of reasonable pluralism' in the face of which government must be neutral.

But this leads to a question that goes to the heart of political liberalism's claim for the priority of the right over the good: If moral argument or reflection of the kind Rawls deploys enables us to conclude, despite the persistence of conflicting views, that some principles of justice are more reasonable than others, what guarantees that reflection of a similar kind is not possible in the case of moral and religious controversy? If we can reason about controversial principles of distributive justice by seeking a reflective equilibrium, why can we not reason in the same way about conceptions of the good? If it can be shown that some conceptions of the good are more reasonable than others, then the persistence of disagreement would not necessarily amount to a 'fact of reasonable pluralism' that requires government to be neutral.

Consider, for example, the controversy in our public culture about

62 See Rawls, *A Theory of Justice*, esp. pp. 72–5, 100–107, 136–42, 310–15.
63 See ibid., pp. 20–22, 48–52, 120, 577–87.

the moral status of homosexuality, a controversy based on comprehensive moral and religious doctrines. Some maintain that homosexuality is sinful, or at least morally impermissible; others argue that homosexuality is morally permissible, and in some cases gives expression to important human goods. Political liberalism insists that neither of these views about the morality of homosexuality should play a role in public debates about justice or rights. Government must be neutral with respect to them. This means that those who abhor homosexuality may not seek to embody their view in law; it also means that proponents of gay rights may not base their arguments on the notion that homosexuality is morally defensible. From the standpoint of political liberalism, each of these approaches would wrongly base the right on some conception of the good; each would fail to respect the 'fact of reasonable pluralism' about comprehensive moralities.

But does the disagreement in our society about the moral status of homosexuality constitute a 'fact of reasonable pluralism' any more than does the disagreement about distributive justice? According to political liberalism, the libertarian's objection to the difference principle does not constitute a 'fact of reasonable pluralism' that requires government neutrality, because there are good reasons to conclude, on due reflection, that the arguments for the difference principle are more convincing than the ones that support libertarianism. But is it not possible to conclude, with equal or greater confidence, that on due reflection, the arguments for the moral permissibility of homosexuality are more convincing than the arguments against it? Consistent with the search for a reflective equilibrium among principles and considered judgments, such reflection might proceed by assessing the reasons advanced by those who assert the moral inferiority of homosexual to heterosexual relations.

Those who consider homosexuality immoral might argue, for example, that homosexuality cannot fulfill the highest end of human sexuality, the good of procreation.[64] To this it might be replied that many heterosexual relations also do not fulfill this end, such as con-

---

64 In this paragraph, I draw on some of the arguments for and against the morality of homosexuality that appear in Stephen Macedo, 'The New Natural Lawyers,' *Harvard Crimson*, Oct. 29, 1993; Harvey C. Mansfield, 'Saving Liberalism from Liberals,' *Harvard Crimson*, Nov. 8, 1993; and John Finnis and Martha Nussbaum, 'Is Homosexuality Wrong? A Philosophical Exchange,' 209 *New Republic,* pp. 12–13 (1993).

tracepted sex, or sex among sterile couples, or sex among partners beyond the age of reproduction. This might suggest that the good of procreation, important though it is, is not necessary to the moral worth of human sexual relations; the moral worth of sexuality might also consist in the love and responsibility it expresses, and these goods are possible in homosexual as well as heterosexual relations. Opponents might reply that homosexuals are often promiscuous, and hence less likely to realize the goods of love and responsibility. The reply to this claim might consist in an empirical showing to the contrary, or in the observation that the existence of promiscuity does not argue against the moral worth of homosexuality as such, only against certain instances of it.[65] Heterosexuals also engage in promiscuity and other practices at odds with the goods that confer on sexuality its moral worth, but this fact does not lead us to abhor heterosexuality as such. And so on.

My point is not to offer a full argument for the moral permissibility of homosexuality, only to suggest the way such an argument might proceed. Like Rawls' argument for the difference principle, it might proceed by seeking a reflective equilibrium between our principles and considered judgments, adjusting each in the light of the other. That the argument for the morality of homosexuality, unlike the argument for the difference principle, addresses claims about human ends and conceptions of the good does not mean that the same method of moral reasoning cannot proceed. It is unlikely, of course, that such moral reasoning would produce conclusive or irrefutable answers to moral and religious controversies. But as Rawls acknowledges, such reasoning does not produce irrefutable answers to questions of justice either; a more modest notion of justification is appropriate. 'In philosophy questions at the most fundamental level are not usually settled by conclusive argument', writes Rawls, referring to arguments about justice. 'What is obvious to some persons and accepted as a basic idea is unintelligible to others. The way to resolve the matter is to consider after due reflection which view, when fully

---

65 An alternative line of reply might undertake to defend promiscuity and to deny that the goods of love and responsibility are necessary to the moral worth of sexuality. From this point of view, the line of argument I suggest mistakenly seeks to defend the moral legitimacy of homosexuality by way of an analogy with heterosexuality. See Bonnie Honig, *Political Theory and the Displacement of Politics*, pp. 186–95 (1993).

worked out, offers the most coherent and convincing account.'[66] The same could be said of arguments about comprehensive moralities.

If it is possible to reason about the good as well as the right, then political liberalism's claim for the asymmetry between the right and good is undermined. For political liberalism, this asymmetry rests on the assumption that our moral and religious disagreements reflect a 'fact of reasonable pluralism' that our disagreements about justice do not. What enables Rawls to maintain that our disagreements about distributive justice do not amount to a 'fact of reasonable pluralism' is the strength of the arguments he advances on behalf of the difference principle and against libertarianism. But the same could be said of other controversies – including, conceivably, some moral and religious controversies. The public culture of democratic societies includes controversies about justice and comprehensive moralities alike. If government can affirm the justice of redistributive policies even in the face of disagreement by libertarians, why cannot government affirm in law, say, the moral legitimacy of homosexuality, even in the face of disagreement by those who regard homosexuality as sin?[67] Is Milton Friedman's objection to redistributive policies a less 'reasonable pluralism' than Pat Robertson's objection to gay rights?

With morality as with justice, the mere fact of disagreement is no evidence of the 'reasonable pluralism' that gives rise to the demand that government must be neutral. There is no reason in principle why in any given case, we might not conclude that, on due reflection, some moral or religious doctrines are more plausible than others. In such cases, we would not expect all disagreement to disappear, nor would we rule out the possibility that further deliberation might one day lead us to revise our view. But neither would we have grounds to insist that our deliberations about justice and rights may make no reference to moral or religious ideals.

The Limits of Liberal Public Reason. Whether it is possible to reason our way to agreement on any given moral or political controversy is not

---

66 Rawls, *Political Liberalism*, p. 53.
67 It is possible to argue for certain gay rights on grounds that neither affirm nor deny the morality of homosexuality. The question here is whether government is justified in supporting laws or policies (gay marriage, for example) on grounds that affirm the moral legitimacy of homosexuality.

something we can know until we try. This is why it cannot be said in advance that controversies about comprehensive moralities reflect a 'fact of reasonable pluralism' that controversies about justice do not. Whether a moral or political controversy reflects reasonable but incompatible conceptions of the good, or whether it can be resolved by due reflection and deliberation, can only be determined by reflecting and deliberating. But this raises another difficulty with political liberalism. For the political life it describes leaves little room for the kind of public deliberation necessary to test the plausibility of contending comprehensive moralities – to persuade others of the merits of our moral ideals, to be persuaded by others of the merits of theirs.

Although political liberalism upholds the right to freedom of speech, it severely limits the kinds of arguments that are legitimate contributions to political debate, especially debate about constitutional essentials and basic justice.[68] This limitation reflects the priority of the right over the good. Not only may government not endorse one or another conception of the good, but citizens may not even introduce into political discourse their comprehensive moral or religious convictions, at least when debating matters of justice and rights.[69] Rawls maintains that this limitation is required by the 'ideal of public reason'. According to this ideal, political discourse should be conducted solely in terms of 'political values' all citizens can reasonably be expected to accept. Since citizens of democratic societies do not share comprehensive moral and religious conceptions, public reason should not refer to such conceptions.

The limits of public reason do not apply, Rawls allows, to our personal deliberations about political questions, or to the discussions we may have as members of associations such as churches and universities, where 'religious, philosophical, and moral considerations' may properly play a role.

But the ideal of public reason does hold for citizens when they engage in political advocacy in the public forum, and thus for members of political

---

68 Rawls states that the limits of public reason apply to all discussion involving constitutional essentials and basic justice. As for other political questions, he writes that 'it is usually highly desirable to settle political questions by invoking the values of public reason. Yet this may not always be so.' See Rawls, *Political Liberalism*, pp. 214–15.

69 Ibid., pp. 10, 15, 215, 224, 254.

parties and for candidates in their campaigns and for other groups who support them. It holds equally for how citizens are to vote in elections when constitutional essentials and matters of basic justice are at stake. Thus, the ideal of public reason not only governs the public discourse of elections insofar as the issues involve those fundamental questions, but also how citizens are to cast their vote on these questions.[70]

How can we know whether our political arguments meet the requirements of public reason, suitably shorn of any reliance on moral or religious convictions? Rawls offers a novel test: 'To check whether we are following public reason we might ask: how would our argument strike us presented in the form of a supreme court opinion?'[71] For citizens of a democracy to allow their political discourse about fundamental questions to be informed by moral and religious ideals is no more legitimate, Rawls suggests, than for a judge to read his or her moral and religious beliefs into the Constitution.

The restrictive character of this notion of public reason can be seen by considering the sorts of political arguments it would rule out. In the debate about abortion rights, those who believe that the fetus is a person from the moment of conception and that abortion is therefore murder could not seek to persuade their fellow citizens of this view in open political debate. Nor could they vote for a law that would restrict abortion on the basis of this moral or religious conviction. Although adherents of the Catholic teaching on abortion could discuss the issue of abortion rights in religious terms within their church, they could not do so in a political campaign, or on the floor of the state legislature, or in the halls of Congress. Nor for that matter could opponents of the Catholic teaching on abortion argue their case in the political arena. Relevant though it clearly is to the question of abortion rights, Catholic moral doctrine cannot be debated in the political arena defined by political liberalism.

The restrictive character of liberal public reason can also be seen in the debate about gay rights. At first glance, these restrictions might seem a service to toleration. Those who consider homosexuality immoral and therefore unworthy of the privacy rights accorded heterosexual intimacy could not legitimately voice their views in public debate. Nor could they act on their belief by voting against laws that would protect gay men and lesbians from discrimination. These beliefs reflect comprehensive moral and religious convictions and so may not play a part in political discourse about matters of justice.

But the demands of public reason also limit the arguments that can be advanced in support of gay rights, and so restrict the range of reasons that can be invoked on behalf of toleration. Those who oppose antisodomy laws of the kind at issue in *Bowers v. Hardwick*[72] cannot argue that the moral judgments embodied in those laws are wrong, only that the law is wrong to embody any moral judgments at all.[73] Advocates of gay rights cannot contest the substantive moral judgment lying behind antisodomy laws or seek, through open political debate, to persuade their fellow citizens that homosexuality is morally permissible, for any such argument would violate the canons of liberal public reason.

The restrictive character of liberal public reason is also illustrated by the arguments offered by American abolitionists of the 1830s and 1840s. Rooted in evangelical Protestantism, the abolitionist movement argued for the immediate emancipation of the slaves on the grounds that slavery is a heinous sin.[74] Like the argument of some present-day Catholics against abortion rights, the abolitionist case against slavery was explicitly based on a comprehensive moral and religious doctrine.

In a puzzling passage, Rawls deals with the abolitionists' case and claims that their argument against slavery, religious though it was, did not violate the ideal of liberal public reason. When a society is not well ordered, he explains, it may be necessary to resort to comprehensive moralities in order to bring about a society in which public discussion is conducted solely in terms of 'political values'.[75] The religious arguments of the abolitionists can be justified as hastening the day when religious arguments would no longer play a legitimate role in public discourse. The abolitionists 'did not go against the ideal of public reason', Rawls concludes, 'provided they thought, or on reflection would

---

72 478 U.S. 186 (1986).
73 See Michael J. Sandel, 'Moral Argument and Liberal Toleration: Abortion and Homosexuality', 77 *California Law Review*, 521–38 (1989).
74 See James M. McPherson, *Battle Cry of Freedom: The Civil War Era*, p. 8 (1988); Eric Foner, *Politics and Ideology in the Age of the Civil War*, p. 72 (1980); Aileen S. Kraditor, *Means and Ends in American Abolitionism* (1967).
75 Rawls, *Political Liberalism*, p. 251n.

have thought (as they certainly could have thought), that the comprehensive reasons they appealed to were required to give sufficient strength to the political conception to be subsequently realized.'[76]

It is difficult to know what to make of this argument. There is little reason to suppose, and I do not think Rawls means to suggest, that the abolitionists opposed slavery on secular political grounds and simply used religious arguments to win popular support. Nor is there reason to think that the abolitionists sought by their agitation to make a world safe for secular political discourse. Nor can it be assumed that, even in retrospect, the abolitionists would take pride in having contributed, by their religious arguments against slavery, to the emergence of a society inhospitable to religious argument in political debate. If anything, the opposite is more likely: that by advancing religious arguments against so conspicuous an injustice as slavery, the evangelicals who inspired the abolitionist movement were hoping to encourage Americans to view other political questions in moral and religious terms as well. In any case, it is reasonable to suppose that the abolitionists meant what they said, that slavery is wrong because it is contrary to God's law, a heinous sin, and that this is the reason it should be ended. Absent some extraordinary assumptions, it is difficult to interpret their argument as consistent with the priority of the right over the good, or with the ideal of public reason advanced by political liberalism.

The cases of abortion, gay rights, and abolitionism illustrate the severe restrictions liberal public reason would impose on political debate. Rawls argues that these restrictions are justified as essential to the maintenance of a just society, in which citizens are governed by principles they may reasonably be expected to endorse, even in the light of their conflicting comprehensive moralities. Although public reason requires that citizens decide fundamental political questions without reference 'to the whole truth as they see it',[77] this restriction is justified by the political values, such as civility and mutual respect, that it makes possible. '[T]he political values realized by a well-ordered constitutional regime are very great values and not easily overriden and the ideals they express are not to be lightly aban-

---

76 Ibid., p. 251.   77 Ibid., p. 216.

doned.'[78] Rawls compares his case for restrictive public reason with the case for restrictive rules of evidence in criminal trials. There too we agree to decide without reference to the whole truth as we may know it – through illegally obtained evidence, for example – in order to advance other goods.[79]

The analogy between liberal public reason and restrictive rules of evidence is instructive. Setting aside the whole truth as we know it carries moral and political costs, for criminal trials and for public reason alike. Whether those costs are worth incurring depends on how significant they are compared to the goods they make possible, and whether those goods can be secured in some other way. To assess restrictive rules of evidence, for example, we need to know how many criminals go free as a result and whether less restrictive rules would unduly burden innocent persons suspected of a crime, lead to undesirable law-enforcement practices, violate important ideals such as respect for privacy (exclusionary rule) and spousal intimacy (spousal privilege), and so on. We arrive at rules of evidence by weighing the importance of deciding in the light of the whole truth against the importance of the ideals that would be sacrificed if all evidence were admissible.

Similarly, to assess restrictive rules of public reason, we need to weigh their moral and political cost against the political values they are said to make possible; we must also ask whether these political values – of toleration, civility, and mutual respect – could be achieved under less restrictive rules of public reason. Although political liberalism refuses to weigh the political values it affirms against competing values that may arise from within comprehensive moralities, the case for restrictive rules of public reason must presuppose some such comparison.

The costs of liberal public reason are of two kinds. The strictly moral costs depend on the validity and importance of the moral and religious doctrines liberal public reason requires us to set aside when deciding questions of justice. These costs will necessarily vary from case to case. They will be at their highest when a political conception of justice sanctions toleration of a grave moral wrong, such as slavery

78 Ibid., p. 218.   79 Ibid., pp. 218–19.

in the case of Douglas' argument for popular sovereignty. In the case of abortion, the moral cost of bracketing is high if the Catholic doctrine is correct; otherwise it is much lower. This suggests that, even given the moral and political importance of toleration, the argument for tolerating a given practice must take some account of the moral status of the practice, as well as the good of avoiding social conflict, letting people decide for themselves, and so on.

This way of thinking about the moral cost of liberal public reason is admittedly at odds with political liberalism itself. Although Rawls repeatedly states that a political conception of justice expresses values that normally outweigh whatever other values conflict with them,[80] he also insists that this involves no substantive comparison of the political values to the moral and religious values they override:

We need not consider the claims of political justice against the claims of this or that comprehensive view; nor need we say that political values are intrinsically more important than other values and that is why the latter are overridden. Having to say that is just what we hope to avoid.[81]

But since political liberalism allows that comprehensive moral and religious doctrines can be true, such comparisons cannot reasonably be avoided.

Beyond the moral costs of liberal public reason are certain political costs. These costs are becoming increasingly apparent in the politics of those countries, notably the United States, whose public discourse most closely approximates the ideal of public reason advanced by political liberalism. With a few notable exceptions, such as the civil rights movement, American political discourse in recent decades has come to reflect the liberal resolve that government be neutral on moral and religious questions, that fundamental questions of public policy be debated and decided without reference to any particular conception of the good.[82]

But democratic politics cannot long abide a public life as abstract and decorous, as detached from moral purposes, as Supreme Court opinions are supposed to be. A politics that brackets morality and reli-

---

80 Ibid., pp. 138, 146, 156, 218.   81 Ibid., p. 157.
82 I elaborate this claim in Michael J. Sandel, *Democracy's Discontent: America in Search of a Public Philosophy* (1996).

gion too thoroughly soon generates disenchantment. Where political discourse lacks moral resonance, the yearning for a public life of larger meanings finds undesirable expressions. Groups like the 'moral majority' and the Christian right seek to clothe the naked public square with narrow, intolerant moralisms. Fundamentalists rush in where liberals fear to tread. The disenchantment also assumes more secular forms. Absent a political agenda that addresses the moral dimension of public questions, public attention becomes riveted on the private vices of public officials. Public discourse becomes increasingly preoccupied with the scandalous, the sensational, and the confessional as purveyed by tabloids, talk shows, and eventually the mainstream media as well.

It cannot be said that the public philosophy of political liberalism is wholly responsible for these tendencies. But its vision of public reason is too spare to contain the moral energies of a vital democratic life. It thus creates a moral void that opens the way for the intolerant, the trivial, and other misguided moralisms.

If liberal public reason is too restrictive, it remains to ask whether a more spacious public reason would sacrifice the ideals that political liberalism seeks to promote, notably mutual respect among citizens who hold conflicting moral and religious views. Here it is necessary to distinguish two conceptions of mutual respect. On the liberal conception, we respect our fellow citizen's moral and religious convictions by ignoring them (for political purposes), by leaving them undisturbed, by carrying on political debate without reference to them. To admit moral and religious ideals into political debate about justice would undermine mutual respect in this sense.

But this is not the only, or perhaps even the most plausible, way of understanding the mutual respect on which democratic citizenship depends. On a different conception of respect – call it the deliberative conception – we respect our fellow citizen's moral and religious convictions by engaging, or attending to, them – sometimes by challenging and contesting them, sometimes by listening and learning from them – especially when those convictions bear on important political questions. There is no guarantee that a deliberative mode of respect will lead in any given case to agreement with, or even appreciation of, the moral and religious convictions of others. It is always possible that learning more about a moral or religious doctrine will lead us to like it less. But the respect of deliberation and engagement affords a more spacious public reason than liberalism allows. It is also a more suitable ideal for a pluralist society. To the extent that our moral and religious disagreements reflect the ultimate plurality of human goods, a deliberative mode of respect will better enable us to appreciate the distinctive goods our different lives express.

Bibliography

PART I

Listed are all references indicated in the text as well as some works whose influence is present in the text although not referred to directly.

Ackerman, B.A. 1980. *Social Justice in the Liberal State*, New Haven
Arendt, H. 1958. *The Human Condition*, Chicago
Aristotle. *Nicomachean Ethics*, translated by D. Ross, 1925. London
    Politics, ed. E. Barker, 1946. London
Atiyah, P.S. 1979. *The Rise and Fall of Freedom of Contract*, Oxford
Barker, E., ed. 1948. *Social Contract*, New York
Bartlet, V. 1915. The Biblical and early Christian idea of property. In *Property: Its Duties and Rights*, ed. C. Gore, London
Beer, S. 1966. Liberalism and the national idea, *The Public Interest* (Fall) No. 5, 70–82
Bell, D. 1973. *The Coming of Post-Industrial Society*, Harmondsworth
Bickel, A.M. 1975. *The Morality of Consent*, New Haven
Dworkin, R. 1977a. *Taking Rights Seriously*, London
    1977b. Why Bakke has no case, *New York Review of Books* (November 10), 11–15
    1978. Liberalism. In *Public and Private Morality*, ed. S. Hampshire, pp. 113–43. Cambridge
Feinberg, J. 1970. *Doing and Deserving*, Princeton
Frankfurt, H. 1971. Freedom of the will and the concept of a person, *Journal of Philosophy* 68, 5–20
Fried, C. 1978. *Right and Wrong*, Cambridge
    1981. *Contract as Promise*, Cambridge
Hampshire, S. 1959. *Thought and Action*, London
    1972. Spinoza and the idea of freedom. In *Freedom of Mind*, pp. 183–209. London
    1977. *Two Theories of Morality*, Oxford
    1978. Morality and pessimism. In *Public and Private Morality*, ed. S. Hampshire, pp. 1–22. Cambridge
Hart, H.L.A. 1979. Between utility and rights. In *The Idea of Freedom*, ed. A. Ryan, pp. 77–98. Oxford

Hegel, G.W.F. 1807. *Phenomenology of Spirit,* translated by A.V. Miller, 1977. Oxford

    1821. *Philosophy of Right,* translated by T.M. Knox, 1952. London

    1899. *The Philosophy of History,* translated by J. Sibree, 1956. New York

Hume, D. 1739. *A Treatise of Human Nature,* 2nd edn, ed. L.A. Selby-Bigge, 1978. Oxford

    1777. *An Enquiry Concerning the Principles of Morals,* 1966 edn, La Salle, Illinois

Kant, I. 1781. *Critique of Pure Reason,* 1st edn, translated by N. Kemp Smith, 1929. London

    1785. *Groundwork of the Metaphysics of Morals,* translated by H.J. Paton, 1956. New York

    1787. *Critique of Pure Reason,* 2nd edn, translated by N. Kemp Smith, 1929. London

    1788. *Critique of Practical Reason,* translated by L.W. Beck, 1956. Indianapolis

    1793. On the common saying: 'this may be true in theory, but it does not apply in practice'. In *Kant's Political Writings,* ed. H. Reiss, 1970, pp. 61–92. Cambridge

    1797. *The Metaphysical Elements of Justice,* translated by J. Ladd, 1965. Indianapolis

Kronman, A. 1980. Contract law and distributive justice, *Yale Law Journal* 89, 472–511

Locke, J. 1690. *Treatise of Civil Government,* ed. C.L. Sherman, 1937. New York

Lyons, D. n.d. Nature and soundness of the contract and coherence arguments. In *Reading Rawls,* ed. N. Daniels, pp. 141–68. New York

MacIntyre, A. 1967. Egoism and altruism. In *Encyclopedia of Philosophy,* ed. P. Edwards, vol. ii, pp. 462–6. New York

    1981. *After Virtue,* Notre Dame

Marx, K. *Early Writings,* translated by R. Livingstone and G. Benton, 1975. Harmondsworth

Mill, J.S. 1849. *On Liberty.* In *The Utilitarians,* 1973, pp. 473–600. Garden City.

    1863. *Utilitarianism.* In *The Utilitarians,* 1973, pp. 399–472

Murdoch, I. 1970. The idea of perfection. In *The Sovereignty of Good,* pp. 1–45. London

Nagel, T. 1973. Rawls on justice. In *Reading Rawls,* ed. N. Daniels, pp. 1–15. New York

Nozick, R. 1972. Coercion. In *Philosophy, Politics, and Society,* 4th series, eds P. Laslett, W.G. Runciman, and Q. Skinner, pp. 101–35.

    1974. *Anarchy, State, and Utopia,* New York

Bibliography

Oakeshott, M. 1962. *Rationalism in Politics,* London
Pitkin, H. 1965. Obligation and consent – I, *American Political Science Review* 66, 990–9
Rawls, J. 1971. *A Theory of Justice,* Oxford
  1972. Reply to Lyons and Teitelman, *Journal of Philosophy* 69, 556–7
  1975. Fairness to goodness, *Philosophical Review* 84, 536–54
  1977. The basic structure as subject, *American Philosophical Quarterly* 14, 159–65
  1979. A well-ordered society. In *Philosophy, Politics, and Society,* 5th series, eds P. Laslett and J. Fishkin, pp. 6–20. Oxford
  1980. Kantian constructivism in moral theory, *Journal of Philosophy* 77, 515–72
Spinoza, B. 1670. *A Theologico-Political Treatise,* translated by R.H.M. Elwes, 1951. New York
  1677. *The Ethics,* translated by R.H.M. Elwes. In *The Rationalists,* 1960, pp. 179–408. Garden City
Strauss, L. 1953. *Natural Right and History,* Chicago
Taylor, C. 1975. *Hegel,* Cambridge
  1977. What is human agency? In *The Self: Psychological and Philosophical Issues,* ed. T. Mischel, pp. 103–35. Oxford
Unger, R. 1975. *Knowledge and Politics,* New York
Wolin, S. 1960. *Politics and Vision,* Boston

PART II

The following works offer critical responses to the first edition of *Liberalism and the Limits of Justice,* or discussion of related issues:

Allen, Jonathan. 1992. Liberals, communitarians, and political theory, *South African Journal of Philosophy* 11:77–91.
Avineri, Shlomo, and Avner de-Shalit, eds. 1992. *Communitarians and Individualism.* Oxford: Oxford University Press.
Badhwar, Neera K. 1996. Moral agency, commitment, and impartiality. In *The Communitarian Challenge to Liberalism,* ed. Ellen Frankel Paul, Fred D. Miller, Jr., and Jeffrey Paul, pp. 1–26. Cambridge: Cambridge University Press.
Baker, C. Edwin. 1985. Sandel on Rawls, *University of Pennsylvania Law Review* 133:895–928.
Bell, Daniel. 1993. *Communitarianism and Its Critics.* Oxford: Clarendon Press.
Benhabib, Sheyla. 1992. Autonomy, modernity and community: Communitarianism and critical social theory in dialogue. In *Situating the*

Self: Gender, Community, and Postmodernism in Contemporary Ethics, pp. 68–88. New York: Routledge.

Berten, André, Pablo da Silveira, and Hervé Pourtois, eds. 1997. *Libéraux et Communautariens.* Paris: Presses Universitaires de France.

Borgmann, Albert. 1989. Technology and the crisis of liberalism: Reflections on Michael J. Sandel's work. In *Technological Transformation: Contextual and Conceptual Implications,* ed. Edmund F. Byrne and Joseph C. Pitt, pp. 105–22. Dordrecht: Kluwer Academic Publishers.

Buchanan, Allen E. 1989. Assessing the communitarian critique of liberalism, *Ethics* 99:852–82.

Caney, Simon. 1991. Sandel's critique of the primacy of justice: A liberal rejoinder, *British Journal of Political Science* 21:511–22.

——— 1992. Liberalism and communitarianism: A misconceived debate, *Political Studies* 40:273–90.

Delaney, C.F., ed. 1994. *The Liberalism-Communitarianism Debate.* Lanham, Md.: Rowman & Littlefield.

Doppelt, Gerald. 1989. Is Rawls's Kantian liberalism coherent and defensible? *Ethics* 99:815–51.

Douglass, R. Bruce, Gerald M. Mara, and Henry S. Richardson, eds. 1990. *Liberalism and the Good.* New York: Routledge.

Feinberg, Joel. 1988. *Harmless Wrongdoing,* vol. 4 of *The Moral Limits of the Criminal Law,* 4 vols. New York: Oxford University Press.

——— 1988. Liberalism, community and tradition, *Tikkun* May–June:38–41, 116–120.

Ferrara, Alessandro, ed. 1992. *Comunitarismo e Liberalismo.* Rome: Editori Riuniti.

Frazer, Elizabeth and Nicola Lacey. 1993. *The Politics of Community: A Feminist Critique of the Liberal-Communitarian Debate.* Toronto: University of Toronto Press.

Friedman, Jeffrey. 1994. The politics of communitarianism, *Critical Review* 8:297–340.

Friedman, Marilyn. 1989. Feminism and modern friendship: Dislocating the community, *Ethics* 99:275–90.

Gardbaum, Stephen A. 1992. Law, politics, and the claims of community, *Michigan Law Review* 90:685–760.

——— 1996. Liberalism, autonomy, and moral conflict, *Stanford Law Review* 48:385–417.

Gerber, Leslie, E. 1990. The man who mistook his wife for a transcendental subject, *First Things* 2:36–41.

Gill, Emily R. 1986. Goods, virtues, and the constitution of the self. In *Liberals on Liberalism,* ed. Alfonso J. Damico, pp. 111–28. Totowa, N.J.: Rowman & Littlefield.

Gilman, James E. 1994. Compassion and public covenant: Christian faith in public life, *Journal of Church and State* 36:747–71.

Gutmann, Amy. 1985. Communitarian critics of liberalism, *Philosophy and Public Affairs* 14:308–22

Hekman, Susan. 1992. The embodiment of the subject: Feminism and the communitarian critique of liberalism, *Journal of Politics* 54:1098–1119.

Hirsch, H.N. 1986. The threnody of liberalism, *Political Theory* 14:423–49.

Holmes, Stephen. 1993. *The Anatomy of Antiliberalism*. Cambridge, Mass.: Harvard University Press.

Honig, Bonnie. 1993. *Political Theory and the Displacement of Politics*. Ithaca, N.Y.: Cornell University Press.

Iroegbu, Pantaleon. 1991. La pensée de Rawls face au défi communautarien, *Revue Philosophique de Louvain* 89:113–28.

Kukathas, Chandran. 1996. Liberalism, communitarianism, and political community. In *The Communitarian Challenge to Liberalism*, ed. Ellen Frankel Paul, Fred D. Miller, Jr., and Jeffrey Paul, pp. 105–36. Cambridge: Cambridge University Press.

Kukathas, Chandran, and Philip Pettit. 1990. *Rawls: A Theory of Justice and its Critics*. Stanford, Calif.: Stanford University Press.

Kymlicka, Will. 1988. Liberalism and communitarianism, *Canadian Journal of Philosophy* 18:181–204.

   1988. Rawls on teleology and deontology, *Philosophy and Public Affairs* 17:173–90.

   1989. *Liberalism, Community and Culture*. Oxford: Clarendon Press.

   1990. *Contemporary Political Philosophy: An Introduction*. Oxford: Clarendon Press.

Larmore, Charles E. 1987. *Patterns of Moral Complexity*. Cambridge: Cambridge University Press.

Lasch, Christopher. 1986. The communitarian critique of liberalism, *Soundings* 69:60–76.

Lund, William R. 1993. Communitarian politics and the problem of equality, *Political Research Quarterly* 46:577–601.

Macedo, Stephen. 1990. *Liberal Virtues: Citizenship, Virtue, and Community in Liberal Constitutionalism*. Oxford: Clarendon Press.

MacIntyre, Alasdair. 1984. Is patriotism a virtue? Findley Lecture, University of Kansas.

   1988. *Whose Justice? Which Rationality?* Notre Dame, Ind.: University of Notre Dame Press.

Meyer, Michael J. 1992. Rights between friends, *Journal of Philosophy* 89:467–84.

Miller, David. 1989. In what sense must socialism be communitarian? *Social Philosophy and Policy* 6:57–73.

Moore, Michael S. 1989. Sandelian antiliberalism, *California Law Review* 77:539–51.

Mosher, Michael A. 1991. Boundary revisions: The deconstruction of moral personality in Rawls, Nozick, Sandel and Parfit, *Political Studies* 39:287–303.

Mouffe, Chantal. 1988. American liberalism and its critics: Rawls, Taylor, Sandel and Walzer, *Praxis International* 8:193–206.

Mulhall, Stephen. 1987. The theoretical foundations of liberalism, *Archives Européennes de Sociologie* 28:269–95.

Mulhall, Stephen, and Adam Swift. 1992. *Liberals and Communitarians*. Oxford: Blackwell.

——— 1993. Liberalisms and communitarianisms: Whose misconception? *Political Studies* 41:650–6.

Neal, Patrick. 1987. A liberal theory of the good? *Canadian Journal of Philosophy* 17:567–82.

Okin, Susan, 1989. *Justice, Gender, and the Family*. New York: Basic Books.

Paul, Ellen Frankel, Fred D. Miller, Jr., and Jeffrey Paul, eds. 1996. *The Communitarian Challenge to Liberalism*. Cambridge: Cambridge University Press.

Paul, Jeffrey, and Fred D. Miller, Jr. Communitarian and liberal theories of the good, *Review of Metaphysics* 43:803–31.

Post, Robert. 1989. Tradition, the self, and substantive due process: A comment on Michael Sandel, *California Law Review* 77:553–60.

Rasmussen, David, ed. 1990. *Universalism vs. Communitarianism: Contemporary Debates in Ethics*. Cambridge, Mass.: MIT Press.

Rawls, John. 1985. Justice as fairness: Political not metaphysical, *Philosophy and Public Affairs* 14:223–51.

——— 1987. The idea of an overlapping consensus, *Oxford Journal of Legal Studies* 7:1–25.

——— 1987. The priority of right and ideas of the good, *Philosophy and Public Affairs* 17:251–76.

——— 1993. *Political Liberalism*. New York: Columbia University Press.

Regan, Milton C., Jr. 1985. Community and justice in constitutional theory, *Wisconsin Law Review* 1073–1133.

Rorty, Richard. 1988. The priority of democracy to philosophy. In *The Virginia Statute of Religious Freedom*, ed. Merrill D. Peterson and Robert C. Vaughan, pp. 257–82. Cambridge: Cambridge University Press.

Rosenblum, Nancy [L.] 1987. *Another Liberalism: Romanticism and the Reconstruction of Liberal Thought*. Cambridge, Mass.: Harvard University Press.

Rosenblum, Nancy L., ed. 1989. *Liberalism and the Moral Life*. Cambridge, Mass.: Harvard University Press.

Sandel, Michael J. 1984. The procedural republic and the unencumbered self, *Political Theory* 12:81–96.

1989. Moral argument and liberal toleration: Abortion and homosexuality, *California Law Review* 77:521–38.

1996. *Democracy's Discontent: America in Search of a Public Philosophy*. Cambridge, Mass.: Harvard University Press.

Sandel, Michael J., ed. 1984. *Liberalism and Its Critics*. Oxford: Blackwell.

Scheffler, Samuel. 1992. Responsibility, reactive attitudes, and liberalism in philosophy and politics, *Philosophy and Public Affairs* 21:299–323.

Sher, George. 1989. Three grades of social involvement, *Philosophy and Public Affairs* 18:133–58.

Simon, Thomas W. 1994. The theoretical marginalization of the disadvantaged: A liberal/communitarian failing. In *The Liberalism-Communitarianism Debate*, ed. C.F. Delaney, pp. 103–36 Lanham, Md.: Rowman & Littlefield.

Sorell, Tom. 1991. Self, society, and Kantian impersonality, *Monist* 74:30–43.

Sypnowich, Christine. 1993. Justice, community, and the antinomies of feminist theory, *Political Theory* 21:484–506.

Tamir, Yael. 1993. *Liberal Nationalism*. Princeton, N.J.: Princeton University Press.

Taylor, Charles. 1985. *Philosophical Papers*. 2 vols. Cambridge: Cambridge University Press.

1987. Cross-purposes: The liberal-communitarian debate. In *Liberalism and the Moral Life*, ed. Nancy L. Rosenblum, pp. 159–82. Cambridge, Mass.: Harvard University Press.

1989. *Sources of the Self: The Making of the Modern Identity*. Cambridge, Mass.: Harvard University Press.

Tessman, Lisa. 1995. Who are my people? Communitarianism and the interlocking of oppressions, *International Studies in Philosophy* 27:105–17.

Thigpen, Robert B., and Lyle A. Downing. 1987. Liberalism and the communitarian critique, *American Journal of Political Science* 31:637–55.

Tomasi, John. 1991. Individual rights and community virtues, *Ethics* 101:521–36.

1994. Community in the minimal state, *Critical Review* 8:285–96.

Urbinati, Nadia. 1992. Il ritorno alla comunità nella filosofia Americana contemporanea, *Giornale Critico Della Filosofia Italiana* 12:518–35.

Velek, Josef. 1995. Communitarian criticism of the liberal self and liberal community according to Michael Sandel, *Filosoficky Casopis* 43:265–71.

Waldron, Jeremy. 1988. When justice replaces affection: The need for rights, *Harvard Journal of Law and Public Policy* 11:625–47.

1993. Particular values and critical morality. In *Liberal Rights,* pp. 168–202. Cambridge: Cambridge University Press.

Wallach, John R. 1987. Liberals, communitarians, and the tasks of political theory, *Political Theory* 15:581–611.

Walzer, Michael. 1983. *Spheres of Justice: A Defense of Pluralism and Equality.* New York: Basic Books.

1990. The communitarian critique of liberalism, *Political Theory* 18:6–24.

Young, Iris M. 1986. The ideal of community and the politics of difference, *Social Theory and Practice* 12:1–26.

Index